Theology at the Void

THEOLOGY

AT THE

VOID

The Retrieval of Experience

Thomas M. Kelly

UNIVERSITY OF NOTRE DAME PRESS
Notre Dame, Indiana

Manufactured in the United States of America

Library of Congress Cataloging-in-Publication Data
Kelly, Thomas M., 1969–
Theology at the void : the retrieval of experience / Thomas M. Kelly.
p. cm.
Includes bibliographical references and index.
ISBN 0-268-03352-8 (alk. paper) — ISBN 0-268-03353-6 (pbk. : alk. paper)
1. Experience (Religion)   2. Postmodernism—Religious aspects—Christianity.
3. Language and languages—Religious aspects—Christianity.
4. Schleiermacher, Friedrich, 1768–1834—Contributions in concept
of religious experience. I. Title.
BR110 . K373 2002
230 — dc21
2001004257

for

MICHAEL J. BUCKLEY, S.J.,

&

REV. MICHAEL J. HIMES

Priests, Mentors, Friends

Deconstruction is a counter-movement to such attempts of "modernist conceit." It reveals these efforts as futile attempts—compulsive defenses against the "void"—the reality of life which has turned the hallelujahs of Easter sunrise into a perplexity before the empty tomb.

—Carl A. Raschke, "The Deconstruction of God"

What grounds man's openness and his reaching out in the unlimited expanse of his transcendence cannot be nothingness, an absolutely empty void. For to assert that of a void would make absolutely no sense.

—Karl Rahner, *Foundations of Christian Faith*

Contents

Acknowledgments

I thank the members of the Department of Theology at Boston College for their support, understanding, and encouragement during my doctoral studies, especially John Darr, Steve Pope, Don Dietrich, Bob Daly, S. J., and Louis Roy, O. P. I thank Brian Hughes for suggesting that I look at the work of George Steiner, Richard Miller for his careful reading and suggestions concerning the Rahner chapter, and Sean Sennott for suggesting the cover art. I thank Wayne Proudfoot and George Lindbeck for carefully reading and responding to chapters on their thought. I thank William Neenan, S. J., for his concrete support and encouragement. Words could never capture my gratitude to Michael J. Buckley, S. J., and Michael J. Himes, but they know of it. I especially thank my wife, Lisa, without whom this work would have been impossible, for being my strength, my love, and my comfort. I thank Andrew and Michael for being my balance. Finally, I thank Jeffrey Gainey, associate director of the University of Notre Dame Press, for his interest, his honesty, and his humor.

Preface

The following work tries to tell a story. Within that story is a response to a contemporary problem in theology. It is a story that, ultimately, tries to answer the question, both intellectually and existentially, of whether we move toward nothing or whether we move toward something—in inquiry, in human hope and love, in being. It is a story that comprises many phases but that centers on three questions. What is human being? What is language? What is theology? Five significant thinkers from various religious and academic perspectives have asked, and answered, those questions. Their responses make up the story line of this work.

The story begins with Friedrich Schleiermacher, who frames an understanding of human experience, language, and theology to articulate and explicate the Christian faith. Two contemporary thinkers take issue with the presuppositions of Schleiermacher's inquiry and thus reject it. They do so because they find it dependent upon a culturally limited theological anthropology. An appeal to experience for theology, as framed by Schleiermacher, is the product of a prior belief system or ideology. And while there may be theological claims and counterclaims, the issues determining such differences are, finally, philosophical, hermeneutical, and anthropological. This is the problem. Which approach is legitimate inquiry into some very serious questions? For the postmodern thinkers in this story, there is no priority to experience; rather, languages and cultural systems construct the very particular experience referenced. This critique of the conjunction between experience and language by postmodernity, and its impact upon the nature of theology, is the contemporary problem that this work proposes to examine.

The brief and general introduction begins with a general reflection on postmodernism in both its "radical" and its more "moderate" manifestations. It explains the book's selection among the critics of Schleiermacher and prepares for the analysis of two exemplary postmodern critiques of Schleiermacher's work. These critiques concentrate their dissatisfaction on

Schleiermacher's treatment of the human subject, the anatomy of "experi-ence" and its relationship to language, and the nature of theological inquiry. This introduction is preparatory for the first moment of the story, Schleier-macher's unique conjoining of experience, language, and theological inquiry.

The method for telling this story depends upon the tension between Schleiermacher's approach and a postmodern one. This tension is acknowl-edged, and both sides are subsumed in a response to each. Thus, this account will trace the emergence and development of the problem through progressive contradictions to one possible resolution. This is not the only resolution but rather a viable alternative to both the nineteenth-century "turn to the subject" and contemporary postmodernism. The first moment of this story is consti-tuted by Schleiermacher's project, the second by the postmodern critique, and the third by suggestions for resolution through the works of George Steiner and Karl Rahner. Ultimately, an understanding of "experience" can be retrieved that adequately addresses contemporary theological concerns.

The first chapter on Schleiermacher's theology will explore the "classical" nexus between the experience of God, its relation to language, and the pur-pose of theological inquiry. The method and result of his project can be termed the "turn to the subject" in theology. I will argue that this turn to the subject in Schleiermacher's thought occurs in three major stages. First, it occurs in the *apologia* for religion. Second, it occurs in the later theological appropriation of an experiential starting point for dogmatic theology. Finally, it occurs in a theological treatment of doctrine enabled by a turn to the sub-ject in hermeneutics. Schleiermacher's threefold turn to the subject—in reli-gion, in dogmatics, and in hermeneutics—highlights the issues that will be explored and severely evaluated by the postmodern critique. These issues include but are not limited to (1) the universal nature of the human subject, evident in the appeal to an experience of God that claims to be accessible to all; (2) the priority and independence of "experience" over the vehicle for its expression—that is, over language; and (3) the character of theology. By way of response, two authors will represent the (moderate) postmodern critique of Schleiermacher's project.

In the book *Religious Experience*, Wayne Proudfoot frames a postmodern approach to a theory of religion. In *The Nature of Doctrine*, George Lindbeck offers a postmodern approach to a theory of Christian doctrine. Despite their many differences, the authors share critical points of disagreement with Schleiermacher's mode of theological inquiry. Both postmodern responses reject elements of a "common humanity" or any appeal to a common human "experience." Both authors subscribe to a constructive or formative theory of language and an understanding of "experience" as a kind of knowledge. Finally, both advocate what will later be characterized as a "theoretical" approach to the study of religion and doctrine.

Proudfoot and Lindbeck bring very different agendas to their critique of Schleiermacher's approach to the topic of "religious experience." Further, each is representative of the contemporary problem—one from within theology and the other from an "extrinsic" or "nonconfessional" school of theory engaged in the study of religion. The three critiques they advance on the topics mentioned represent postmodern themes decisively at odds with Schleiermacher's project. It is precisely this contradiction—the postmodern countering of the nineteenth-century turn to the subject—that defines contemporary arguments concerning religious experience and theological inquiry.

George Steiner, in his recent work *Real Presences,* considers that the postmodern critiques provide a valuable counterbalance to Schleiermacher's project but are finally incoherent. And with his analysis, this story enters into the third moment of its examination of these questions. For Steiner, postmodernism uses for its critique all the mechanics of language, meaning, and external linguistic reference while claiming to discard them. More important, Steiner understands postmodernism fundamentally as an a priori rejection of the theological. This is so because postmodernism misunderstands the nature of language and its relation to human experience. For Steiner, language embodies an encounter with and response to an "other." This encounter can be one of "real presence": a coming up against something that is not the self (or constructed by the self) that makes claims upon the self through the reality of aesthetic experience. Such an encounter reveals both language and human experience to be aboriginally self-transcendent. The postmodern assertion of language boundaries is thus countered by demonstrating that both language and experience condition each other— and that both move the subject beyond the self. Steiner's work suggests that at the basis of the contemporary problem surrounding the experience of God, language, and theological inquiry is an incoherent metaphysical anthropology. There is something rather than nothing, as manifested through the experience of art, literature, and music. Thus, the issue between Steiner and postmodernity is a particular conception of language and experience. He will argue that the relation of these two topics, however finally designated, directly corresponds to an understanding of the human condition either as confined to its own determinate origins or as open and able to experience the "other." Steiner's general critique of postmodernism is helpful, but the theological consequences of what he terms "verification transcendence" are unacceptable for Christian theology. Overall, Steiner does supply a legitimate alternative to postmodern anthropology and linguistic theory. By appropriating such an alternative, one can turn to a specific response from within Christian theology.

Karl Rahner provides a viable *theological* alternative to both Schleiermacher and postmodernism, and with this theologian the problem at the heart of this story moves toward a possible resolution. Rahner's approach to theology emerges from, and addresses, the human subject, the relationship of experience and language, and the nature and function of theology. He formulates a coherent explication of the experience of God: its actual meaning, its relation to language, and its consequences for theological inquiry. His works take seriously humanity's appropriation of language, humanity's place in history, the formative aspects of culture, and the theological importance of the particular. Conversely, he avoids a fundamentalism of another kind—that of finitude, of time boundedness, of spatiotemporal relativity. If the productive moments of the various stages of this story can be brought into a higher synthesis, one can be closer to the truths of an inherently relational faith. More important, one can approach the formulation of theology in terms of *mystery* properly understood. Ultimately, this will lead to a consideration of the Trinity as perhaps the most misunderstood but critically important doctrine in Christianity.

In summary, this work proposes to tell a story. In the process it hopes to frame and address a contemporary problem in systematic theology. The story has as its plot a development of how human beings understand themselves, their language, and the nature of their inquiry about God. The problem that drives this inquiry is the contradiction between Schleiermacher's turn to the subject—with all its assumptions regarding religious experience, the relation of religious experience to language, and theology—and the postmodern critique of that turn and its assumptions. This work will move through three moments. The postmodern critique is based on Schleiermacher's view of language, a particular understanding of experience, and a particular conception of the purpose of theology. Three topics emerge from the intersection of Schleiermacher's project and the postmodern critique to control this plot and provide the basis for a thematic comparison: (1) the understanding of the human subject/experience, (2) the relationship between language and experience, and (3) the nature of theological inquiry. George Steiner will offer a possibility for moving beyond the more radical anthropological elements of the postmodern critique. Karl Rahner will indicate one theological alternative that is sensitive both to the postmodern critique and to the nature of a foundational theology. This alternative provides a conclusion to the story that can serve as a response to what is today an outstanding contradiction.

Introduction:
Postmodernism(s)
and Theology

If deconstruction is branded as nihilistic, it should be noted that it does naught but reveal the inherent nihilism of its host discipline. Where the body is, there shall the eagles gather. It is fitting today that deconstruction should spread throughout the corpus (or "corpse") of theology, because the theological mind has been responsible for the modern elevation of the linguistic signifier, which Derrida's "play of difference" exposes as a phantom, a veiled abyss, a nothingness. In Derrida's words: "the age of the sign is essentially theological."

—Carl A. Raschke, "The Deconstruction of God"

A general overview of postmodernism makes intelligible the specific critiques of Schleiermacher's experiential starting point for theological inquiry. Thus, the following overview is preparatory for two contemporary critiques of Schleiermacher's project. Like any "movement," postmodernism is variously defined, and its starting point is critically argued. This overview, consequently, will give a general sense of the postmodern undertaking— enough to introduce the nature of its critique.[1] It goes without saying that any overview of such a vast movement as "postmodernism" will always be deficient because the movement is still contemporary and changing. The purpose of this quite limited section is to explore how postmodernism has influenced a very particular theological approach.

Foundationalists such as Schleiermacher, as well as many other Protestant and Catholic theologians, begin their inquiry from an established principle. This overview will suggest a basic trajectory of thought that is contrary to such an approach. Postmodernity must, therefore, first be seen as a critique of foundationalism. This analysis will further explore the postmodern critique as it is actually applied. The terms *deconstruction* and *postmodernism* will be used interchangeably when referring to the negation with which both movements begin their critiques of traditional (foundational) theology. While both methods negate a traditional approach to various fields, postmodernism usually attempts to "correct" the traditional approach with what is put forward following the negation. The postmodern approach, at least in its moderate forms, is constructive because it suggests possibilities, albeit limited ones, for traditional theology. Deconstruction or, as termed here, strong postmodernism simply critiques dated or naive modes of philosophy, art, literature, theology, and so forth. The value of the method lies in exposing the inadequacies of these attempts at modernist control.

Deconstruction arose in response to two presuppositions that undergird modern Western thought—linguistic formalism and anthropological reductionism.[2] The codification of language into "precise structures of meaning" and the illusion that "man" is anything other than "an invention of language" have prompted a move to free both language and "person" from human-centered inquiry altogether.[3] Both, according to deconstructionists, represent attempts by humanity "to 'construct' [its] own world with the materials of introspection and rational analysis, then live comfortably within it."[4] Deconstruction, conversely, is a countermovement to such attempts of "modernist conceit." Fred Lawrence captures the "modernist conceit" quite well in the following description of modernist anthropology:

In the context of the modern project, the premodern notion of the soul as the form of the living body, endowing it with natural and inevitable inclinations that point beyond the person toward a hierarchy of ends or goods, is simply eliminated. In its place is installed the subject as object, which is imagined to be a unitary ego capable of deploying disengaged reason's rigor and proof as a means of carrying out the project of mastery and control of human and subhuman nature. This truncated model of the self is dominated by the crucial and highly questionable idea of consciousness conceived of as an internal, reflexive perception that leads ineluctably to the modern image of the subject as primary object, whether in the form of Descartes' disengaged reason or of Locke's punctual individual subject.[5]

Deconstruction, according to Carl Raschke, "reveals these efforts as futile attempts—compulsive defenses against the 'void'—the reality of life which has turned the hallelujahs of Easter sunrise into a perplexity before the empty tomb."[6] "The movement of deconstruction has set about to show that the cathedral of modern intellect is but a mirage in cloud-cuckooland. Neither language nor human self-awareness conceals any thread of reference to things as they are."[7] Such an assertion, renouncing any human ability to know reality (a construct as well), defines the paradox of deconstruction. The use of reason annihilates the possibility of reasoning. Clearly, the critique of Western thought by deconstruction or, as termed here, radical postmodernism essentially takes place on the foundational level in the areas of anthropology and epistemology. Both are essential to any description of the human subject; hence, both constitute areas of severe disagreement between "postmodernism" broadly understood and certain approaches to theology. This disagreement becomes clearer when one considers the postmodern critique of the role of reason in theology.

Thomas Guarino begins his article "Between Foundations and Nihilism: Is Phronesis the Via Media for Theology?" with the question: "What type of rationality is proper to theology as a discipline?"[8] A broad range of answers greets this question today, from a nihilism that undercuts itself to a naive fundamentalism that is blind to its own insufficiencies. Each has profound consequences for any theological inquiry, for each operates from deeply held presuppositions concerning the human subject. Admitting that rationality is not a univocal term, Guarino asserts that "a particular understanding of the way reason is used, or a denial of reason's capacities, will affect one's conception of revelation, how it is received, and the type of truth or falsity predicated for it."[9]

But the postmodern critique of "foundationalism" is not only a debate concerning epistemology. Postmodernism aims to undercut theological approaches that are generally optimistic concerning the human possibility of encountering the divine (a construct) from within human experience itself. These approaches have been present throughout the history of theology.

They presume both a universal human experience or subjectivity, however understood, and a view of language that communicates *but does not constitute* such experience. Thus, any epistemological critique has, at its core, a specific view of the human subject (or nonsubject) as a whole. The targets of the postmodern critiques are the totalizing universal theological anthropologies (and their attendant epistemologies) asserted by authors in many traditions that underlie various approaches to theology. Within this general anthropological critique of the capabilities of the human subject can be found the more specific critique concerning human knowing—and, even more specifically, the establishment of a foundation from which to do theology.

> Traditional "foundationalist" thought, whether of the classical metaphysical or modern transcendental variety, has come on hard times of late. Its critics resist the foundationalist compulsion to establish some first principle, Archimedean point, or ahistorical matrix from which to begin the search for rigorous and objective knowledge. The search for ultimate and determinate ontological or epistemological grounds guides virtually the entire tradition of Western thought, wholly enveloping the Platonic-Thomistic-Cartesian-Kantian-Husserlian axis. It attempts, once and for all, to "stop the show" by means of assorted foundational *archai* or *principia*, such as *esse, ousia, eidos, res cogitans, Wille zur Macht*, etc.[10]

Foundationalism (i.e., a mode of thought grounded by an appeal to some first principle) and similar hermeneutical trajectories have grounded much traditional Catholic and Protestant systematic theology. Generally speaking, this approach assumes a common humanity to which the universal or totalizing vision is accessible. Consequently, foundationalism presumes that real knowledge is accessible to the believer, however one is situated in history. The human being has access to "Truth," in part because of the intelligibility of "reality." This conviction is particularly evident when systematic theology interprets both the biblical corpus and received doctrinal texts and posits the possibility of the transmittal of "Truth," and specifically revelation, through history. Bernard Lonergan, Karl Rahner, and Walter Kasper, to name but a few prominent contemporary Catholic thinkers, all use "a foundationalist ontology in order to undergird a theology which supports both the referential nature of doctrinal statements as well as their integral and continuous transmission."[11]

Opposed to such foundationalism—a foundationalism evident in any universal claim regarding human experience—is the postmodern critique. One must make a distinction between moderate and strong postmodernism, for they differ radically on how seriously they question the possibility of encountering Truth. Guarino states that "as I will use the terms, 'moderate postmodernism' indicates nonfoundationalist thought which seeks a rationality appropriate to our postmetaphysical, post-transcendental age; 'strong postmodernism' is more radical inasmuch as it appears to involve an outright rejection of rationality of any kind."[12] Both movements within postmodernism define themselves over and against "modernism," that is, against any attempt "to construct some grand narrative or over-arching theoretical system, one of the *grand recits* of history such as the 'dialectics of the Spirit' or the 'emancipation of the rational.'"[13] In the sharpest contrast to such an approach is the strong postmodern critique.

> The postmodern rebels against all ontotheological meta-narratives and protological-eschatological schemas. It accentuates and celebrates the heteromorphous nature of discourse and life.
>
> Epistemic systematizations and totalizing visions are at base, ontotheological and isomorphic illusions which ultimately seek the obliteration of heterogeneity and *differe(a)nce.* Metaphysics in particular and foundationalism in general are unblinking attempts at congruency and commensurability.[14]

As Fredric Jameson puts it, "The very concept of 'truth' itself is part of the (now discarded) metaphysical baggage. . . . There exists only sheer heteronomy and the emergence of random and unrelated subsystems of all kinds."[15]

Such extreme claims seem to preclude dialogue or even consideration of dialogue for theological purposes, for they undercut even themselves. But why put forward an argument against anything if all reality is "random and unrelated"? How does one reasonably assert there is no rationality? Strong postmodernism will challenge the "contemporary 'subjectivism'" (Heidegger's phrase), the "massive illusion of self-reference," and by this negation it will free "meaning" from its rigid strictures to a "pure movement, the overflowing self-effacement of language."[16]

Both the "divine word" (the agenda of theology) and "human speech" (the subject matter of anthropology) are born of what Derrida denotes as Western man's endemic "logocentrism." In place of all versions of the illusory transcendental signified, or what he elsewhere terms merely "presence" or the "tutelary meaning," Derrida proffers the unlimited "play" of signification itself.[17]

For radical postmodernism, the "semantic notion of the transcendental signified" stems from the "authoritarian sentiment of an eternal and immutable logos permeating the universe" that results in a "spurious meta-physics of self-reference."[18] Language, as that which communicates meaning, and any human subjectivity which may discern such meaning, represent nothing less than the diminishment of both. The core of the radical postmodern critique is a view of language and anthropology as antihuman. Fixed meaning, for anything, is accomplished only by the illusions of a semantic origin or a semantic end. It results in the destruction of the self-moving, creative flow of language, which makes discourse and "the phenomenality of the world, including our own self-awareness, ripples in the void, shudders across a sea of emptiness."[19] This supports a nonreferential view of language: "The spectrum of signification is open at both ends; at no point in the sign-process can we say that the 'meaning' of a sentence, or a text, has been secured."[20] Meaning, therefore, is *difference,* "the moment of difference, the divorce of familiar and alien connotations, the disengagement between the formal lexicon and language as untrammeled, creative force."[21] It is within this difference that a "trace" of meaning is left. "A trace is 'evidence' of something that paradoxically is not present at hand, but conspicuous through its absence. The trace is deposited by the movement of *différance.*"[22]

The moderate postmodern position attempts to utilize rationality and affirms a type of "meaning" but confines it to narrow and paradigm-bound perimeters. Its critique of foundationalist efforts is specifically concerned with the problems of language and history. Of particular concern is the assumption that one can get beyond the self and enter into the meaning of the text through time and culture in a way which can lead to "real" or "objective" knowledge. Any such assumption is marked by dated understandings of language and history, as well as of the human subjectivity determined by both. This is especially true if, according to the postmodern understanding, the relationship between language and experience places language as an absolute requirement and precondition for experience. If language is the boundary-world that confines and determines one's experience, then much that was previously thought accessible (other cultures, historical works in other languages, the thought of the ancients, etc.) is hidden, and our knowledge is revealed as mere projection of the self and its needs. Postmodernism, consequently, severely limits what and how one knows through time and space. The following assertions would be descriptive of moderate postmodernism:

> [I]t takes into serious consideration fundamental postmodern concerns such as the radicalness of historicity, the pervasiveness of ideology, the decentered subject, the rejection of transcendentalism, the encompassing horizons of absence, and the subsequent avoidance of *Identitatsphilosophie.*

> . . . [I]t must be unceasingly stated that reason is exercised in circumstances which are thoroughly finite, conditioned, and historical.

> The moderate postmodern trajectory has appropriated these themes from Heidegger and Wittgenstein, but without giving them the decidedly Nietzschean and antirational flavor of the stronger trajectory. So, the radicalness of historicity, the forestructure of understanding, and the linguisticality of thought are all prominent themes among the moderate postmodernists.[23]

The moderate postmodern approach still presents serious difficulties for much "classical" theology. It finds problematic basic affirmations about the human subject. The human subject is determined by human language and history paradigms, and any thought that these might be transcended is pure fantasy. More specifically, moderate postmodernism finds problematic (if it does not preclude it altogether) the role of language and history in the transmittal of any truth through time and space, let alone the truth of biblical or doctrinal statements. All of this is opposed to the tendency of foundationalist thought to use reason "as the instrument of foundationalist ontology, ruthlessly enforcing transcultural absolutes and relentlessly dominating through the mythology of universal truths."[24]

In its present state, according to Guarino, moderate postmodernism "involves fundamental ontological presuppositions which militate against the type of truth which appears to be integrally linked to a Catholic theology of revelation."[25] What is possible, at least for theology, is a nuanced theological foundationalism "salubriously chastened by postmodernism" that incorporates "the broad horizons of historicity, facticity and paradigm-bound rationality even while maintaining the metaphysical or transcendental subject."[26] Whether and how this might be accomplished will constitute the question for the last section of the present work.

Taking the postmodern critique seriously, and hence emphasizing the limiting role of language and history, is also a concern for David Tracy. The pervasiveness of the postmodern critique partly explains the interest in its challenge.

> If theology is to continue to have a systematically apologetic task, and if that task is to prove adequate to the contemporary postmodern situation, then new criteria for the task are needed. Traditional modern fundamental theologies relied too exclusively on transcendental inquiry—and, too often, models of that inquiry not explicitly related to the questions of language (and thereby plurality and historicity) and questions of history (and thereby ambiguity and postmodern suspicion, not merely modern critique).[27]

Tracy accepts parts of the postmodern critique because of the real need, heretofore largely neglected, to attend to the specifics of history, historicity, and language when doing theology. Only with a method sensitive to the limits of language and history can one understand oneself "as a subject active in history."[28] Anything less than the recognition of these elements fails to take into account the human being as being human *in history*. The admission of one's historical boundaries certainly limits the understanding of historical texts. But the opposite, a move into *ahistoricism*, is even more damaging. Tracy views with greater alarm the faults of an all-encompassing foundationalism that fails to take into account any difference in language or history: in other words, fundamentalism.

Two examples of fundamentalist thought, Romanticism and positivism, serve to illustrate this danger. Both approaches presuppose that language and, subsequently, history are instruments at our disposal. "The romantic uses language to express or represent some deep, nonlinguistic truth inside the self, especially the self of the romantic genius through whom the cosmos expresses itself."[29] The positivist "uses language to articulate and communicate scientific results as facts rather than interpretations."[30] Both approaches view language as secondary to reality, understanding, and history. Fundamentalism is the error of egocentrism in control of an ahistorical, prelinguistic "meaning" and its communication. Paradoxically, Tracy states that "artists—like Kafka with words, Rodin with bronze, and Duncan with dance—may render a new experience or help us name a felt but previously undefined experience." This reference to "a felt but previously undefined experience" is not developed, though if it is meant to designate an immediate prelinguistic experience, it is certainly at odds with a moderate postmodern theory of language, which views language as constructing all experience and such immediacy as not really possible. Fundamentalism, consequently, is not confined only to past approaches to epistemology and hermeneutics. It can be found in contemporary strands of deconstructionism as well.[31]

> The favorite illusion of some deconstructionist thinkers is that they have so freed themselves from history and society that they alone can enjoy the energizing experience of language deconstructing itself. But this is at least as familiar an illusion of Western intellectuals as any claim to full self-presence. It is an illusion challenged by their own rhetorizing of structuralist grammar. It is the illusion that history and society can be kept at bay while we all enjoy the surf of the signifiers. But history and society do not wait upon us. History and society engulf us even as we speak and write.[32]

Against such radical fundamentalism, in both traditional and deconstructionist thought, Tracy describes postmodernity as an "ethics of resistance." "[I]t is resistance, above all, to more of the same, the same unquestioned sameness of the modern turn to the subject, the modern over-belief in the search for a perfect method, the modern social evolutionary narrative whereby all is finally and endlessly more of the self-same."[33]

What now determines all intellectual categories is the postmodern turn to the other and the different—the other and different that were not only neglected by modernist thinkers but even suppressed in an attempt to achieve uniformity of thought and congruity of result. The classical "turn to the subject" is rejected. This new approach immediately eschews all sameness epitomized by overarching systems that ignore difference while trying to achieve the goals of resolution or identity. What was once ignored or at least deemphasized in modernity's quest for all-encompassing claims of identity—difference in language and history—now becomes the determining factor for inquiry. The emphasis on the other and the different calls into question the "grand narrative" of the dominant culture—in our case, the "social evolutionary narrative of modernity." The postmodern critique, for Tracy, is a wake-up call for theologians to respond and utilize contemporary intellectual movements for the benefit of theology: "God's shattering otherness, the neighbor's irreducible otherness, the othering reality of 'revelation,' not the consoling modern communality of 'religion,' all these expressions of otherness come now in new postmodern and post-neoorthodox forms to demand the serious attention of all thoughtful theologians."[34]

An embrace of aspects of the postmodernist critique of theology ultimately benefits theology, for, as Tracy states, "Any transcendental mode of inquiry (like Husserl's) will function well if, and only if, it can account for its own linguistic and historical essence."[35] How a transcendental mode of inquiry might account for its own "linguistic and historical essence" and still maintain its claims in light of the postmodern critique will be explored later. First, it is necessary to view, in its full development, the "turn to the subject" originating in the theology of Friedrich Schleiermacher.

CHAPTER ONE

Schleiermacher and the Turn to the Subject

Thinking, therefore, that what I rejoiced to have found, would, if put in writing, be welcome to some readers, of this very matter, and of some others, I have written the following treatise, in the person of one who strives to lift his mind to the contemplation of God, and seeks to understand what he believes.

—Anselm, *Proslogion*

There lies before me, at this moment, the *Preface* with which I accompanied this work on its first appearance nine years ago. And just because I do not intend to reprint it, I dwell with pleasure on the wish expressed at its conclusion— namely, that, if possible by its own contents, but if not, then by the antagonism which its imperfections must excite, the book might contribute to an ever clearer understanding as to the meaning of our Evangelical Faith.

—Schleiermacher, Preface, *The Christian Faith*

Schleiermacher's theological project tried to retrieve into the vastly differ- ent world of modernity the Anselmian tradition of faith seeking under- standing. The preface to the second edition of *The Christian Faith* set forth this attempt as the guiding goal of this theological inquiry: that the work might contribute to a clearer understanding [*Verständigung*] of the content [*Inhalt*] of the Evangelical faith [*evangelischen Glaubens*]. So on the title page of the first and second German editions Schleiermacher appropriated for himself the maxim of Anselm, a text in which faith and understanding are joined to a third critical term, *experience:* "Nor do I seek to understand [*intel- ligere*] in order that I may believe [*credere*], but I believe in order that I may

11

understand. —For he who does not believe does not experience [*experietur*], and he who does not experience, does not understand."[1]

Experience, faith, and understanding—the medieval theologian supplied the nineteenth-century theologian with the terms that were to constitute the character of his project. Schleiermacher would not repeat or even simply continue the Anselmian tradition; rather, he would transpose it into the world of German Lutheran theology and Enlightenment religious skepticism.

Though often misinterpreted as attempting to establish some objective experiential locus from which religion could be justified, Schleiermacher actually sought a deeper understanding of religion from within Christian life itself. The *fides quaerens intellectum* of Anselm would be transposed into Schleiermacher's dogmatic theology as piety seeking meaning. The experience of God, articulated as the feeling of absolute dependence, leads to a search for knowledge and understanding of the Evangelical faith. Through the experience of piety, in the context of dogmatic theology, Schleiermacher sought a greater understanding of the doctrine articulated in the Evangelical faith in its normative texts. These three variables—experience, faith, and understanding—indicate the problem and the challenge that Schleiermacher's project sought to address. How could these three variables be framed in an effort to understand Evangelical faith in terms of modernity? Schleiermacher's response came in three major works consisting of a new reimagination of religion, a new articulation of dogmatic theology, and a groundbreaking effort in a theory of hermeneutics.[2]

The dominant view of religion as irrelevant to the Romantic search for true humanity was perhaps Schleiermacher's greatest challenge. It prompted his emphasis on "experience." This emphasis would dictate a turn to the subject in his first major work, *On Religion: Speeches to Its Cultured Despisers.*[3] The predominant view of faith that Schleiermacher sought to change was no less of a challenge, for he found that Enlightenment skepticism and rationalism had reduced faith to sterile dogmatic affirmations concerning its object. Such an excessively rationalistic faith, characteristic of modernity, would be rejected. Instead, a subjective, relational faith emerging from human experience would redefine the content of dogmatic theology. But it was not just faith that was the object of exploration, it was Evangelical faith: that is, Lutheran faith, the faith of the Church. Schleiermacher would radically reorient the content of faith by first making it existentially vital to what was truly human. He attempted this reorientation of the content of faith in his major dogmatic work, *The Christian Faith.*[4]

If the need to attend to "experience" dictated the turn to the subject and "faith" indicated the Evangelical faith of the Lutheran Church, "understanding" became interpretation—of religious experience, of Christian dogma, of interpretation itself (i.e., of hermeneutics). How historical texts determined the content of faith became the issue. This prompted an effort by Schleiermacher to develop a new theory of interpretation. The theory would be crucial for the translation of biblical and doctrinal texts, which, in turn, could serve to maintain and increase the piety upon which the Church was grounded. This new effort in interpretation was made possible through the *Hermeneutics.*[5] In each of Schleiermacher's major works (the *Speeches, The Christian Faith,* and the *Hermeneutics*), three critical concerns are always present—experience, faith, and understanding. At times the emphasis falls more on one than on the others, but the three are always present together.

Schleiermacher's project can be understood best through an examination of the turn to the subject in each of these works. The first embodies a turn to the subject through "experience" in a defense of "religion." *On Religion: Speeches to Its Cultured Despisers* introduces a threefold "turn to the subject." I would argue that this turn is partly responsible for the contemporary perimeters of the discussion of experience, its relation to language, and the nature of theological inquiry.[6] The second work, *The Christian Faith,* reframes the content of "faith" through a turn to the subject in the context of dogmatic theology. The third work, the *Hermeneutics,* offers a new approach to human "understanding" through a turn to the subject in an effort to systematize a theory of interpretation.

"RELIGION" AND THE TURN TO THE SUBJECT

The audience and the problem addressed in the *Speeches* require a radical reformulation of religion. The audience for the *Speeches* are those identified in its title as the "Cultured Despisers." They do not struggle or rebel against religion but simply view it as utterly inconsequential to their busy lives.[7] Schleiermacher suggests his view of their attitude and a hint at a possible solution near the beginning of the work:

> I know that you worship the deity in holy silence just as little as you
> visit the forsaken temples, that in your tasteful dwellings there are no
> other household gods than the maxims of the sages and the songs of
> the poets, and that humanity and fatherland, art and science (for you
> imagine yourself capable of all of this) have taken possession of your
> minds so completely that no room is left over for the eternal and holy
> being that for you lies beyond the world, and that you have no feelings
> for and with it.[8]

The Romantic energy of those whom the *Speeches* addresses is focused on
humanity with all its possibilities. "Religion" is irrelevant for the attainment
of true humanity. This marginalization of religion follows from the conviction that the "eternal and holy being" is at a distance. God is "out there"
and therefore not accessible or relevant "here." The unrelatedness of God
has consigned his existence to irrelevance. The distance between God and
humanity implies a lack of any direct encounter with or experience of God that
might lead the audience to believe that "religion" could be understood otherwise. The perception of the holy and eternal being as "out there" and the
view of the human as categorically "here" dominate this audience's view of
religion and close off any possible openness to the "divine."

This attitude is more taken for granted than argued. It dictates that traditional theological apologetics make a radical reversal. A turn to the subjective
experience of religion over its objective expression becomes of utmost importance. An apologetic method focused on the subjective discloses the essence
of the human being as directly related to divine reality. If the audience can be
encouraged to reimagine religion from an experience within the human condition, the chasm between God "out there" and humanity "here" will be nar-
rowed significantly. This new apologetic focus dictates an approach that
emphasizes a basic phenomenology of human existence. Only within a general understanding of human existence can the "essence of religion" be perceived as constitutive of the human being. Thus, Schleiermacher can say, "Let
us repair to humanity, that we may find the material for religion."[9]

Throughout the *Speeches* the humanizing effect of religion is emphasized
in general. The Church, as a communal realization of this, is emphasized in
particular.[10] The goal of the *Speeches* is to defend religion from within religion itself: that is, to re-present the nature of religion and better capture its
essence *for the times.* The essence of religion, says the *Speeches,* needs to be

distinguished from the broken attempts at living it out in the world: "Let us, then, I beg you, examine whence your contempt properly originates, from the individual or the whole? Does it start with differing types and sects of religion as they have been in the world or from the concept itself?"[11]

A defense of religion from within the very idea of religion itself is Schleiermacher's first goal. Drawing members to the Evangelical faith or, minimally, at least to a better view of the Church, is also important.[12] While arguments to the intellect might fail for a variety of reasons, Schleiermacher knows that membership in the Christian community allows one the possibility to experience the essence of religion that is so thoroughly misunderstood. In a letter to Henrietta Herz in April 1799, just before the completion of the *Speeches*, he writes of his efforts concerning the fourth speech, "On the Social Element in Religion, or, On Church and Priesthood": "I will entirely recast the fourth; for there ought to be something more elevating in it than you all seem to have found; and it must be my fault that you have not found it. The Church ought to be the most exalted of all human institutions and concerns, and I must work out a representation of it as such."[13]

Before this uplifting function of the Church can be realized, Schleiermacher must articulate an understanding of human existence in which an experience of God is both accessible and normative. This is the key to the appeal to human experience in defense of religion. He will try to reimagine and ground religion within a Kantian construct. Whatever objective data are dealt with by the mind are experienced through the forms and concepts conferred by the subject.[14] But Schleiermacher goes even further by grounding his method in the human experience of God that occurs in the interiority of the subject and is accessible through simple reflection on the fact of existence. This becomes the comprehensive principle by which religion is redefined.[15] It is this appeal to inner experience that made Schleiermacher's apology for religion so effective.

Thus Schleiermacher states:

What I assert and what I should like to establish for religion include the following: It springs necessarily and by itself from the *interior* of every better soul, it has its own province in the mind in which it reigns sovereign, and it is worthy of moving the noblest and the most excellent by means of its innermost power and by having its innermost essence known by them.[16]

The "essence of religion" possesses its "own province" and emerges from the interiority of each human being.[17] It is this specific province of interiority that distinguishes religion from classical metaphysics and Christian morality. Such a distinction serves to avoid the past mistake of conflating religion with either or both. This, in turn, prompts a turn toward the subject, to the "interior of every better soul" where the essence of religion resides.[18]

The nature of religion is not found in speculation put forward by the "schools." It is not found in a metaphysics divorced from the real that originates from "nurseries of the dead letter," nor in a morality.[19] Rather, former understandings of "religion" must be avoided. "I ask, therefore, that turning away from all that is usually called religion you aim your attention only at these individual intimations and moods that you will find in all expressions and noble deeds of God-inspired persons."[20] True religion is different from organized sects and their interminable conflicts. True religion is the possibility for an elevated and true humanity. It is not a stifling system of outdated rules and regulations or the dark, historical conflicts resulting from confessional infighting.[21]

This reimagination of religion allows one to understand religion, not for what it can accomplish in terms of either imparting a certain power or supporting a particular moral end, but simply for what it is in itself.[22] This bypasses a utilitarian argument for "religion" and directly contrasts with traditional presentations that emphasize either metaphysical information or ethical usefulness.[23]

> If you put yourselves on the highest standpoint of metaphysics and morals, you will find that both have the same subject as religion, namely, the universe and the relationship of humanity to it. This similarity has long since been a basis of manifold aberrations; metaphysics and morals have therefore invaded religion on many occasions, and much that belongs to religion has concealed itself in metaphysics or morals under an unseemly form. But shall you, for this reason, believe that it is identical with the one or the other? I know that your instinct tells the contrary, and it also follows from your opinions; for you never admit that religion walks with the firm step of which metaphysics is capable, and you do not forget to observe diligently that there are quite a few ugly immoral blemishes on its history.[24]

Metaphysics loses the meaning of religion in its *excessive* rationalization of "essences," "natures," "reasons," and "deductions." Morality uses, and sometimes misuses, the universe "to derive duties" and construct codes of laws. When confused with "religion," both result in human constructions aimed at bringing clarity to existence either through a classification of being or through a code of laws. "Religion," conversely,

> does not wish to determine and explain the universe according to its nature as does metaphysics; it does not desire to continue the universe's development and perfect it by the power of freedom and the divine free choice of a human being as does morals. Religion's essence is neither thinking nor acting, but intuition and feeling.[25]

This does not preclude knowing and doing as essential to human nature and even essential to the expression of the experience of religion: "Only when it places itself next to both of them is the common ground perfectly filled out and human nature completed from this dimension. Religion shows itself to you as the necessary and indispensable third next to those two, as their natural counterpart, not slighter in worth and splendor than you wish of them."[26] And again: "Praxis is an art, speculation is a science, religion is the sensibility and taste for the infinite. Without religion, how can praxis rise above the common circle of adventurous and customary forms? How can speculation become anything better than a stiff and barren skeleton?"[27] The turn away from objects in terms of either metaphysics (knowledge) or morality (praxis) dictates a turn to the subject. It is in the interior experience of being human that the essence of religion can be discovered.

Humanity possesses two orientations or forces that define it. "The one strives to draw into itself everything that surrounds it, ensnaring it in its own life and, wherever possible, wholly absorbing it into its innermost being."[28] A human being internalizes elements that surround his or her existence, and these elements, which include language and learned behavior, actually come to constitute him or her to a certain degree. This absorbing force is counterbalanced by another that "longs to extend its own inner-self ever further, thereby permeating and imparting to everything from within, while never being exhausted itself."[29] This aspect of being human transcends the particular to participate in the universal. The first drive "strives after individual things that bend toward it; it is quieted so long as it has grasped one of them."[30] The second drive "overlooks individual things and manifestations just because it penetrates them and finds everywhere only the forces and entities on which its own force breaks; it wants to penetrate and to fill everything with reason and freedom, and thus it proceeds directly to the infinite and at all times seeks and produces freedom and coherence, power and law, right and suitability."[31]

These general orientations define human being: one moves to absorb the finite and particular, while the other strives to penetrate the infinite and universal. These "two original functions of spiritual nature" are present in every human being in an infinite variety. If the drive that strives to absorb individual things entirely dominates, a materialism and a deification of the individual occur that never move "beyond perceptions of the individual phenomenon."[32] If the drive that transcends the individual completely dominates— if an "uncultivated enthusiasm" reigns supreme—the result is a restless flitting toward empty ideals.

But when both forces combine in "a fruitful manner," as they do, for example, in extraordinary historical figures, such figures can actually function as mediators between limited reality and infinite possibility: "Thus they become heroes, lawgivers, inventors, conquerors of nature, and benevolent genies who quietly create and disseminate a nobler happiness. By their mere existence such people prove themselves to be ambassadors of God and mediators between limited man and infinite humanity."[33] The mediators' "force of attraction," counterbalanced by their "spiritual penetration," serves to wake people from their monotony and inspire them to a "better humanity."[34] Those who move deeper into the finite/infinite dialectic through flights of the spirit and attempt to record such a movement through creative dynamism epitomize the most effective mediators. "Such people are true priests of the Most High, for they bring deity closer to those who normally grasp only the finite and trivial."[35] This mediation of a better humanity is only possible through what is most neglected by the audience of the *Speeches*—religion.

Thus, religion elevates the human activities of both speculation (metaphysics) and praxis (morality) because religion precedes and informs both of them. It does so through two specific faculties—intuition and feeling. Intuition and feeling discern the finite and infinite dimensions of reality. If "everything finite exists only through the determination of its limits, which must, as it were, 'be cut out of' the infinite," then intuition and feeling make accessible a definition of religion.[36] When these two terms are understood correctly, religion can be properly conceived.

Schleiermacher asserts in the *Speeches* that "everything must proceed from intuition, and those who lack the desire to intuit the infinite have no touchstone and indeed need none in order to know whether they have given any respectable thought to the matter."[37] Intuition in general is "the immediate perception, nothing more."[38] It proceeds "from an influence of the intuited on the one who intuits from an original and independent action of the former, which is then grasped, apprehended, and conceived by the latter according to one's own nature."[39] We intuit, not the nature of things, "but their action upon [us]."[40] Furthermore, we intuit not only isolated effects but also the interrelatedness of the universe. This is the essence of religion.

> The universe exists in uninterrupted activity and reveals itself to us every moment. Every form that it brings forth, every being to which it gives a separate existence according to the fullness of life, every occurrence that spills forth from its rich, ever-fruitful womb, is an action of the same upon us. Thus to accept everything individual as a part of the whole and everything limited as a representation of the infinite is religion.[41]

Religion begins with what is actually given to the subject who accepts and apprehends it in a particular way. Furthermore, intuition includes a propensity or drive that, "if oriented to the infinite, places the mind in unlimited freedom; only religion saves it from the most ignominious fetters of opinion and desire."[42] The intuition out of which religion emerges is an immediate perception of the action of the universe upon oneself. If this is continually sought and correctly oriented, it releases the mind in unlimited freedom. This unlimited freedom is the experience of the infinite, an experience of wholeness, completeness, of that in which nothing is lacking and all is given. Religion "is infinite in all respects, an infinity of matter and form, of being, of vision, and of knowledge about it."[43] Participation in this possibility of wholeness is made possible through feeling.

Feeling, the companion term of *intuition* in the *Speeches*, is intimately connected with intuition. The two terms cannot be understood without each other.

> Finally, to complete the general picture of religion, recall that every intuition is, by its very nature, connected with a feeling. Your senses mediate the connection between the object and yourselves; the same influence of

the object, which reveals its existence to you, must stimulate them in various ways and produce a change in your inner-consciousness. This feeling, of which you are frequently scarcely aware, can in other cases grow
to such intensity that you forget both the object and yourselves because
of it; your whole nervous system can be so permeated by it that for a
long time that sensation alone dominates and resounds and resists the
effect of other impressions. But that an action is brought forth in you,
that the internally generated activity of your spirit is set in motion,
surely you will not ascribe this to the influence of external objects?[44]

The object of intuition moves to the inner-consciousness via the senses and
results in the emergence of "feeling." The intensity of certain feelings points
toward the "internal" generation of activity: that is, to the generation of feeling
from a source that transcends any possible external finite object. Certain "feelings" originate elsewhere. Because the human is "scarcely aware" of feeling as
the product of external stimulation, there is even less awareness of its source in
moments of heightened inner-consciousness. The difficulty in grasping this
"feeling" is evident in how it is described. Both words—*intuition* and *feeling*—
describe a single experience, which for the purpose of explication, must be distinguished as two "moments" in an effort to recapture its parts.
    Experiences of interiority, or of the "inner self," present serious problems
for communication. The paradox of experience, however conceived as a theological source, lies in the difficulty of communicating internal events and
their phenomena. This difficulty requires the recognition that an experience
and the subsequent reflection upon that experience are two different realities.[45] "[P]ermit me first for a moment to mourn the fact that I cannot speak
of both [intuition and feeling] other than separately."[46] The original, unified,
and prelinguistic experience is distinct from and inaccessible to thought and
speech. But it is present in intuition and feeling. This original experience separates naturally into two aspects immediately upon reflection—a reflection
through which it necessarily moves before any communication in speech is
possible. Paradoxically, language communicates (always insufficiently) a
level of interiority that is prior to and exclusive of linguistic structuring. This
fact always results in only partial translations of the original "experience."

The finest spirit of religion is thereby lost for my speech, and I can dis-
close its innermost secret only unsteadily and uncertainly. But *reflection*

necessarily separates both; and who can speak about something that belongs to consciousness without first going through this medium. Not only when we communicate an inner action of the mind, but even when we merely turn it into material for contemplation within ourselves and wish to raise it to lucid consciousness, this unavoidable separation immediately occurs.[47]

The experience of religion cannot be enclosed in reflection or through the expression of such reflection in language. Both reflection and language are simply insufficient. Not only does language fail to describe this experience approximately, it cannot even find the possibility—it is "lost to my speech." Thus, the description of the experience of religion in the *Speeches* is always suggestive—and never satisfactory. There is a tension between an original experience and the process of reflection and communication that follows.

That first mysterious moment that occurs in every sensory perception, before intuition and feeling have separated, where sense and its objects have, as it were, flowed into one another and become one, before both turn back to their original position—I know how indescribable it is and how quickly it passes away. But I wish that you were able to hold onto it and also recognize it again in the higher and divine religious activity of the mind. Would that I could and might express it, at least indicate it, without having to desecrate it![48]

At the secondary level, one's reflection reveals that one intuits/feels acted upon by the world—and, in some cases, that one does not feel completely at one's own disposal. This primary, unified experience is prior to any differentiation between subject and object. Differentiation occurs only at the secondary level.[49] For example, when reflecting on a reality that comes into contact with our individual existence, "the simplest matter separates itself into two opposing elements, the one combining into an image of an object (intuition), the other penetrating to the center of our being, there to effervesce with our original drives and to develop a transient feeling."[50] This unified experience is spoken of in two parts.[51]

"Dependence," for Schleiermacher, emerges directly from a correct interpretation of feeling, which previously was "thoroughly misunderstood."[52] When feeling is properly understood, "our self, . . . in comparison with the universe, disappears into infinite smallness." The result of such a realization is "true unaffected humility." This revelation of our place in the universe prompts a new understanding of other human beings.

> When we also perceive our fellow creatures in the intuition of the world and it is clear to us how each of them without distinction is his own representation of humanity just as we are, and how we would have to dispense with intuiting this humanity without the existence of each one, what is more natural than to embrace them all with heartfelt love and affection without any distinction of disposition and spiritual power?[53]

The dual realization of one's distinct place in the universe and one's gratitude for the existence of others results in the feeling of *dependence.* It is the realization that one's "self" is only a part of the whole and that the whole is necessary for "self." If others are necessary for the realization of our own finitude and smallness, then each person is necessary for any true experience of religion. Human beings mediate an awareness of the divine. Dependence acknowledges that the "autonomous" self is, in fact, not autonomous. Rather, the self is deeply indebted to others for the possibility of "religion," which elevates the subject to a better humanity.

Such a description of human existence is ultimately confirmed by a biblical source. It was Adam's experience of humanity through which "God" became accessible: "In the flesh and bone of his bone (Eve) he discovered humanity, and in humanity the world; from this moment on he became capable of hearing the voice of the deity and of answering it, and the most sacrilegious transgression of its laws from now on no longer precluded him from association with the eternal being."[54] Only through an encounter with others can the human encounter God. Without Eve, Adam could not have associated with the Eternal. The possibility of having a "feeling of dependence" diminishes greatly if one refuses to encounter others. Those who "fortify and surround themselves with many external deeds, so that they might conduct their isolated lives" have refused an openness to give themselves over to a dependence that can actually free them.[55]

Isolated lives cannot come to an awareness of the intuition of the universe. "Religion" does not occur solely between the individual and divine reality. Thus, the interhuman dimension of experience is not only important but necessary for "true religion."

This is why both are so deeply and indissolubly connected, longing for religion is what helps him to the enjoyment of religion. Each person embraces most ardently the one in whom the world is reflected most clearly and purely; each loves most tenderly the one in whom he believes he finds everything brought together that he himself lacks for the completion of humanity. Therefore, let us repair to humanity, that we may find the material for religion.[56]

The communal or relational element in the *Speeches* is vital for the defense of religion. First, the discussion of religion occurs for the individual (something morality is excessively consumed with) in direct relation to the communal. Loving another is described in *revelational* terms ("the one in whom the world is reflected most clearly and purely") and establishes the condition for the possibility of religion as well as later introducing the possibility of an ultimate human mediator to the divine.[57] This directly leads to one implicit Christological reference—the "rejected concept" of a human who could be "the mediator between your limited way of thinking and the eternal limits of the world."[58]

The humanizing dimension in the communal aspect of this reimagination of "religion" is crucial for an audience that lacks interest in the topic. "Bring them back to religion. . . . Religion is not the servant of morals or anything else that is an object of human action, but the indispensable friend and their unexceptional advocate and intermediary with humanity."[59] The argument of the *Speeches* directly connects the universe to inner subjectivity. Knowledge and experience of one lead to the other. This ultimately moves toward a glimpse of infinity through the feeling of dependence that elevates humanity. Individual experience can include an ever-deeper realization of the divine that moves one closer to human interdependence.

In summary, "religion," which traditionally pertained to faith, revelation, and its relationship to morality and metaphysics, has undergone a major reformulation in Schleiermacher's *Speeches*. Religion is not the "system" of speculation that the audience assumes it to be but is instead that which makes possible anything really human. "I have shown you what religion actually is. Have you found anything therein that would be unworthy of your highest human formation?"[60]

A turn away from objects (metaphysics) and actions (morals) results in a turn to the subject's interior experience. The human subject is the actualization of two distinct forces. One force draws reality within and is concerned with the particular and finite, while the other transcends external material reality and is concerned with the universal and infinite. The essence of religion, consequently, is conceived in the unity of intuition and feeling—each corresponding to an aforementioned force.

Intuition and *feeling* designate a unified, original, prereflexive experience that emerges from the interiority of a person in the encounter with the world. And though language may attempt to describe and communicate such an experience, it is finally insufficient. For this experience is not only prior to language but is prior even to subject/object differentiation. Furthermore, this experience is universal: it is accessible to every human being. It will thus serve as the comprehensive principle through which *religion* is redefined. A person's particular religious "sense" is higher when a gratitude for the revelatory value of other human beings is realized in dependence. The role of "mediator" is given to those gifted enough to reveal true knowledge concerning the relation of the human and the divine. The Church is the community of people who share a similar approach to the divine through the experience of intuition/feeling and its resulting feeling of dependence.[61] The task of the *Speeches*, consequently, is apologetical. It hopes to redefine religion as that which humanizes the human while rejecting previous notions deemed unacceptable by its "despisers."[62]

Three topics emerge from the *Speeches* that will figure in all subsequent sections. The first is an understanding of the experience of the infinite as something universal. In principle, the experience of intuition/feeling is accessible to all. There is an essential experience of being human that all people share and from which religion may emerge. For the *Speeches*, a specific understanding of human being makes possible the location of the "essence of religion" in human interiority. Thus, there is an essential relation between the human and the divine. This location of the essence of religion is made intelligible by the second topic: the description of the particular "experience" and its relationship to language and thought.

The essence of religion is articulated through language. A priority is assumed for experience, while language is understood as, ultimately, descriptive. Language can facilitate the recognition of a particular experience of the infinite, but it does not constitute such experience. This conception of the relationship of experience to language makes possible an appeal to an experience of God that is foundational as well as accessible to the reader/hearer of the *Speeches*. Simple reflection on inner-consciousness in the context of community allows one immediate access to the experience of "religion."

The nature of theology, the third topic, emerges from, informs, and in part determines the previous two topics. The apologetical nature of the theological task determines an argument that takes seriously the audience—the "despisers." It does so by framing the elevation of the human condition as the possibility for true "religion." Thus, what "religion" gives human beings is a comprehensive principle by which all religious statements can be evaluated and understood. This presupposes an absolute subject, experience as prior to language, and a particular understanding of religion that will deeply affect the nature of theology. How this can be applied to a specifically Christian Church becomes the function of dogmatic theology.

Focused as it is on "religion," the *Speeches* fails to provide a sufficient basis for a specifically *Christian* dogmatic starting point for theology. It does provide the basis for construing religion independently of any particular appeal to extrinsic religious authority.[63] But it is insufficient for a systematic explication of Christian doctrine. Only the last ten pages of the *Speeches* directly address Christianity, and that section leaves more questions than helpful answers.[64] The problems associated with the latter points, evident toward the conclusion of the *Speeches*, are addressed by the second moment of Schleiermacher's project—a turn to the subject through the content of "faith" in his major work of dogmatic theology, *The Christian Faith*.

"DOGMATIC THEOLOGY" AND THE TURN TO THE SUBJECT

The audience for *The Christian Faith*, the "leaders" of the Church, were those who combined the necessary skills of learning and research with the vital practical skills of preaching and teaching. Their challenge was to teach and preach a new content of faith. Their goal was to make it existentially relevant to Christian piety and free from meaningless and useless dogma and to put aside the sterility of an outdated, objective faith in favor of a more immediate, subjective faith. Pastors, theologians, and advanced seminary students were offered a radically new way of ministering to their respective communities. Dogmatic theology, for Schleiermacher, was theology that maintained and cultivated communal piety. *The Christian Faith* tried to offer the best method by which that might be accomplished. Its first task was to redefine

Church. Its second task was to offer an interpretation of human existence through which the experiential emphasis on communal piety could be developed as the guideline for doctrinal understanding and assessment.

According to Schleiermacher, the Church had concerned itself for too long with exterior objects and actions in terms of either metaphysics or morality. One had to instead turn inward to rediscover the purpose of "Church." The cultivation and communication of piety would become the sole purpose of Church. The "feeling of dependence" that had been described in the *Speeches* would mature. It would come to designate the experience of God at the most advanced stage of religion: the "feeling of absolute dependence," the essence of piety, described in *The Christian Faith*. This highest stage of self-consciousness was the necessary dogmatic transposition of what had begun as a general defense of "religion" in the *Speeches*. The content of faith could now be redefined and understood in terms of this experience of God.

Schleiermacher acknowledged the priority of faith in this quest for deeper understanding. He emphasized the feeling of absolute dependence and faith. The context of faith is made up of the unity between the individual experience of God and the Christian community.

> Our proposition says nothing of any intermediate link between faith and participation in the Christian communion, and is accordingly to be taken as directly combining the two, so that faith of itself carries with it that participation; and not only as depending on the spontaneous activity of the man who has become a believer, but also as depending on the spontaneous activity of the communion (Church), as the source from which the testimony proceeded for the awakening of faith.[65]

Faith, defined by Schleiermacher, is "nothing but the certainty concerning the feeling of absolute dependence."[66] This certainty comes only through participation in the Christian community. "To participate in Christian communion means to seek in Christ's institution an approximation to the above-described state of absolute facility and constancy of religious emotions."[67] What is necessary for this faith is (1) to realize the need for redemption and (2) to acknowledge that this has occurred in Christ.[68] While the feeling of absolute dependence may occur outside the community, any *certainty* regarding the redemptive efficacy of this experience does not. Preaching initiates this discovery of needing redemption and finding it in Christ.

Communal piety occupies a central position in *The Christian Faith*. Dogmatic theology maintains, regulates, and advances Christian piety at the present time. Human love builds to the possibility of experiencing God at the highest level of self-consciousness, the feeling of absolute dependence, and is most fully realized in a Christian community of shared piety. Piety seeking the meaning of the Evangelical faith is a search that presupposes such faith and membership in that community. For this reason Schleiermacher can say with Anselm, "I do not seek to understand so that I may believe, but I believe so that I may understand; and what is more, I believe that unless I do believe I shall not understand."[69] But Schleiermacher concentrates on piety as occurring *coterminously* with the believing and *before* the search for understanding, in the experiencing of belief in community. The experience of God, the feeling of absolute dependence, can culminate in the certainty of faith. This can then lead to greater understanding. If the people of Schleiermacher's time could experience God through communal piety, both belief and understanding would benefit.

In *On the Glaubenslehre: Letters to Lücke,* Schleiermacher states that the goal of the introduction is "to establish a principle for determining what is valid in all the modifications of Christian self-consciousness and what is not present except within that consciousness."[70] The prolegomena (sections 2–31) of this work, defined as philosophical theology, does three things. It identifies the theological discipline and its sources; it offers a new articulation of human subjectivity; and, finally, it further differentiates communal manifestations of "piety." Schleiermacher specifies at length that this philosophical theology should not be confused with dogmatic theology.[71]

Theology, for Schleiermacher, is first of all positive.[72] It is not merely theoretical, empirical, or speculative; rather, it refers to actual historical experience. Such experience occurs within given social relationships, and reflection upon it serves a definite practical function. Overall, theology is conceived as a three-part coherent whole: "*Historical* theology is the actual corpus of theological study which is connected with science by means of *philosophical* theology and with the active life by means of *practical* theology."[73]

The prolegomena, the philosophical theology, establishes the foundation upon which the understanding of dogmatic theology rests in *The Christian Faith*. Specifically, it is the apologetical aspect of philosophical theology that investigates "the distinctive nature of Christianity, and likewise of Protestantism."[74] If dogmatic theology addresses the current God-consciousness of the Church, philosophical theology first defines the presuppositions for such an address. What is the Church? What is the human being? What draws the individual to the Church, and how does one arrive at such a conception? The Church is central to the nature of being human, and being human necessarily includes piety. Thus, in the context of the Church, this piety as constitutive of the human being is the object of dogmatic theology. "Since Dogmatics is a theological discipline, and thus pertains solely to the Christian Church, we can only explain what it is when we have become clear as to the conception of the Christian Church."[75]

A "definition of Dogmatics" first depends upon the "conception of the Christian Church, in order to define in accordance therewith what Dogmatics should be and should do within that Church."[76] The concept of Church is derived from "Ethics," "since in every case the 'Church' is a society which originates only through free human action and which can only through such continue to exist."[77] The application of "borrowed propositions, i.e., propositions which belong to other scientific studies, in this case to Ethics, Philosophy of Religion, and Apologetics," further defines communal piety.[78]

The promotion of piety in the context of Church is the purpose of dogmatic theology.[79] Therefore, a specific understanding of the essence of the Church is necessary to explain the nature of piety inherent to the human subject. The particular description of human existence in turn requires an articulation of the experience of God rooted in human existence and consistent with the description given. This experience of God will be the comprehensive principle for how *Church* will be understood. Most important for the dogmatic task, the experience of God—that is, Christian piety—becomes the principle that determines the assessment of all relevant doctrine.

The Church is "nothing but a communion or association relating to religion or piety."[80] The Church is not focused on objects (metaphysics), actions (morals), or "outward organization" (state). While these are important, they are not the duties of the Church. Instead, one must turn inward to the experience that constitutes the essence of the Church—piety. This piety is accessible through a new understanding of human subjectivity.

Two concepts are necessary for this examination of piety: feeling and self-consciousness: "The piety which forms the basis of all ecclesiastical communions is, considered purely in itself, neither a Knowing nor a Doing, but a modification of Feeling, or of immediate self-consciousness."[81] Both components are necessary, and they are necessary together, for both speak of the immediate self-consciousness of the subject that is neither objective nor representative nor unconscious. *Feeling* describes the nonobjective sense of this state (i.e., its immediacy), while *self-consciousness* describes an ongoing prerepresentational awareness of it. Together, the two point to a state of self-consciousness that is prior to representative consciousness even of the self.

For Schleiermacher, knowing and feeling on the one hand and doing on the other constitute the total consciousness of the human subject.[82] Knowing and feeling are the forms of consciousness that signify "an abiding-in-self," while doing signifies a "passing-beyond-self."[83] The subject (self) therefore lives reality through these two aspects of being—that through which reality is received and that through which action is performed.[84] Because "feeling" occurs totally in the realm of receptivity, it is completely an "abiding-in-self," and "in this sense it stands alone in antithesis to the other two—knowing and doing."[85] Feeling is described *analogously* as a self-consciousness that is immediate, and though immediate self-consciousness and feeling are not synonymous, they are equivalent: that is, they point to a similar experience.

> [T]o the term "self-consciousness" is added the determining epithet "immediate," lest anyone should think of a kind of self-consciousness which is not feeling at all; as, e.g., when the name of self-consciousness is given to that consciousness of self which is more like an objective consciousness, being a representation of oneself, and thus mediated by self-contemplation.[86]

The prereflexive nature of feeling, or immediate self-consciousness, are found in joy and sorrow as genuine states of immediate self-consciousness. At the moment when reflection encounters those same "mental phases," an entirely different phenomenon occurs:

> In the first place, it is *everybody's experience* [italics added] that there are moments in which all thinking and willing retreat behind a self-consciousness of one form or another; but, in the second place, that at times this same form of self-consciousness persists unaltered during a series of diverse acts of thinking and willing, taking up no relation to these, and thus not being in the proper sense even an accompaniment of them. Thus joy and sorrow—those mental phases which are always so important in the realm of religion—are genuine states of feeling,

in the proper sense explained above; whereas self-approval and self-reproach, apart from their subsequently passing into joy and sorrow, belong in themselves rather to the objective self-consciousness of self, as results from analytic contemplation.[87]

With this observation, one that will be a constant throughout this work, is an experience so common that general appeal can be made to it. References are continually made to "every self-consciousness,"[88] to individuals who in general "resemble each other in variable degrees,"[89] and to the tendency of the human mind "to give rise to religious emotions."[90] All these references point toward an understanding of a universal human subjectivity grounding religion. "For every man has in him all another man has, but it is all differently determined; and the greatest similarity is only a diminishing or (relatively) vanishing difference."[91] Piety, which is a particular determination of "feeling," together with knowing and doing, constitutes the unity that is "the essence of the subject itself."[92]

Within this common nature, piety is a particular determination of "feeling," though it is not isolated from the other two elements, for "it will fall to piety to stimulate knowing and doing, and every moment in which piety has a predominant place will contain within itself one or both of these in germ."[93] The relationship of piety to knowing and doing is important, for the argument for "God-consciousness" is grounded upon it: "[T]here are both a Knowing and a Doing which pertain to piety, but neither of these constitutes the essence of piety: they only pertain to it inasmuch as the stirred-up Feeling sometimes comes to rest in a thinking which fixes it, sometimes discharges itself in an action which expresses it."[94] Strictly speaking, piety remains essentially a state of feeling, though all modes of human consciousness are affected. If no subordination is intended, piety could be understood as "the state in which knowing, feeling, and doing are combined."[95] The unity of these various elements is the "essence of the subject itself, which manifests itself in those severally distinct forms, and is thus, to give it a name which in this particular is permissible, their common foundation."[96] Thus, in the subject, Christian piety is directly linked to Christian belief and Christian action, but it is not equivalent to either. For example, if piety "did consist in Knowing . . . the most perfect master of Christian Dogmatics would always be likewise the most pious Christian. And no one will admit this to be the case."[97] Piety maintains its own integrity in the interiority of the human condition. It not only undergirds all thinking and willing but can also be prereflexively unrelated: that is, it is dependent on neither thinking nor willing for its existence. Piety is prereflexively informative of both. When it emerges, it can make any living moment a religious one. While this piety claims a particular aspect of interiority for its own, there are various representations of it. To allow piety to be a useful element for grounding the content of faith, it is first necessary to delineate exactly what is common to all its variations. "The common element in all howsoever diverse expressions of piety, by which these are conjointly distinguished from all other feelings, or, in other words, the self-identical essence of piety is this: the consciousness of being absolutely dependent, or, which is the same thing, of being in relation with God."[98]

The three elements of the soul have been identified, and piety has been seen as a determination of feeling. But how can piety be articulated so as to be informative and normative? The once-used term *dependence* from the *Speeches* is now transposed into *The Christian Faith* more specifically and in greater detail to indicate a "feeling of absolute dependence." The same difficulty of isolating and describing a particular consciousness apart from knowing and doing—that is, prior to language—is again evident.

> If, however, word and idea are always originally one, and the term "God" therefore presupposes an idea, then we shall simply say that this idea, which is nothing more than the expression of the feeling of absolute dependence, is the most direct reflection upon it and the most original idea with which we are here concerned, and is quite independent of original knowledge (properly so called), and conditioned only by our feeling of absolute dependence.[99]

Being in relation to God, a particular determination of feeling, is expressed through language and thought. This is especially true when this God-consciousness originates in an interiority that is prereflexive and prelinguistic. But how can the actual describe the possible—prior to actuality? First, one must recognize that the experience or essence of piety cannot be isolated in a particular moment as such; second, it is only because of *change* (i.e., causality) that we are able to identify it at all.

Two critical aspects of existence dominate every state of consciousness. The first is an awareness of the subject's unchanging identity. The second is an awareness of the subject's ever-changing state of being.[100] "The Ego in itself can be represented objectively; but every consciousness of self is at the same time the consciousness of a variable state of being."[101] Thus, in every human subject there are two elements, "a self-caused element" and a "non-self-caused element," or a "Being and a Having-by-some-means-come-to-be." "The latter of these presupposes for every self-consciousness another factor besides the Ego, a factor which is the source [*woher*] of the particular determination, and without which the self-consciousness would not be precisely what it is."[102] Change indicates that we determine and *are determined,* we act and *are acted upon,* we go out of ourselves and *receive into ourselves.* The movement out of ourselves is activity designated as "freedom." The receptivity of outside forces moving inward is designated as "dependence."[103] This movement out of ourselves is freedom because it "expresses the existence of the subject for itself." The receptivity is identified as dependence because it expresses a "co-existence with an Other."[104] What is common to all diverse representations of piety, therefore, is the consciousness of our dependence. *Whether we receive or act, both depend on something first being given to the subject.* There is a priority to reception.

> But as we never do exist except along with an Other, so even in every outward-tending self-consciousness the element of receptivity, in some way or other affected, is the primary one; and even the self-consciousness which accompanies an action, while it predominantly expresses spontaneous movement and activity, is always related to a prior moment of affective receptivity, through which the original "agility" received its direction.[105]

This give-and-receive existence, this total self-consciousness, is a "reciprocity between the subject and the corresponding Other."[106] There is the self and the Other. Therefore, life in varying degrees is an acting and a being acted upon. Within this finite world the balance might shift dramatically, but it never reaches an absolute state, for even "towards all the forces of Nature—even, we may say, towards the heavenly bodies—we ourselves do, in the same sense in which they influence us, exercise a counter-influence, however minute."[107]

Within the finite world there is neither an absolute freedom nor an absolute dependence, for we can invariably influence something or someone, however minutely, and likewise may be influenced. Absolute freedom is impossible, for if the feeling of freedom "expresses a forth-going activity, this activity must have an object which has been given to us, and this could not have taken place without an influence of the object upon our receptivity."[108] In this sense, a feeling of dependence always accompanies a moment of freedom. The inverse may seem to be true, but then Schleiermacher asserts the comprehensive principle that determines his entire system of dogmatic theology:

> Hence a feeling of absolute dependence, strictly speaking, cannot exist in a single moment as such, because such a moment is always determined, as it regards its total content, by what is given, and thus by objects towards which we have a feeling of freedom. But the self-consciousness which accompanies all our activity, and therefore, since that is never zero, accompanies our whole existence, and negatives absolute freedom is itself precisely a consciousness of absolute dependence; for it is the consciousness that the whole of our spontaneous activity comes from a source outside of us in just the same sense in which anything towards which we should have a feeling of absolute freedom must have proceeded entirely from ourselves. But without any feeling of freedom a feeling of absolute dependence would not be possible.[109]

The source of this essence of piety, this feeling of absolute dependence, can be designated as God, for "the Whence of our receptive and active existence, as implied in this self-consciousness, is to be designated by the word 'God,' and this is for us the really original signification of that word."[110] Absolute dependence includes "all others in itself"; it combines the "God-consciousness in the self-consciousness" in such a way that the two can never be separated.[111]

The feeling of absolute dependence is the common element in all diverse expressions of piety. It is the copresence of God in the immediate self-consciousness of the subject. This is explicitly given in one's experience of existing as one who determines and is determined. Thus, one experiences always and absolutely a dependence on an Other through a determination of "feeling" that grounds both knowing and doing. This Other is designated with the name God. It is in this way that "God is given to us in feeling in an original way."[112]

The "feeling of absolute dependence," the essence of piety in *The Christian Faith*, is also of the essence of the human.[113] And though it is isolated in a description of the individual human being, it has a direct connection to the social nature of the human as well. Piety necessitates community, which, in turn, informs, maintains, and cultivates piety. The possibility of dogmatic theology occurs in the transition from individual piety (which never happens in solitude) to the communal realization of piety in "Church." "The religious self-consciousness, like every essential element in human nature, leads necessarily in its development to fellowship or communion; a communion which, on the one hand, is variable and fluid, and, on the other hand, has definite limits, i.e., is a Church."[114]

The religious self-consciousness is essential to human nature. It is not merely accidental. "Fellowship is demanded by the *consciousness of kind* which dwells in every man, and which finds its satisfaction only when he steps forth beyond the limits of his own personality and takes up the facts of other personalities into his own."[115] Everything "inward" is eventually expressed "outward" and becomes a "revelation of the inward." Expression of interiority is a hallmark of the human condition. The human being is social by nature. The movement "outward" is not a choice but rather the product of an "inward agitation." The need to share one's self begins with bare expression and moves into a living imitation prompted by a consciousness of kind. All people participate in this process of both expressing and perceiving and are therefore always "involved in a multifarious communion of feeling, as a condition quite in conformity with [their] nature."[116] While the feeling of absolute dependence is of the essence for the individual human, it is first awakened, *though not initially constituted or caused*, through expression and utterance in community. "As regards the feeling of absolute dependence in particular, everyone will know that it was first awakened in him in the same way, by the communicative and stimulative power of expression or utterance."[117]

The feeling of absolute dependence is realized through a living imitation of its communal expression and not in solitude. Initially, this communion is "variable and fluid," but as the sensible self-consciousness unites more intensely with religious emotions, "each person's religious emotions have more affinity with those of one of his fellows than with those of another, and thus communion of religious feeling comes to him more easily with the former than the latter."[118] One is not repelled from another communion "absolutely" but only as a matter of preference. Communions will inevitably stress varying degrees of relation between the sensible self-consciousness and religious emotions.

The example of a family, as that which shares a similar intensity of feeling, epitomizes a communion of religious self-consciousness. The members of a family share a particular kinship. They associate certain emotions with certain occasions. They are, therefore, able to share them more easily with each other than with strangers. The individuals who are social by nature, and the family that shares a similar dynamic of religious life and communion, together evolve naturally into the possibility for the basis of "Church."[119] Thus, the Church's essential business is the maintenance, regulation, and advancement of piety. This gives rise to dogmatic theology, which monitors the communal religious self-consciousness at a given time. It also interprets both historical doctrines and contemporary developments for the advancement of Christian piety.

In summary, the argument in the introduction to *The Christian Faith* bears a remarkable similarity to the argument found in the *Speeches*. Both begin with a turning away from prominent conceptions of their subjects—religion (*Speeches*) and Church doctrine (*The Christian Faith*). This turn requires an emphasis on the interiority of human existence. *Intuition/feeling*, the pre-reflexive, comprehensive, and unified principle argued in the *Speeches*, is transposed as *piety* in *The Christian Faith*. Both efforts maintain the priority of experience over language: that is, both the experience of intuition/feeling and the feeling of absolute dependence are expressed, though never adequately captured, by language.[120]

In the *Speeches*, true religion becomes possible through movement toward an encounter with humanity that is revelatory. This is transposed in *The Christian Faith* when communal piety is construed as the direct result of religious consciousness. Religious consciousness, in turn, is nurtured by communal piety. In the *Speeches*, the term true "religion" is an "Other," which is transposed in *The Christian Faith* as the Whence of "piety." Both religion and piety lead to the communal realization of "feeling," that is, to the Church. The Church, in turn, makes accessible religion and piety to others outside its boundaries.

The confessional appropriation of an experiential starting point for a defense of "religion" becomes the comprehensive principle that defines an introduction to dogmatic theology. Understanding how the essence of religion and the essence of piety are situated in these works is critical for understanding Schleiermacher's theological project—a piety that seeks understanding of the Evangelical faith. This core experiential principle further differentiates all aspects of religion and theology.

But the specifically dogmatic task is not yet accomplished. How is it possible to interpret doctrines that have *not* originated from the contemporary

God-consciousness while still remaining true to the task of dogmatic theology as a Church discipline? How can piety be maintained, advanced, and regulated with the incorporation of "received" doctrines that do not necessarily speak to the God-consciousness of a particular time? And finally, how might this interpretation of doctrine be realized in a way that moves the various Christian denominations toward a deeper unity?[121]

This concern for doctrinal reconciliation between the Lutheran and Reformed traditions is one controlling aspect of Schleiermacher's overall project. The particular approach to doctrine, which is identified in the preface to *The Christian Faith* as "free and conciliatory," stresses the fluidity of meaning and emerges from a desire to serve two ends—the piety of the Church and the possibility of denominational reconciliation. The problem of interpreting and applying doctrine in the Church introduces the third moment in Schleiermacher's project—a turn to the subject through a particular approach to "understanding," namely hermeneutics.[122]

"Hermeneutics" and the Turn to the Subject

Schleiermacher's theory of hermeneutics can be gleaned mainly from handwritten manuscripts that served as notes for his teaching.[123] The audience for these manuscripts consisted of seminary students working to become ministers with the necessary balance of theoretical and practical skills. In part, their job was to help maintain, regulate, and advance the piety in their communities of faith through preaching the proper interpretation and presentation of doctrine. This had become increasingly difficult as traditional interpretations of dogma, divorced as they were from contemporary piety, became obstacles, and even sometimes injurious, to faith. Traditional methods of interpretation demanded that outdated doctrines be lifted from their historical context and accepted or rejected *in toto*. This, of course, caused incalculable damage to Christian piety. A proper hermeneutics for the selection and interpretation of necessary doctrines became critically important for these aspiring ministers and scholars.

The study of human understanding and interpretation was a task pursued throughout Schleiermacher's career. Prior to this work, the rules for translation and interpretation varied with the subject matter. What was called for now was a theory of hermeneutics that could serve as a universal "art" for understanding. While the broad principles would be applicable in all disciplines, they would be applied differently as the subject matter demanded.[124] The application of this new theory of hermeneutics within dogmatic theology completes the turn to the subject by extending this "turn" to the interpretation of texts through the mind of the authoring subject. This allows historical doctrines to contribute to the maintenance and cultivation of communal piety (i.e., dogmatic theology).

The theory of hermeneutics applied in *The Christian Faith* must be understood as uniting two kinds of historical theology. Schleiermacher's overarching schema of theology as a three-part organic whole, composed of philosophical, historical, and practical theology, employs hermeneutics specifically in the area of exegetical theology.[125] Any investigation of doctrine must first complete the exegetical task of attaining the correct understanding of "those writings which contain the normative representation of Christianity [and] which form the New Testament canon of the Christian Church."[126] "Normative" is not based on a fixed, immutable formula, and the "Protestant Church necessarily claims to be continually occupied in determining the canon more exactly; and this is the greatest exegetical-theological task for higher criticism."[127] Thus, hermeneutics is necessary for the move from exegetical theology to practical theology via dogmatic theology.[128]

Dogmatic theology is successful insofar as it increases the level of piety, and hence the possibility of redemption in the Christian community. The theologian is to gauge the Christian self-consciousness current at a given time and to mediate doctrine for the community in such a way that the increase of piety is served. Thus, historical truths must be mediated so as to speak directly to the piety of a given community. This mediation dictates a theory of interpretation that makes accessible the original intentions of the doctrinal authors.

The application of hermeneutics in dogmatic theology allows for three tasks. First, it makes possible a translation of all or parts of doctrines from historical texts directly to the Christian self-consciousness of the day. Second, it makes possible a judgment of which doctrines are to figure prominently and why. Finally, it allows for an interpretation of texts that increases the potential for confessional reconciliation. These three hermeneutical tasks will accomplish the overall goal of dogmatic theology—separating useless and even harmful dogma from necessary dogma in order to increase the piety of the Church.[129] A particular approach to the interpretation of texts, that is, a theory of hermeneutics, sets the criteria for and the method that accomplishes the separation, preservation, and advancement of essential material.

Propositions 15, 19, and 30 in the philosophy of religion section of *The Christian Faith* determine the purpose and scope of dogmatic theology:

§15. Christian doctrines are accounts of the Christian religious affections (*gemütszustände*) set forth in speech.

§19. Dogmatic Theology is the science which systematizes the doctrine prevalent in a Christian Church at a given time.

§30. All propositions which the system of Christian doctrine has to establish can be regarded either as descriptions of human states, or as conceptions of divine attributes and modes of actions, or as utterances regarding the constitution of the world; and all three forms have always subsisted alongside each other.[130]

In *The Christian Faith*, the ecclesiastical value of dogmatic propositions is measured by their capacity to increase the feeling of absolute dependence amongst believers.[131] This increase in Christian affections (i.e., the growing awareness and healing acceptance of the feeling of absolute dependence) makes accessible the redemptive activity of Christ and the Spirit in the context of the Christian community as previously defined—that is, in Church. Redemption is the goal of membership in the Christian community.[132] The proper interpretation of doctrines and their application to the God-consciousness of the community are critical for the realization of this goal.

Schleiermacher's hermeneutical theory insists that the explication of doctrine can change as long as two elements are maintained: the intention of the author(s) is preserved, and the doctrine speaks to the piety of the community and increases such piety for greater redemptive efficacy.[133] The relation and balance of these two moments will be of central importance in the evaluation of any doctrine.

The acquired understanding of the language, context, and purpose of a work, as well as the accessibility to the mind of the author, together make up the two aspects of interpretation. An early aphorism identifies these two aspects of hermeneutical theory (i.e., the grammatical and the technical):

Strictly speaking, grammatical interpretation is the objective side; technical the subjective. Consequently, grammatical interpretation plays a negative role in hermeneutical construction, marking the boundaries; technical interpretation is positive. These two sides of interpretation cannot always coincide, for that would presuppose both a complete knowledge of and completely correct use of language. The "art" lies in knowing when one side should give way to the other.[134]

Interpretation of received doctrine must adequately address these two aspects of interpretation for a successful translation of a text. First, an understanding of the objective realities of language, grammar, and syntax is necessary to discern a doctrine's content and historical relevance. This aspect of hermeneutics sets the boundaries for the subjective, technical component of interpretation, in which the intention of the author(s) is discerned and preserved in a new articulation of the doctrine. This subjective component, sometimes referenced as the "divinatory" moment, is critical for doctrinal reformulation. If the author's intention is so bound up in the historical circumstance in which a particular doctrine was initiated, its usefulness for the Christian self-consciousness of another day will be extremely limited. It is here that a theory of hermeneutics signals the full development of the turn to the subject in dogmatic theology and allows for the completion of Schleiermacher's overall project.

This "art" of interpretation is vital for understanding the dogmatic theological enterprise as well as the approach to language employed by Schleiermacher. The possibility for this new theological method emerges from an experiential starting point for theology. The experience occurs in the prelinguistic interiority of human subjectivity. To correctly discern this interiority or, in the case of hermeneutics, the interiority (intentions) of the mind of the author(s), the two mutually influencing moments of interpretation must be applied. The complex relationship between thoughts, language, and interpretation is evident in the description of both moments. "Just as every act of speaking is related to both the totality of language and the totality of the speaker's thoughts, so understanding a speech always involves two moments: to understand what is said in the context of the language with its possibilities, and to understand it as a fact in the thinking of the speaker."[135] The first aspect of this two-part process, grammatical interpretation, is "the art of finding the precise sense [*Sinn*] of a given statement from its language and with the help of its language."[136] This can be accomplished only if "one should construe the meaning from the total pre-given value of language and the heritage common to the author and his reader, for only by reference to this is interpretation possible."[137] Knowledge of languages and cultural particularities is vital for the successful completion of the grammatical component. The second or divinatory component of hermeneutics appeals to the intention within the mind of the author.

> Who would move in the company of exceptionally gifted persons without endeavoring to hear "between" their words, just as we read between the lines of original or tightly written books? Who does not try in a meaningful conversation, which may in certain respects be an important act, to lift out its main points, to try to grasp its internal coherence, to pursue all its subtle intimation further?[138]

The result of such efforts leads to a kind of certainty different from the critical certainty that results from a solid grammatical grasp of a text.[139] This is a "divinatory certainty which arises when an interpreter delves as deeply as possible into an author's state of mind [*Verfassung*]."[140] Both the grammatical and the divinatory moments mutually condition one another. The divinatory component, for example, is dependent upon one's grammatical grasp of language and culture. Only together do they approximate the best interpretation possible.

Little of what is proposed in the two-part process of hermeneutics is fixed, other than the grammatical rules and linguistic limits of the text that one is required to work within. Constant emphasis is given to an inability to understand any work definitively, finally, or completely. Even if both aspects of interpretation are performed quite well, even when "we may be fully convinced of our view, . . . it would be futile to try to pass this account off as demonstration."[141] Schleiermacher tentatively, and over time, proposes principles that have become part of the contemporary study of hermeneutics. But the inexactness of this two-part "science" is unmistakable and largely due to a particular understanding of language.

> Each side [grammatical and divinatory] is itself an art. For each side constructs something finite and definite from something infinite and indefinite. Language is infinite because every element is determinable in

a special way by other elements. This statement also applies to psychological interpretation, for every intuition of a person is itself infinite. Moreover, external influences on a person will have ramifications which trail off to infinity. Such a construction, however, cannot be made by means of rules which may be applied with self-evident certainty.[142]

The two aspects of hermeneutics are always interwoven and therefore not clearly distinct.

It has been argued that Schleiermacher has a preference for the divinatory aspect of his hermeneutics and deemphasizes the grammatical component, especially later in his career.[143] This develops, according to the translator of the *Hermeneutics*, from the philosophical view that "presupposed a discrepancy between the ideal, inner essence and the outer appearance" of a given text.[144] "Thus the text could not be seen as the direct manifestation of inner mental process but something given up to the empirical exigencies of language. Ultimately, then, the task of hermeneutics came to be that of transcending language in order to get at the inner process. It is still necessary to go through language, but language is no longer seen as fully equivalent to thought."[145]

Both the grammatical and divinatory aspects of this hermeneutical theory are operative in the doctrinal reformulation accomplished throughout *The Christian Faith*. The traditional presentation of a doctrine is given in its original language and then contextualized. Usually, this contextualization consists of an explanation of what the doctrine says within the historical conditions that gave rise to it. Often, forms of heresy or serious disagreements concerning an existing doctrine will then be mentioned.[146] The divinatory aspect then attempts to discern the intention of the author, church, or council responsible for initially promulgating the doctrine. The results of this exegetical theology within hermeneutics are then transferred to its capacity to speak to the God-consciousness of the contemporary Church, i.e., to dogmatic theology. Within both the grammatical and divinatory phases, the judgment concerning a doctrine's historical "boundedness" is made. Is a particular doctrine so immersed in its original time period that it has little or no relevance for today? Are the terms used in the doctrine "translatable" for effective doctrine: in other words, can they speak to, and increase the piety of, the contemporary faith community? The answer to these questions depends partly on the contextualization already established in the grammatical phase and partly on the discernment of the intention of the author in the divinatory phase. Occasionally, the contextualizing necessary for the grammatical component is obscured by the overlapping divinatory component. This results in a preference, evident at times, for the divinatory component.

One classic application of Schleiermacher's theory of hermeneutics put forth in his dogmatic theology illustrates this preference: the proposed reformulation of the doctrine of the Trinity. This doctrine represents a particularly difficult challenge for Schleiermacher's project. Certain aspects of the traditional doctrine of God are necessary for Schleiermacher's soteriology, namely that Christ and the Spirit as divine are essential for redemptive efficacy. At the same time, the traditional doctrine of the Trinity possesses an outdated language and structure and a logical complexity that is harmful to the piety of the Church. Thus, the challenge is to glean from the traditional doctrine only what is necessary for the increase of contemporary piety and thus redemption.[147]

APPLIED HERMENEUTICS: THE TRINITY

The concluding propositions of *The Christian Faith* (propositions 170–172) call for a reappraisal of the formulation and interpretation of the doctrine of the Trinity.[148] This reappraisal is necessary in light of the historical context of the original doctrine and the needs of the (then) contemporary Church. According to proposition 170, "All that is essential in this Second Aspect of the Second Part of our exposition is also posited in what is essential in the doctrine of the Trinity; but this doctrine itself, as ecclesiastically framed, is not an immediate utterance concerning the Christian self-consciousness, but only a combination of several such utterances."[149] The doctrine of the Trinity, as traditionally presented, is far removed from the daily piety (immediate utterance concerning Christian self-consciousness) to which dogmatic theology ministers. Its reformulation is necessary to save it from being dispensed with completely. Hints of dissatisfaction with the doctrine of the Trinity have been evident throughout *The Christian Faith*. Whenever the divine character of Christ or the Spirit is encountered, for example, the technical difficulties associated with words like *person, essence,* and *hypostasis* must be recognized as barriers to their acceptance. These are usually dispensed with because of the confusion they create.[150] Furthermore, the logical problem of the three-and-one paradox continually arises throughout *The Christian Faith.* In part this is due to key presuppositions of philosophical theology developed in the introduction. Thus, the traditional doctrine of the Trinity is put aside in favor of other understandings of the doctrine of God.

The *necessary* elements of the traditional doctrine of the Trinity include the union of the Divine Essence with human nature in the personality of Christ and in the common Spirit of the Church; "therewith the whole view of Christianity set forth in our Church teaching stands and falls."[151] All other formulations, especially those concerned with an "immanent" Trinity with its persons and essences, are far removed from the religious consciousness and hence are not the proper object of dogmatic theology. The essential points of the doctrine, namely "the being of God in Christ and in the Christian Church," are independent of the traditional doctrine of the Trinity and directly related to the religious consciousness. Hence, these two elements, as opposed to the traditional emphasis on inner-Trinitarian processions and relations, form the centerpiece of Schleiermacher's reinterpretation of the doctrine of the Trinity.

According to proposition 171, "The ecclesiastical doctrine of the Trinity demands that we think of each of the three Persons as equal to the Divine Essence, and vice versa, and each of the three Persons as equal to the others. Yet we cannot do either the one or the other, but can only represent the unity of the Essence as less than the three Persons, or vice versa."[152] The traditional doctrine of the Trinity asserts the equality of the three Persons and the unity of the Divine Essence as a whole. But, in fact, this is not possible. For when the definitions of human freedom and dependence that ground philosophical theology in the "Introduction" are followed through to their logical conclusions, anything that is begotten by or that proceeds from anything else is clearly dependent: that is, it is caused. If dependence is framed in accordance with a *change* in being, then causality is the signifier of dependence. Anything dependent is clearly not equal, for it depends either upon the Other who begot it into being or upon the Other from which it proceeds. Therefore, the traditional doctrine is logically contradictory and harmful to Christian piety, for one must either err on the side of subordinationism and hold that the Father is greater than the Son and Spirit or on the side of a Unitarianism and hold that the Divine Essence is greater than the individual parts that constitute it. Neither route is acceptable for a soteriology that requires an equality to the Divine Essence in Christ and the Spirit for the possibility of redemption. The traditional doctrine first fails to satisfy the explicit criteria of speaking directly to the religious consciousness (proposition 170). Its second failure is of a philosophical nature. The Trinity logically contradicts itself when the definitions of freedom and dependence, framed as they are in terms of causality, are operative from the earlier section of philosophical theology (proposition 171).

Throughout *The Christian Faith* as a whole, the technical aspect of this doctrine has been indirectly addressed. Ultimately, technical criticism of the language of the Trinity insists on a view of the doctrine as outdated. The traditional formulation of the doctrine is so tied to its historical context that it is of little or no value anymore.

> If we reflect, on the one hand, that the formulae now accepted in the doctrine of the Trinity originated at a time when Christendom was still being recruited by mass-conversion from heathendom, and consider how easily, when it became necessary to speak of a plurality or distinction in God, unconscious echoes of what is pagan could find their way in, it is not surprising that the descriptions of such plurality should from the start have been vacillating and liable to misconception, and such as were no longer suited to later times, when no further admixture of heathenism was to be feared.[153]

Note the divinatory aspect of interpretation that establishes the intention or purpose of the doctrine in the context in which it was formulated. Once this context is understood and the reason for the formulation is decisively determined as proper only to that historical period, a reformulation of the doctrine can commence.

The actual language of the original doctrine of the Trinity is defined by a historical context of mass pagan conversion. The goal of this doctrine was to encounter the dominant pagan polytheism of the day and to provide a viable, understandable doctrine of God as an alternative to it. The *intention* of the early formulators of the traditional doctrine of the Trinity was to frame a coherent soteriology through a doctrine of God with the schema of the Trinity. Hence, the Trinity was a resultant soteriological construction aimed at fulfilling a prior need—namely, how to explain the redemption of the world effected by Jesus Christ. This was put forth over and against the dominant polytheistic tendencies of that time. This, at least, pagans could recognize and accept. But since the context of this doctrinal development has obviously and radically changed, so has the relevancy of the traditional Trinitarian language and schema. Therefore, the traditional doctrine of the Trinity must be radically altered to serve better the contemporary piety of the Christian Church. The intention of the authors, however, was to teach Christians more about the redemptive efficacy of Christ and the Church. That intention will be preserved in the suggestions for reformulation.

If the maintenance, regulation, and advancement of piety in Christian self-consciousness *at the present time* is the determining criterion by which all doctrine is judged, it is clear that the doctrine of the Trinity has failed to meet this criterion for the God-consciousness of Schleiermacher's Church. In some cases it has even harmed it.[154] "It is here as with the doctrine of God in general; many not merely profess to be but actually think they are opposed to every belief in God, when in fact they are simply repelled by ordinary presentations of the subject, but have by no means parted with all those spiritual affections which spring from the God-consciousness."[155] This response to the doctrine of the Trinity is necessary because the doctrine, as it stands, does not meet the criterion for its inclusion into dogmatic theology. This criterion for dogmatics is concerned primarily with divine operation over and distinct from divine being. The feeling of absolute dependence, or being in relation to God, stresses the effects of divine action in the context of Church as a requirement for any relevant doctrine.

> We have the God-consciousness given in our self-consciousness along with our consciousness of the world; hence we have no formula for the being of God in Himself as distinct from the being of God in the world, and should have to borrow any such formula from speculation, and so prove disloyal to the character of the discipline at which we are working.[156]

Schleiermacher's aversion to speculation arises from a desire to speak not only directly to the Christian consciousness of his day, to which he was minister and theologian, but also from a need to justify religious belief in a manner that can withstand Kantian scrutiny. "Knowledge" of God ties the judgments of experience to perception, which is always accompanied by the prereflexive "sensation" articulated in the feeling of absolute dependence.[157] Put differently, the feeling of absolute dependence is the middle term between the noumenal and the phenomenal. This is the link between the finite and the infinite, of which we can really know only the side of the finite. Hence, Christian doctrine is concerned with the *actions* or operations—the *effects* of divine causality "here" as opposed to the inaccessibility of the divine *being* "there." All Christian doctrine is ultimately measured against this experiential middle term.

Isolated aspects of the doctrine of the Trinity do measure up to the criterion for doctrinal relevancy. The life of Christ and the redemption possible through him, the ongoing activity of the Spirit in the context of Christian community, and God as creator and term of the feeling of absolute dependence are but a few. These elements of the Trinity, as it encounters the world, are necessary for Christian piety, but any discussion of their origination and inner relations, namely the Trinity in itself, becomes mere speculation. Ultimately, in the traditional doctrine of the Trinity, these isolated aspects (of the Trinity as it encounters the world) combine with other propositions and fail to speak to the primary level of God-consciousness as such. The desire to peel away layers of speculation that corrupt the doctrine of God leaves Schleiermacher with the divine in Christ and the divine Spirit in the community of believers. Both "presences" are equal with the divine essence itself. This avoids a discussion of persons in the one God that inevitably errs either on the side of subordinationism or tri-theism. It also avoids a Unitarianism that deprives the person of Christ and the Spirit of the adequate divinity necessary for fellowship with God and, ultimately, for the redemptive transformation of the believing community.

SUMMARY AND EVALUATION

Schleiermacher's project began with a turn to the subject in "experience" through a reimagination of "religion." This led to an experiential starting point for understanding the content of Christian doctrine. This, in turn, demanded a theory of "understanding" that included both objective and subjective elements. All three components together bespeak the Anselmian project of faith seeking understanding—that is, piety (certainty in the feeling of absolute dependence) seeking a greater understanding of the Evangelical faith within the context of modernity. The connection of Schleiermacher's apologetics, dogmatics, and hermeneutics with the turn inward to experience, to the essence of piety, and to the mind of the authoring subject highlights the specific topics taken up by modern-day critics. A careful illustration of the developing turn to the subject in Schleiermacher's overall project has provided the basis for understanding the object of the postmodern critique.

Three topics emerge from all sections of Schleiermacher's project that dictate the particular critiques. These topics are: (1) an experience of God that is, in principle, universally accessible to all human beings; (2) the relationship of such an experience as prior to (and thus expressed through) language; and (3) the purpose of theological inquiry as essentially descriptive and apologetical of an accessible universal truth claim.

Some positive and negative implications of Schleiermacher's project have become evident. The relevancy of doctrine for the community that receives them is always maintained. Unfortunately, this can occur as a result of severing the original doctrine from its context and "preserving" what can be discerned of the intention of the original author(s). The subjective element in both aspects of the hermeneutics, though especially in the divinatory phase in which the intention or mind of the author(s) is discovered, cannot be overlooked. Is such an approach too optimistic? Could not such an approach simply be a projection of the interpreter's desires?

A tension exists between a mode of received doctrinal articulation (language) and the contemporary needs of a faith community. This tension dictates a view of doctrine and language that is largely *descriptive* in character, that is, the language of doctrine contains a description of doctrine measured by a given faith experience (piety) that it may or may not elicit. The relevancy of all doctrine is consequently determined over and against the determination of feeling that is piety. The hermeneutic process, within the field of exegetical theology, aids a dogmatic theology that stresses doctrinal efficacy over accurate preservation of original doctrinal language.

But is language only descriptive of an experience of piety, or can an experience of piety emerge from language as well? Is it possible to discern the mind or intention of the author, in such a definitive manner, from the historical context through a particular text? Can one effectively separate one's current context, with all its needs and competing agendas, out of one's evaluation of another? Are the grammatical and divinatory aspects of Schleiermacher's hermeneutical theory sufficient for the task of discerning whether a doctrine maintains its legitimacy? If that which immediately and necessarily informs the God-consciousness—the purpose or "essence" of the doctrine—can be maintained (according to Schleiermacher's approach), the description itself can vary through time.[158]

This fluidity of sign and signified is problematic. An approach where "essences" are distinct from their signification, whether it concerns doctrine and language or experience and language, constitutes the first part of the contemporary problematic in systematic theology. The assertion of an interiority prior to language and thought will, consequently, become the focus of postmodern critiques. This understanding of interiority is directly connected to one's understanding of "experience" and its relation to a conception of language in the context or history of that language. The interiority of the mind of the author made accessible in the divinatory aspect of Schleiermacher's hermeneutics presumes a certain understanding of experience and language. The universal experiences of feeling/intuition and absolute dependence also hinge upon a similar presumption.[159] This understanding of "experience" and language, and its affirmation of a common humanity for the persons of the present, is also assumed for persons of history. This, in turn, allows for access to the minds of historical authors through the texts they wrote and knowledge of the historical context in which they lived.

The postmodern critique will question what is perceived to be a decontextualization of experience and language. Can one prescind from history and language *boundaries* to access an "interior" experience that depends on neither?[160] Can "feeling" presume a kind of primacy over/before knowing or doing? Can "feeling" (if it exists at all) be singled out, even for explicative purposes, from those others *definitively?* Can there be, as Niebuhr holds concerning Schleiermacher's project, an "underived self not qualified by or determined by specific objects and energies located in this world"?[161] Can there be any aspect of humanity that qualifies as "common?" The answer from the postmodern critique, with its emphasis on language, history, and difference, is a resounding "No!"

Now it is necessary to view two postmodern efforts, and their attendant critiques of foundationalism, in the areas of theory of religion and theology. Serious attempts to employ moderate postmodern principles in constructing both theories of religion as well as theological doctrines have gained in prominence. Two works embody such efforts: Wayne Proudfoot's *Religious Experience*, winner of the 1986 American Academy of Religion Book Award, and George Lindbeck's *The Nature of Doctrine*. These two works address a theory of religion and a "postliberal" approach to theology.[162] Both authors attempt to constructively apply a method that will serve to highlight the particular approach to the study of religion and theology characterized as postmodern. The three topics that emerged from Schleiermacher's project continue to be critically operative in the encounter between foundationalism and postmodernism—the universality and primordiality of human experience (and an experience of God therein), the relationship between language and experience, and the nature of theological inquiry.[163]

Proudfoot and Lindbeck represent the second part of the unfolding story that is framing the problem under investigation here. Their works embody a response to Schleiermacher's articulation of the experience of God. They will question its relation to theological inquiry. They are critical of the hermeneutics that is necessary for such a project. What emerges from the intersection of these opposing elements—Schleiermacher's project and the postmodern critique—exemplifies the troubled situation marking theology today.

Wayne Proudfoot's
Religious Experience:
A Postmodern Theory
of Religious Experience

During the past two centuries, religious thinkers and scholars of religion have
depended heavily on the concept of religious experience. That concept is a
relatively recent one and was developed and shaped to meet the needs of those
thinkers and scholars. I have tried to subject that concept to scrutiny, to show
why it emerged when it did, and to reflect on the ambiguities in the concept
that permit it to be used both for descriptive and apologetic purposes.

—Proudfoot, *Religious Experience*

Wayne Proudfoot's *Religious Experience* argues for a theory of religion and an
interpretation of the concept of "religious experience" largely based on postmodern presuppositions.[1] Though the methodology is not explicitly identified as postmodern, the following elements allow it to be classified as such.
First, there is a reliance upon Wittgenstein's linguistic theory. Second, there
is the rejection of a "common humanity." Finally, there is an emphasis on the
constitutive function of language and belief as the closed paradigm for any
"experience." All three result in the view of theology as an endeavor born of
human anxiety. These factors place this work squarely within what has been
designated "moderate postmodernism." It also directly counters key elements of Schleiermacher's thought.

Religious Experience illustrates and systematically dismantles Schleiermacher's project. A radically different view of the human subject and, more particularly, of the relationship between "experience" and language permits and even requires this dismantling.

The three topics that emerged in this book's analysis of Schleiermacher—namely, a universal common experience/subjectivity, the relationship of experience and language, and the purpose of theology as essentially descriptive—can serve to locate the major points of disagreement. Proudfoot's approach to these topics is grounded by two major convictions: language is pervasively constructive (or formative) rather than expressive (or descriptive), and the "traditional appeal to religious experience" is a protective strategy employed to block critical inquiry for apologetic purposes. These two convictions frame a thoroughly different understanding of the meaning and function of religious experience. The first denies the theoretical coherence of Schleiermacher's appeal to an immediate religious experience; the second reveals the underlying intention or motive that produced this appeal.

The understanding of language as constructive goes along with a corresponding rejection of any common human experience. Such common human experience is presumed by Schleiermacher and, in fact, grounds his appeal to an experience of God upon which his totalizing vision depends.[2] Human experience cannot bespeak such a commonality because experience itself is completely constituted by diverse paradigm-bound social and cultural factors.[3] A "conceptual theory of emotion," one that requires external stimuli for the possibility of any "internal" emotion, proves the incoherency of Schleiermacher's appeal to an immediate experience. The only legitimate method for analyzing religious experience is provided by a "theory of religion." Only such a theoretical approach can maintain a privileged neutrality outside the "confessional" hermeneutical circle. The definition of religious experience finally attained is a product of all the previous factors. This argument can be instantiated by an inquiry into the phenomenon of mysticism.

The developing argument of *Religious Experience* rejects Schleiermacher's understanding of human subjectivity and its universal appeal to a particular experience within that subjectivity. Consequently, it rejects the priority of experience to language, and it takes issue with how Schleiermacher understands the purpose of theological inquiry. *Religious Experience* argues for a different interpretation of all three topics. Experience is the product of language. Human experience is constituted by and particularized by language and culture.[4] Theological inquiry is evocative and inherently biased toward its own construction of religious experience.

LANGUAGE AND EXPERIENCE

The concept of "religious experience" emerged in the late eighteenth century in an attempt to ground theology in something other than metaphysics, morality, or ecclesiastical authority.[5] Schleiermacher's theology was the first serious attempt to make use of this approach, and his contribution tried to present religion as "an autonomous moment in human experience."[6] This moment was an "experiential moment irreducible to either science or morality, belief or conduct."[7]

> Religion is grounded in a moment of experience that is intrinsically reli-
> gious, so it need not be justified by metaphysical argument, by the kind
> of evidence considered by the proponents of the design argument, or by
> the appeals to its importance for the moral life. Moreover, because reli-
> gion is autonomous, all possible conflict between religion and science or
> morality is precluded. Any attempt to assimilate religion to nonreligious
> phenomena is an attempt to reduce it to something other than it is.
> Reductionism is thus the chief error to be avoided in the study of religion.[8]

But any particular experience (religious or otherwise) is always derived from the subject's language and particular belief history. One can never get beyond the culturally determined use of language to describe a seemingly prereflexive experience. Language is constructive and never simply expressive, so any theological inquiry that begins from "religious experience" and lays claim to a universal reality is fundamentally flawed. Schleiermacher's theology misused language as descriptive even as it employed language constructively.[9] The appeal to an immediate experience independent of language is, therefore, suspect. "Schleiermacher's program required that he show that religious experience is independent in the requisite sense. But concepts, beliefs, and practices are assumed by the descriptions he offers and the instructions he gives for identifying the religious moment in experience."[10]

Schleiermacher's understanding of experience and its linguistic expression first asserted that experience spontaneously manifested itself in language.

As Schleiermacher put it, doctrines were natural expressions of piety in speech. Second, Schleiermacher's use of figurative expression indicated its object "by comparison and delimitation rather than directly."[11] Schleiermacher argued that as cultures develop, so does reflection upon these mental states, and eventually figurative expression is cultivated to the extent that real doctrine is produced. But Schleiermacher's two-part description of the experience of "feeling" and "intuition" in the *Speeches* is dependent itself upon "particular concepts, beliefs, and practices."[12] Thus, the sense of independence that Schleiermacher's "immediacy" requires ultimately collapses, and with it any claim to an immediate experience as such.

Two contrasting views of the relationship between experience and language can be seen to be in tension over this issue. Ernst Cassirer views the ultimate basis of language as feeling at the existential level. As Proudfoot describes Cassirer's thought:

> The intuitive and creative form of myth provides the key by which we may gain access to the original forms of language. The ultimate basis of myth is the primitive power of feeling. Mythical thought does not relate and compare but is captivated by the intuitions of immediate experience (Cassirer, 1946: 32). From these moments of immediacy, a process of increasing objectification takes place. Religious symbols and myths preserve the immediacy and power that have been lost in discursive and scientific language. This power varies inversely with the distance of a linguistic form from immediate experience.[13]

For Ludwig Wittgenstein, in contrast, language a priori structures our experience of reality.[14] Proudfoot, connecting this notion with the Kantian dictum that all knowledge must first come through the imposition of the forms and categories of the mind on the manifold of experience, argues that religious experience becomes a reality only through a particular interpretation of religious belief, which is always constituted by a particular language. Wittgenstein "considers the possibility that some linguistic forms might function as natural expressions and be located on the spectrum with moans, cries, and other involuntary behavior."[15] But once natural expressions are given articulation in a learned language, they become conventional and cease to be natural. Hence, there is no possibility of a private language/ experience. All experience is interpreted experience. Interpretation necessarily includes others who teach one how to interpret. Thus, every interpretation of experience is socially mediated.

> Interpretation takes time and it is a social process. To say that interpretation is triadic rather than dyadic again sets it apart from immediate encounters with symbols or other selves. There is always a third, which mediates between two. An interpreter interprets a text or a fact to another person. I can interpret something to myself, but this relation cannot be reduced. The thing to be interpreted, the one to whom it is interpreted, and the third that mediates or interprets are all necessary to the relation.[16]

Language, consequently, is always that third—the mediator, interpreter, the matrix of all experience. Once natural expressions become ensconced in this learned behavior—behavior that the person fully integrates into established modes of communication—all expression becomes governed by convention. Thus, immediate experiences are not possible, for any appeal to an immediate, revelatory, prelinguistic experience is simply an "attempt to assimilate such obviously linguistic forms to nonlinguistic ones."[17]

This theory of language can be brought to bear instrumentally in a critique of Schleiermacher's understanding of religious language as a descriptive extension of inner states—that is, of religious experiences. "To characterize this expression as natural is to deny that it is governed by convention, and thus to assert that the connection between the religious consciousness and its linguistic expression is independent of cultural influences and constructive thought."[18] For this reason, "Religion must be identified with *feeling or emotion* in order to remove it from the arena in which it is dependent on particular beliefs or claims about the world, vulnerable to conflict with scientific beliefs, and open to the criticisms that Kant leveled against metaphysical speculation."[19]

Proudfoot's identification made between the term *feeling* (*Gefühl*) as understood by a nineteenth-century German theologian and the term *emotion* as understood by a twentieth-century philosopher of religion is critical at this point of his critique. The question that inevitably arises—was Schleiermacher referring to "emotions"?—is not an issue for Proudfoot. With a constructive (postmodern) relationship posited between language and experience, "attitudes, emotions, and beliefs are intentional."[20] At issue is a particular theory of emotion and its causes.

Contemporary and traditional theories of emotion can be drawn upon for analyzing the components of religious experience. According to Hume, "the passions are simple and therefore assume no conceptual or interpretive framework."[21] While words can suggest or incompletely describe an experience, they never fully recapture or exhaustively describe any particular experience. In this sense, "thoughts are extrinsic to emotions."[22] Second, for Hume, "the connection between an emotion and its object is a causal one."[23] Only by experience "can we know that certain emotions are associated with certain objects and thoughts."[24]

Conversely, Aristotle argues that "thought allows one to identify both the object of the emotion and the grounds on which it is based.[25] Without reference to both the object and grounds, an emotion cannot be identified."[26] Aristotle's chief discussion of emotions takes place in the *Rhetoric* where "he is addressing the practical question of how specific emotions can be aroused."[27] With this goal in mind, "[s]pecific cognitive structures and capacities for judgment must be presumed for certain kinds of emotions to be possible."[28] Emotions must be evoked through the given structures that inform the possibility for the evocation.[29] "In contrast to Hume, Aristotle holds that emotion cannot be discriminated from other mental states without the attention to the appropriate object and the beliefs that provide relevant grounds for the emotion. Reference to concepts and thoughts is required for the specification of an emotional state."[30] These, in turn, depend upon an interpretive framework that "assumes particular judgments about oneself and the world."[31] "Each of Aristotle's examples suggests that emotions assume and are in part constituted by concepts and judgments. To say that a concept is constitutive of an emotion is to say that the emotion cannot be specified without reference to that concept."[32] Therefore, the "relation between an emotion and its object is a conceptual or logical one," and three requirements become necessary to specify an emotion.[33] First, one must identify the state of mind that refers to the quality of feeling—though to specify that alone is insufficient. Second, one must discover the appropriate object of the emotion. Finally, one must identify the ground for the emotion.

Previously the "felt quality" and the "intentional object" had been sufficient to describe religious experience. These alone are now insufficient. Without a reference to concepts and interpretive frameworks, identification of any emotion becomes theoretically implausible. Concepts construct, in their identity, seemingly immediate experiences. Consequently, experiences described by St. Paul, John Wesley, or Schleiermacher are "religious" not because of any existential (causal) element but because of their shared belief (conceptual) in a God that predated their particular experiences. Even about Rudolph Otto, it can be stated:

> What purports to be a neutral phenomenological description is actually a dogmatic formula designed to evoke or to create a particular sort of experience. By ruling out certain kinds of explanations, the formula guarantees that any experience so identified will not be explicable in naturalistic terms. Thus an explanatory criterion is built into the identifying description, and warnings about reductionism are invoked to protect that criterion.[34]

"Primary states" or "original experiences" are derived from external language and concepts. "The intentional character of these states is sometimes represented by saying that they are always directed toward objects."[35] This is the case with both the "sense of the infinite" in the *Speeches* and the "feeling of absolute dependence" in *The Christian Faith*. A conceptual theory of emotion will designate both "immediate" experiences as emotions. Therefore, according to Proudfoot, "Schleiermacher's claim that piety is prior to and unaffected by any concepts or thoughts is incompatible with his characterization of it."[36]

> No distinguishing mark enables us to identify some language or behavior as expressive. We take it to be expressive if we think that it provides evidence for the ascription of the state that we take it to express. To label something an expression is to make and to license such an inference. We speak of expressing emotions, attitudes, and beliefs, but not pangs, twitches, or even a sensation of warmth. For something to be expressed, it must have a conceptual component.[37]

Schleiermacher's interpretation of "feeling" is incoherent because it confuses "psychological and logical priority."[38] Logically, "feeling" must flow in the channels set by concepts and beliefs, even though psychologically it may seem immediate.[39] This becomes more clear as one understands the nature of primary religious language.

Primary religious language can be "the expression of a deeply entrenched moment of consciousness."[40] But Schleiermacher errs in presenting this moment as independent of thought and belief—that is, as presuppositionless. No experience occurs independently of language. Thus, the source of confusion in the appeal to an immediate self-consciousness is the mixing of the phenomenological and theoretical senses of *immediate.* This confusion stems from misunderstanding both the role of language and the boundaries of human reason. In essence, "we have no direct grasp of the objects of our experience."[41] This is so because "[w]e have no access to any uninterpreted given."[42] The finite limit of our understanding is thoroughly determined. "There are no data unshaped by the forms of sense and the categories of judgment, and those forms and categories cannot be legitimately employed to yield knowledge that transcends our experience."[43] The experience Schleiermacher attends to is "immediate" and is known only by acquaintance, but the language used to express it requires specific concepts. Thus, the appeal to this experience is evocative or constructive—not merely, if at all, descriptive. "Confusion arises, however, when language that is meant to function evocatively is also presented as analysis or as a theoretical account of religious experience."[44]

The purpose of Schleiermacher's universal claim to an immediate experience of God is not to describe such an experience but actually to create, and hence advance, that experience to the reader. Phenomenology, in the guise of the theoretical, characterizes his claim about religious experience. This evocative role of theological language is explicitly operative in thought that assumes a common humanity necessary for its universal claims.

"Common Humanity" versus a Theory of Doubt

Theologies claiming universal truths often appeal to a common experience, a kind of experience that is accessible at some level to all. Likewise, the ascription of meaning as intrinsic to a religious experience implies a common understanding of an experience that is capable of being shared universally. Given a common essence of humanity, a deeply entrenched moment of consciousness that is immediate and revelatory for one must be possible universally.

A constructive theory of language obviates any common humanity in that sense, for "[T]here are no natural expressions of inner states in the sense of the direct manifestations that Schleiermacher's theory requires."[45] For Proudfoot, experience presupposes judgments. Judgments presuppose concepts. Concepts are produced in a social context by an endless variety of historical and linguistic factors. Since these constitutive elements of human experience differ radically among individuals, even among members of a close community, natural expressions or universal claims of immediacy are never identical. Thus, "piety" is never exactly the same for any two people, let alone for human beings of radically different cultures.[46]

A particular view of hermeneutics grounds this opposition to a universally accessible experience that is made possible by a common humanity. A theory of interpretation favoring the "pragmatic tradition" emerges, which maintains that language and history, a priori, determine or identify all experience of human being.[47] This approach effectively inhibits any appeal to a common judgment of meaning delivered by any particular experience. "Religious experience" becomes a concept. It is a kind of knowledge dependent upon particular beliefs, and nothing more.

Interpretation—that is, the understanding of texts, myths, and other cultural products—is "the method required for grasping the rules that govern a certain system of symbols or conventional practices."[48] Interpretation, for example, includes the understanding of the rule of grammar that one applies to a text. Two traditions of interpretation prominent in the history of Western thought—the "hermeneutic" and the "pragmatic"—have been critically operational in analyses of religious experience.[49] A brief review of both traditions is necessary to clarify the respective contributions of both schools.

The hermeneutic tradition argues for an approach to human history and culture markedly different from that used in the study of "natural" phenomena. The pragmatic approach, conversely, holds that the "processes of inquiry and inference are invariant with respect to the object of study."[50] Each tradition offers positive and negative contributions to the understanding of religious experience.

The hermeneutic tradition's positive insight is "that an experience, emotion, intention, action or belief must be identified under a description that accords with the rules governing the subject's language and behavior."[51] But this tradition errs in asserting that one can know an experience only "by sharing it, evoking it in oneself, applying it, or by participating in it in some way."[52] Thus, Proudfoot finds the hermeneutic tradition guilty of assuming a common humanity from which certain experiences can be designated as universal.[53]

Schleiermacher's work on interpretation is the foundation of the hermeneutic tradition. His first, "grammatical" moment was an understanding of the language, culture, and social context in which a text was situated. The second, "divinatory" moment constituted the heart of Schleiermacher's hermeneutics; it sought to understand the mind of the author through an analysis of the author's style and intentions. Its exercise was accomplished by an immediate intuition made possible through participation in direct acquaintance with the author's experience.

> The assumption of a common humanity guarantees that it will always be possible for the interpreter to cultivate himself in such a way as to be able to elicit in his own mind the experience expressed by the author of the text on which he is working. When that happens, interpreter and author meet, the interpreter "turns himself into the author," and the individuality expressed in the text is immediately grasped.[54]

But no such "common humanity" exists.[55] The linguistic and historical plurality that conditions humanity must be taken seriously. Language and history construct every individual experience. Thus, any common attribution denies elements of real difference determinative of every human subject. This will result in a radical rejection of Schleiermacher's appeal to religious experience. It denies the possibility of understanding anyone's "religious experience"—for every experience is so specific to a person's language and history that little or nothing about it can qualify as "common." The analysis of religious experience, then, must be of a descriptive nature: while the scholar may analyze a given description (concept) of religious experience, there is no access to the verity of the *term* of the experience as such.

The pragmatic tradition of hermeneutics is said to originate with the early Charles Sanders Peirce. His arguments include an "attack on foundationalism" and a pragmatic theory of meaning and inquiry "inspired by the procedures of the experimentalist."[56] The early Peirce critiqued all forms of foundationalism in epistemology. He denied any possibility of intuitive cognition and immediate self-consciousness. This resulted in a theory of inquiry motivated by subjective doubt. One must note Peirce's change from this position, but it remains important for the critique of immediate religious experience.[57]

The only evidence that some moment of consciousness is immediate and intuitive is our feeling that it is such—and this is clearly insufficient. An intuition is "a cognition not determined by a previous cognition of the same object, and therefore so determined by something out of consciousness."[58]

Self-knowledge is possible only through "hypothetical reasoning from external facts. None of our cognitions is immediately given, or uninterpreted."[59] Identifying a feeling as immediate when it is in a hidden way dependent upon other cognitions is a widespread misperception. The only way to trust that anything is immediate is to be certain it was an intuition "as opposed to an assumption or opinion that was the result of education, cultural habits, or social influence."[60]

Knowledge of objects necessitates a reflection on knowledge of ourselves—the former actually becomes the possibility for the latter. The early Peirce denies any immediate self-consciousness in self-knowledge and instead views it as "the product of inference." He asserts that "the only way to investigate a psychological question is by inference from external facts, and that all ascriptions to ourselves of internal states must be construed as hypotheses to explain those facts."[61] These first two denials, of intuitive cognition and of immediate self-consciousness, entail that no uninterpreted experience exists. What results is a theory of doubt that avoids any appeal to intuition and claims that "inquiry is elicited by real doubt, and its purpose is to settle opinion and fix belief."[62] Any appeal to an experience of "interiority" for the process of inquiry is clearly mistaken, for it presumes an immediate consciousness uninformed by external references.

The pragmatic tradition, for its part, fails to take sufficient account of "the distinctive problems posed by the interpretation of texts and practices."[63] Testing hypotheses, for example, "is not always appropriate for the task of understanding the thoughts or practices of another."[64] But positively, the pragmatic tradition realizes that all observation is theory laden and that even the way our assumptions and questions are shaped is established prior to the inquiry. "In this context, interpretation means not the decoding of texts or cultural symbols, but the construction and assessment of hypotheses. Reflection on the conduct of inquiry and the interpretation of experience has been central to the pragmatic tradition."[65]

Whatever its limitations, the pragmatic tradition is clear on one point—there is no immediate self-consciousness because all data originate from the external. Any claim of "immediacy" must then be identified as an "emotion" due to its conceptual reliance upon the externals of language and history. Thus, a conceptual theory of emotion, emerging from a postmodern theory of language, grounds the pragmatic approach to interpretation as it critiques Schleiermacher's appeal to an immediate experience of God.

Schleiermacher's appeal to an experience of God for the basis of theological understanding is articulated *from within* a particular belief system. What is needed is an analysis of religious experience *from without,* one that can distinguish between the various and sometimes contradictory articulations of religious experience. This analysis, made from some distance, can separate the theoretical from the phenomenological and the psychological from the analytical because it has no agenda outside of explicating the concept. Hence, theory is preferable to theology for an accurate analysis of religious experience.

THEORY VERSUS THEOLOGY

Because language is constructive and a universal experience empirically implausible, a coherent analysis of religious experience(s) can be accomplished only through a "theory of religion." The theorist, in this sense of the word, maintains a distance from the phenomenon to sort and analyze the given data responsibly. Schleiermacher is guilty of the exact distortion attributed to the traditional view of religious experience: namely, that since assumed beliefs or concepts constitute religious experience, those who promulgate the very belief system they participate in simply make universal their own particular experience. Therefore, disconnected theorists—those outside the particular belief system within which the experience is situated— are better positioned to evaluate religious experience. Those not invested in a particular piety are better suited to analyze the piety of others. The inadequate critique of Freudian reductionism by D. Z. Phillips is a case in point: "The characterizations of religious belief offered by Phillips are as inadequate as his accounts of the theories of others. The problem arises from his attempt to attribute to believers the neutrality appropriate for the scholar describing religious beliefs."[66]

The theorist of religious experience walks a fine line—"we want to identify certain experiences as religious without committing ourselves to endorsing the claims that are constitutive of those experiences."[67] Professional analysis, combined with personal distance, is the preferred method. Consequently, the description of religious experience will not be aimed at any "essence" of religious experience, for there is no essence. Rather, the aim is to explicate the concept. While "experience" covers a wide variety of phenomena from dreams to extraordinary states, "to call something an experience requires that it be specified under a description that can be plausibly ascribed to the person to whom we attribute the experience."[68] In any description of religious experience one must carefully distinguish between "ascribed to the person" and "employed by the person."

Descriptions of religious experience "must employ only concepts in the subject's repertoire, and any background beliefs or desires presupposed by the attribution of the experience to the subject must be plausibly ascribed to the subject."[69] Therefore, an experience is properly religious only if the subject deems it to have "religious significance or import." This is determined to the extent that the subject is convinced that "the experience could not be accounted for without reference to religious beliefs."[70] "A religious experience is an experience that is identified by its subject as religious, and this identification must be based, not on the subject matter or content of the experience, but on its noetic quality or its significance for the truth of religious beliefs."[71]

"Reductionism" has long been the accusation of those in the field of religion who are threatened by historical, psychological, or sociological explanations of the origins of religious phenomena.[72] A careful distinction between the types of reductionism addresses the concerns of those who fear the critiques of "neutral" theorists. At issue is the way in which the theorist identifies a particular experience. The theorist must identify the experience of another with the concepts and beliefs that have informed that subject's experience.[73] But this does not mean that the theorist and the subject need to agree on the cause of the experience. Descriptive and explanatory reduction delineate the distinction between what is and is not acceptable for the theorist:

> *Descriptive reduction* is the failure to *identify* an emotion, practice, or experience under the description by which the subject identifies it. This is indeed unacceptable. To describe an experience in nonreligious terms when the subject himself describes it in religious terms is to misidentify the experience, or to attend to another experience altogether. . . .
>
> *Explanatory reduction* consists in offering an *explanation* of an experience in terms that are not those of the subject and that might not meet his approval. This is perfectly justifiable and is, in fact, normal procedure. The explanation stands or falls according to how well it can account for all the available evidence.[74]

The reaction to reductionism from within the religious establishment by those who advocate a particular religious experience has conflated these two kinds of reductionism. The first is an obfuscation of the experience itself, while the second is a privilege accorded to theorists of any science as they analyze and sort a given field of data. The failure to distinguish between these types of reduction is at the core of protective strategies employed by those who are threatened by the sciences and their impact on religion.

Descriptive reduction is emphasized by opponents of reductionism to insist that all accounts of religious experience confine themselves only to descriptions that would be acceptable to the subject of that experience. This harmonizes with the view that to truly understand an experience, one must know it by direct acquaintance (which implies that at some level such an experience is universally accessible). What opponents of explanatory reduction misunderstand is that while the explanatory hypotheses differ from those of the subject, they are necessary for the theoretical study of religious experience. The theoretical study of religious experience is, perhaps, the only guard against evocation concealed as description: that is, phenomenology in the guise of the theoretical advanced by proponents of particular faith experiences.[75]

Mysticism: An Instantiation of the Postmodern Critique

Just as Schleiermacher's struggle with the doctrine of the Trinity exemplified his hermeneutics for reappropriating certain doctrines for his church, Proudfoot's analysis of the phenomenon of mysticism can illustrate his approach to religious experience. Using the categories of William James, and relying heavily on the thought of Steven Katz, Proudfoot reveals the core elements of mystical experience to be essentially constructive.[76]

There is no fixed meaning for the term *religious experience* that is "based on universally shared intuitions."[77] Even James's *sense* or *consciousness* that runs through the *Varieties of Religious Experience* has "the epistemic status of hypotheses."[78] For example, the presence of someone else sensed in a room would be, not a feeling, but a thought, hunch, or guess that results in a feeling. The priority of concepts over direct sensation is central to Proudfoot's understanding of mysticism:

[S]ense or consciousness is said to be more like a sensation than like an intellectual operation. It is formative of, rather than consequent upon, religious belief. But the examples James gives of a sense of reality or consciousness of a presence suggest that intellectual operations are involved, and that what he has called a sense is really a thought or belief. He proposes that questions of origin and questions of evaluation be radically separated in the study of religious experience. But his observation that experience is characterized by a noetic quality similar to that of sense perception suggests that matters of assessment and explanation cannot be kept as clearly distinct as he would like.[79]

A distinction between a description (descriptive reduction) of an experience and the attribution of its cause (explanatory reduction) must be made. The believer has unique access to the first. But the second part is open to the interpretation of the (neutral) theorist who, understanding language as an a priori, analyzes the description of the experience to discern its linguistic or conceptual cause. A theorist of religious experience evaluates the empirical data (description) and ascertains the term of those data. This is not possible for believers, who cannot maintain the proper theoretical distance from the experience and their own belief context to analyze it correctly.

Therefore, while it may seem that mysticism employs certain concepts to describe a particular religious experience, these concepts are actually applied to "restrict the conditions under which an experience can be properly identified as religious so as to guarantee that the experience picked out will not be subject to classification under our ordinary descriptive or explanatory categories."[80] "Ineffability" and "noetic quality," two concepts employed by William James in his description of mystical experience, illustrate this use of religious language.

James's study of the mystical begins with a search for a mystical core between and among various religious traditions. To even begin such a search, he must assume a common humanity. The study also includes distinctions between primary and secondary characteristics of mystical experience (i.e., language is descriptive). But "experience is shaped by a complex pattern of concepts, commitments, and expectations which the mystic brings to it."[81] Thus, beliefs and attitudes that *appear* to flow from religious experience are those that actually form their possibility.

Steven Katz (1978) recognizes that the mystic's experience is conditioned by the complex preexperiential pattern of beliefs, attitudes, and expectations that he brings to it. He illustrates this by contrasting the Jewish mystic's nonabsorbative encounter with God, on the one hand, with the unitive experience of some Christian mystics, on the other, and both of these with the insight into the impermanence of all things that constitutes the state of nirvana for the Buddhist. The fact that Jewish mystics do not experience union with God is best explained by reference to parameters set by the tradition that has formed their beliefs about persons and God and their expectations for such experience.[82]

Buddhists and Christians cannot have the same experience. The concepts from which an experience is derived and through which it is understood are constitutive of the experience itself. Therefore, it is theoretically implausible to equate cross-cultural descriptions of religious experience even if certain mental and physical traits associated with the experiences appear to be similar.[83] Descriptions of mystical states are formative: that is, they serve as tools for evocation in the reader.

James's "ineffability" may appear to be a "simple property of the experience" that defies expression.[84] But this mistakenly presumes a descriptive understanding of language. "According to him [Katz], the terms *paradox* and *ineffable* are mystifying ploys, serving only to cloak experiences from investigators and to render their comparative study impossible."[85] The terms *ineffable* and *paradoxical* are not imprecise and vague but very precise, and they require a reference to something by which to judge both the ineffable and paradoxical qualities. If both require a reference, references presuppose a symbol system as a context of meaning in which they can be situated. Insofar as this is true, "the ineffability of an experience must result from its logical or grammatical component."[86] For this reason, Katz "calls for a pluralistic account of these experiences and a halt to any search for common characteristics."[87]

Mystical experiences, like all religious experiences, are derived through and from preexperiential beliefs, attitudes, and concepts. Likewise, the religious object is consequent to a presupposed system of metaphysics within which it is already situated. This results in a constant tension between "God" and the God described by us through language. The tension between an indeterminate object and the determinate language used to describe it is a tension that pervades all good theology. Historically, perimeters have been erected to regulate the use of language in reference to a religious object. Anselm's *aliquid quo nihil maius cogitari potest*, Aquinas's *esse*, and Schleiermacher's *whence* function as "placeholders" in these systems of thought whose purpose is to guarantee some degree of ineffability. The refusal to admit any determinate characterization of an experience is therefore a tool, a placeholder, for evoking the experience in others while repelling serious inquiry and analysis. Whether such designations actually point to something "real" that eludes or is prior to language is not considered, for language is the possibility of experience.

"Noetic quality," the second characteristic for identifying mystical experience in the Jamesian view, claims that a religious experience provides some insight or knowledge with a sense of objectivity. One should not focus upon the noetic results of a mystical experience; rather, one should note the role of noesis in shaping those experiences. The preparatory exercises undertaken by mystical seekers in various traditions illustrate this point:

> The mystic's identification of his experience requires a commitment to a certain kind of explanation or, what comes down to the same thing, the exclusion of a particular kind of explanation. He must identify his experience under a certain description, and that description must preclude naturalistic explanation. The assumption that the experience cannot be exhaustively accounted for in naturalistic terms is included in the criteria for identifying an experience as mystical. Not surprisingly, then, it turns out that mystical experiences elude natural explanations.[88]

Mystical experience can be identified either by a description of certain states, with no judgment concerning their origin, or by the argument that naturalistic explanations are insufficient. These two alternatives are prominent in most literature on mysticism, and the second largely owes its existence to Hume's argument that a miracle is only a miracle if it violates the laws of nature.[89] The second view is predominant, for "judgment about these conditions is itself a part of the experience."[90] This is the key to the use of Jamesian categories. Any judgment of a mystical experience presupposes some concept of "naturalistic terms" and the boundaries of the natural. "In each case the point is a logical one having to do with the conditions under which an experience might be identified as mystical, and is independent of the content of particular situations."[91] Therefore, the purpose of describing mystical experiences is to render its description indeterminate. This, in turn, serves as an evocative tool to encourage readers toward a particular faith.[92]

The argument of *Religious Experience* began with an analysis of accounts of "religious experience," mainly in works by Schleiermacher, James, and Otto, all of whom hold a primacy of "feeling" over thought and action.[93] Proudfoot argues for exactly the opposite. The previous authors focus on "immediate" experiences that connect them to the "Infinite" in some sense of relationship. Proudfoot's theoretical approach is concerned with the components of the concept of a particular experience—the individual, human assumptions (i.e., the categories and forms of the mind, including language and beliefs) that one takes into defining a religious experience.

> The experience to which Schleiermacher appeals assumes certain concepts and beliefs. The authority of religious experience rests upon certain judgments about how that experience is to be explained. The noetic quality cited by James is not given in the experience but assumes a tacit judgment about the kind of explanation appropriate for that experience. The authority of religious doctrine or of the religious form of life cannot be disconnected from other concepts and beliefs. Each of these attempts to restrict philosophical or theological reflection to internal analysis, and elucidation fails because the doctrines and experiences to be analyzed assume concepts and beliefs that are not distinctively religious and because the authority of the doctrine or experience assume[s] a tacit explanatory commitment.[94]

This approach is advanced through three arguments. First, language is constitutive of experience, and a conceptual theory of emotion inhibits any reliance upon an "interiority," however conceived. Religious experience is constructed from language and belief. Second, a pragmatic theory of interpretation eclipses any possibility of an appeal to a universal experience/ subjectivity or a common understanding of "experience." Finally, a "neutral" theorist able to sort the given data without being influenced by subjective interests best accomplishes analysis of religious experience. Any experience beyond the analysis applied to the human presuppositions involved (if there is one) remains inaccessible.

This approach to the evaluation of "religious experience" is consistent in works by Proudfoot dating back to the 1970s. *God and Self: Three Types of Philosophy of Religion* advances a definition for philosophy of religion that is similar to the argument made in *Religious Experience:* "It is the rational reconstruction of concepts that originate in the symbols and practices that constitute religious experience. These symbols and practices are those which enable a person or a culture to deal with crises of interpretability as these arise in limiting or boundary situations."[95]

A theorist of religious experience analyzes the linguistic and social factors productive of religious experiences. An account of a religious experience emerges that is free from the agenda of those who wish to promulgate a particular truth claim. "Theology is the same kind of rational reconstruction, but is one in which the conception of God is central."[96] Theology is not a descriptive discipline: that is, a discipline aimed at bringing greater clarity to an existing and accessible truth claim. The world, for the postmodern theorist, is not directly intelligible—hence, neither is any truth claim. "In a post-Kantian context, theology cannot be seen as a direct description of some external world with which we can make direct contact. It is rather an attempt to construct interpretations of God, the self, the world, and appropriate categories for describing our experiences in that world."[97] The role of theology is to construct interpretations of reality as "limit and boundary situations" require. The limits of experience require the construction of the conceptions of God and Self. The self "stands at the limit that is the origin of our acts, and is thus inaccessible to us in our thinking or action."[98] A conception of God "stands at the limit of our ability to imagine the origin and goal of all experience."[99] Human limitation requires the constructions of God and Self to make life bearable. As human experience changes, so will the theology constructive of that belief-experience. Whether and if these conceptions actually correspond to any reality is another question completely—perhaps one that can never be answered—at least for the theorist of religion.

One implication of this theoretical approach to religious experience is realized through what might seem a peculiar omission for a work on religious experience. One notices in the section on mysticism, for example, the lack of primary sources drawn from the "mystical" tradition. Most, if not all, references are secondary. For an inquiry into religious experience, with a chapter on mysticism, not to deal directly with any primary sources of the mystical tradition is fundamentally unacceptable. It will become evident that the role of observer in Proudfoot's definition of *experience* is very important and is responsible for the lack of primary sources.

The postmodern method does not analyze a relational experience in which descriptive accounts are given of a direct or immediate experience of God. It is constrained from saying anything about the *term* of such an experience if it lies outside of language and culture paradigms. Or perhaps the term has been stated quite clearly: the term of religious experience is the accumulation of presuppositions from which a "religious experience" is derived. The final remark on the uniqueness of religious experience supports this assertion. "The distinguishing mark of a religious experience is not the subject matter but the kind of explanation the subject believes is appropriate." This is some-what similar to elements of Feuerbach's thought. Instead of "God" as a pro-jection of the human ideal, now "God" or an experience of "God" is the pro-jection of presupposed beliefs. Essentially, the language/belief paradigm that produces religious experience for the human becomes deified.

Religious Experience exemplifies the use of postmodern presuppositions by a theorist of religion to approach the particular conception of religious expe-rience put forth by Schleiermacher. George Lindbeck offers a *theological* cri-tique of Schleiermacher and of those who possess similar understandings of experience and language.

George Lindbeck's *Nature of Doctrine:* A Postmodern Theological Effort

The problem, as the title of this essay suggests, is not confined to doctrines per se but extends to the notion of religion itself. Theories of religion and of doctrine are interdependent, and deficiencies in one area are inseparable from deficiencies in the other. Furthermore, all the standard theological approaches are unhelpful. The difficulties cannot be solved by, for example, abandoning modern developments and returning to some form of preliberal orthodoxy. A third, a postliberal, way of conceiving religion and religious doctrine is called for.

—Lindbeck, *The Nature of Doctrine*[1]

Two fundamental concerns underlie *The Nature of Doctrine* as it proposes a new, postmodern framework for reconceiving religion and religious doctrine. First, ecumenical endeavors both past and present demand new concepts to remove anomalies present in doctrinal disputes among Christian denominations. These anomalies of concern include the "interrelationship of doctrinal permanence and change, conflict and compatibility, unity and disunity, and variety and uniformity among, but especially within religions."[2] How might religion and doctrine be reinterpreted to allow for real progress on these issues? Second, theology's resistance to using prominent academic methods of analysis isolates it from other recognized and credible sciences. For this reason one must be concerned for the academic status, and hence the legitimacy, of the study of theology.

Religion and religious discourse are slowly removing themselves from contemporary intellectual movements in the academy. "Other sciences" increasingly employ the cultural-linguistic method within their respective fields of study. Consequently, the elaboration of a theoretical framework for religion using this method becomes a primary concern.[3] For a theory of religion, inquiry must be both strictly theoretical and religiously neutral. Any other approach to religion and doctrine will prove to be either provincial or relativistic.

Within this overall method, "theology" becomes a subset of a theory of religion. This latter includes "scholarly activity of second-order reflection on the data of religion (including doctrinal data) and of formulating arguments for or against material positions (including doctrinal ones)."[4] Thus, theology engages in second-order discourse—discourse about the language and grammar of doctrine and their impact on the anatomy of religious experience. This division between first-order discourse (in which truth claims are made) and second-order discourse (which speaks of grammar) becomes critical for the application of this "rule theory" to particular doctrines. Such a distinction allows one to understand doctrines as rules for speaking and thinking about God, while avoiding conflict over first-order truth claims that are often considered timeless absolutes.

According to Lindbeck, one can come to understand the foundations of religion and the role of experience through an analysis of current theological theories of religion and doctrine. Lindbeck's comparisons and critiques of these theories hinge upon a particular understanding of language extended to the notion of religion and its relation to experience and come to focus upon what he claims to be the best approach to doctrinal disputes—the cultural-linguistic method.[5] This method can advance ecumenical efforts and is illustrated by its application to the doctrine of the Trinity.

Three major contentions operate throughout *The Nature of Doctrine* that are similar to those advanced by Proudfoot for a theory of religion. First, current "theological theories of religion" are inadequate. These theories fail to grasp the formative function of language (and, by extension, religion) in the construction of "experience." Thus, these current theological theories erroneously assume a universally accessible human experience required for the imposition of their corresponding universal truth claims. Second, the approach to religion and doctrine through the cultural-linguistic method is the best way to accomplish "doctrinal reconciliation without capitulation" because the application of doctrinal rules, or language about a given topic, can change with a given context. Finally, the cultural-linguistic method allows the purpose of specifically Christian theology to emerge: to aid the biblical narrative in constituting the belief and experience of Christian communities.

RELIGION AND DOCTRINE: CURRENT THEOLOGICAL THEORIES

Current theological theories of religion and doctrine fall into three broad categories. The first category, propositionalism, "emphasizes the cognitive aspects" of religion.[6] The second, or "experiential-expressive" category, emphasizes the experiential aspect of religion almost exclusively. The third category is a combination of these two approaches that considers both the "cognitively propositional and the expressly symbolic dimensions and functions of religion and doctrine . . . as religiously significant and valid."[7] All three theories result in an unsatisfactory formation and maintenance of doctrine. This is so because they ultimately fail to achieve "doctrinal reconciliation without capitulation."[8]

The propositional approach to religion and doctrine occurs exclusively as first-order discourse: it "stresses the ways in which church doctrines function as informative propositions or truth claims about objective realities."[9] Such a method is concerned with the meaningfulness of religious utterances but misunderstands language as corresponding directly to intelligible, universal truth claims. Doctrinal reconciliation without capitulation is impossible in this propositional approach because "if a doctrine is once true, it is always true, and if it is once false, it is always false."[10] The meanings of doctrines remain inflexibly fixed and therefore cannot change "while remaining the same."[11]

The experiential-expressive approach to religion "interprets doctrines as noninformative and nondiscursive symbols of inner feelings, attitudes, or existential orientations."[12] Doctrines express and are continually measured as effective against a prereflexive experience or existential orientation. This approach began with Schleiermacher and is equally unsatisfactory for doctrinal reconciliation. Different and developing existential orientations and experiences are unable to maintain doctrinal consistency. Thus, the elasticity between "meaning" and "doctrines" is quite pronounced under some uses (e.g., Schleiermacher's project), and doctrinal stability becomes unfeasible.

74 THEOLOGY AT THE VOID

The general principle is that insofar as doctrines function as nondiscursive symbols, they are polyvalent in import and therefore subject to
changes of meaning or even to a total loss of meaningfulness, to what
Tillich calls their death. They are not crucial for religious agreement or
disagreement, because these are constituted by harmony or conflict in
underlying feelings, attitudes, existential orientations, or practices, rather
than by what happens on the level of symbolic (including doctrinal)
objectifications.[13]

The third category of theological theories combines the cognitively propositional and experiential-expressive approaches. While this method is able to
"account more fully . . . for both variable and invariable aspects of religious
traditions," the practical application of such an approach continually falls
short of the goal.[14] This is so for two reasons. First, this method lacks the criteria with which to determine "when a given doctrinal development is consistent with the sources of faith,"[15] so it must rely on the magisterium more than
is desirable. Second, the "explanations of how this reconciliation is possible
tend to be too awkward and complex to be easily intelligible or convincing."[16]
The third or hybrid theory, therefore, is also unacceptable.[17]

The hybrid approach to religion can be representatively exemplified
through five of the six theses that Lonergan puts forth in his theory of religion:[18] "(1) Different religions are diverse expressions or objectifications
of a common core experience. (2) The experience, while conscious, may be
unknown on the level of self-conscious reflection. (3) This experience is present in all human beings. (4) In most religions, the experience is the source and
norm of objectifications. (5) The primordial religious experience is God's gift
of love."[19] Lonergan's theory of religion first errs when the "term" of this
experience (he specifically names God as the author of this primordial experience of love), a first-order truth claim, is identified in a confessional sense.
It is unacceptable to reference the "term" because "it is difficult or impossible
to specify" the distinctive features of the core experience.[20] Because it is not
possible to detail concretely this core experience, one should refrain from
using it to assert either its cause or its universal accessibility in human experience. Material points, at least those not empirically specifiable, have no
place in a theory of religion.

If one proceeds to assert this universal human experience, it "becomes
logically and empirically vacuous."[21] The characterization of a core experi-

ence designated as prior to a subject-object differentiation is problematic because the preconceptual and prelinguistic aspects of this experience are unspecifiable. This has a corresponding effect on the experience itself. If an experience is unspecifiable, so is its cause. Thus, what amounts to speculation cannot contribute to sound theoretical or theological inquiry. Because the characterizations of this experience are empirically deficient, confusing, and often quite different among theologians, more problems are created than solved when a common and universal religious experience is used as a basis for theological inquiry or doctrinal formation.

THE CULTURAL-LINGUISTIC METHOD

The previous three categories of theological theory are either too rigid in maintaining doctrinal meaning, too elastic with doctrinal meaning, or simply too complex to be easily intelligible. The theological landscape is effectively cleared of viable options for the goal of doctrinal reconciliation without capitulation. The problems of indeterminacy, ambiguity, and sometimes even contradiction associated with the previous approaches can be adequately addressed only by introducing an alternative—the cultural-linguistic approach. This method addresses the anomalies of doctrinal permanency and change by substantially reinterpreting religion and doctrine.

> It has become customary in a considerable body of anthropological, sociological, and philosophical literature (about which more will be said later) to emphasize neither the cognitive nor the experiential-expressive aspects of religion; rather, emphasis is placed on those respects in which religions resemble languages together with their correlative forms of life and are thus similar to cultures (insofar as these are understood semiotically as reality and value systems—that is, as idioms for the construing of reality and the living of life). The function of church doctrines that becomes most prominent in this perspective is their use, not as expressive symbols or as truth claims, but as communally authoritative rules of discourse, attitude and action. This general way of conceptualizing religion will be called in what follows a "cultural-linguistic" approach, and the implied view of church doctrine will be referred to as a "regulative" or "rule" theory.[22]

A growing number of fields are using the cultural-linguistic method–history, anthropology, sociology, philosophy, criminology, and psychology (Proudfoot is mentioned specifically in terms of conceptual attribution theory).[23] Originators of this approach in their various fields of study include Karl Marx, Max Weber, Emile Durkheim, G. H. Mead, Peter Berger, Ludwig Wittgenstein, Peter Winch, and Clifford Geertz.[24]

Though experiential models continue to be attractive in theological circles, their prominence has receded in the nontheological study of religion and in other disciplines. Academic disciplines in general have bypassed the experiential-expressive approach in favor of a cultural-linguistic method, while those "commending religion to society at large" continue to appeal to religious experience.[25] "Historians, anthropologists, sociologists, and philosophers (with the exception of some phenomenologists) seem increasingly to find the cultural-linguistic approaches congenial."[26] The reason for this difference between the academic and the pastoral is the marketability of the experiential-expressive approach for modern theological and pastoral needs. The experiential-expressive approach and hybrid models of close proximity are prevalent today because the goal of contemporary theology has become the fulfillment of the modern psyche.

> The structures of modernity press individuals to meet God first in the depths of their souls and then, perhaps, if they find something personally congenial, to become part of a tradition or join a church. Their actual behavior may not conform to this model, but it is the way they experience themselves. Thus the traditions of religious thought and practice into which Westerners are most likely to be socialized conceal from them the social origins of their conviction that religion is a highly private and individual matter.[27]

The modern psyche seeks comfort and fulfillment. Religion promises that in the depths of the soul through "religious experiences." The appeal to experience is attractive because it provides an existentially accessible avenue to faith. "Religions are seen as multiple suppliers of different forms of a single commodity needed for transcendent self-expression and self-realization."[28]

One must view with concern the presentation of theology, marketed for modern pastoral needs, through a method at odds with nearly every other academic discipline. A different or opposing method for theological inquiry "tends to ghettoize theology and deprive[s] it of the vitality that comes from close association with the best in non-theological thinking."[29] Other sciences have turned to the cultural-linguistic method for inquiry in their respective fields. Theology can and should do the same.

Unlike most other disciplines in the academy, the discipline of "religious studies" is concerned with a person's relation to an "other" that somehow encounters the human subject. A cultural-linguistic theory, one that prefers categories of formation (language and culture) to categories of relation (depth experience), would appear insufficient to provide the necessary line of thought to frame relationality in the context of religion. It may seem that "the cultural and linguistic approaches are better suited to the non-theological study of religion."[30] This appears to be so because "languages and cultures do not make truth claims, are relative to particular times and places, and are difficult to think of as having transcendent rather than this-worldly origins."[31] This, of course, presupposes the understanding of experience and religion that undergirds the experiential-expressivist approach. At issue is the need to explore and reframe, in greater depth, the relationship between experience (religious or otherwise) and religion.

The cultural-linguistic approach to religion and its relation to "experience" is derived from the language theory of the ever-recurring thought of Ludwig Wittgenstein. The idea that language is constructive of reality is extended to the notion of religion itself. "There are several ways of arguing this. The most ambitious is Wittgenstein's contention that private languages are logically impossible. If so, the same would have to be said regarding private religious experiences (such as the dynamic state of being unrestrictedly in love), which are purportedly independent of any particular language game."[32] For this reason religion, like language, "is similar to an idiom that makes possible the description of realities, the formulation of beliefs, and the experiencing of inner attitudes, feelings, and sentiments."[33] Thus, religion structures reality, but language structures the possibility for religion. Thus, the culture and language that form the human subject elicit (create) certain responses to certain stimuli. This becomes the essence of religion. "First come the objectivities of the religion, its language, doctrines, liturgies, and modes of action, and it is through these that passions are shaped into various kinds of what is called religious experience."[34] This has direct consequences for the new definition of religion proposed. Religion cannot be something universal "arising from within the depths of individuals" (for this assumes a common humanity); rather, religion must be "a variegated set of cultural-linguistic systems that, at least in some cases, differentially shape and produce our most profound sentiments, attitudes, and awareness."[35] While the experiential-expressive approach to religion views itself as a *product* of a religious experience, the cultural-linguistic approach views itself as a *producer* of religious experience.[36]

Experience *qua* experience still has a very important role for the cultural-linguistic method. For traditional experiential-expressivists such as Schleiermacher, and for theologians such as Rahner and Lonergan who combine approaches, experience *qua* experience and the subsequent reflection upon it are two distinct moments.[37] The opposite is true for the cultural-linguistic method.

> We cannot identify, describe, or recognize experience *qua* experience without the use of signs and symbols. These are necessary even for what the depth psychologist speaks of as "unconscious" or "subconscious" experiences, or for what the phenomenologist describes as prereflective ones. In short, it is necessary to have the means of expressing an experience in order to have it, and the richer our expressive or linguistic system, the more subtle, varied, and differentiated can be our experience.[38]

For this reason, "religion is above all an external word, a *verbum externum,* that molds and shapes the self and its world. Language is not an expression or thematization of a preexisting self or of preconceptual experience."[39] Language, viewed as constructive, rejects a correspondence between language and what is "out there" and instead confirms only intertextual reference and a meaning therein. There is no possibility of an encounter with external *reference* or with anything else that transcends the boundaries of one's language or culture paradigm.[40] One's reality and one's language are de facto one and the same—language, and by extension religion, constructs reality.[41]

Religions, like languages, are better seen as "comprehensive interpretive schemes" that structure human experience and the understanding of self and world.[42] They are cultural frameworks "that shape the entirety of life and thought."[43] Religion is not primarily (though perhaps it is secondarily) an array of beliefs concerning the truth or a symbolism of attitudes, feelings, or sentiments. "Instead of deriving external features of a religion from inner experience, it is the inner experiences which are viewed as derivative."[44]

Two critical definitions underlie the cultural-linguistic interpretation of the relation between language and experience. The first pertains to limitations on the definition of experience; the second concerns the order of "mental activities." First, experience considered apart from its communication or symbolization is not possible. That is, an experience and the ability to identify the meaning of it cannot be separated—the latter is the possibility for the former. Experience, in itself, can never be isolated. Practically applied, there are no strictly private experiences because "all symbol systems have their origin in interpersonal relations and social interactions."[45] At issue is the relation between language as sign and a reality signified.

> When one pictures inner experiences as prior to expression and communication, it is natural to think of them in their most basic and elemental form as also prior to conceptualization or symbolization. If, in contrast, expressive and communicative symbols, whether linguistic or non-linguistic, are primary—then, while there are of course nonreflective experiences, there are no uninterpreted or unschematized ones. On this view, the means of communication and expression are a precondition, a kind of quasi-transcendental (i.e., culturally formed) *a priori* for the possibility of experience.[46]
>
> ... Thus language, it seems, shapes domains of human existence and action that are preexperiential.[47]

Language is the condition for the possibility of experience. Without language, outside of language, or beyond language, experience is not available. This assertion is critical for what will follow and is informative of the entire argument that Lindbeck proposes.

Second, the order of mental activities supports this interpretation of language and experience.[48] The first mental intention is "the act whereby we grasp objects." The second intention "is the reflex act of grasping or reflecting on first formal intentions."[49] First-intentional experiences are possible only as "by-products of linguistically or conceptually structured cognitive activities."[50] Thus, one cannot grasp, know, or experience anything without certain tools that are prepossessed by being culturally communicated. This applies to religious experience as well.

This understanding of language and experience has far-reaching consequences. Formerly, "depth experiences in which religions originate according to expressive models are easily pictured as involving communion with or openness to transcendent reality, and this makes it possible to speak of religions as having a certain kind of divine truth and, in their generic aspect, universal validity."[51] Now, with the cultural-linguistic method, there can be no "universal principles or structures—if not metaphysical, then existential, phenomenological, or hermeneutical."[52] There is no possibility of appealing to any one principle or experience participated in by various peoples, even within a relatively closed society. The language and culture that form experience are endlessly diverse; hence, so is every experience. Second, "[t]o the degree that religions are like languages and cultures, they can no more be taught by means of translation than can Chinese or French."[53] The first argument makes a universal appeal to "others" impossible due to the lack of a universal human experience.[54] The second reinforces this view with a particular understanding of language that severely limits a belief system and its attendant "truth claims" to those who share the idiom.[55] Both assertions originate from anthropological (and theological) presuppositions concerning the constitution of human subjectivity. For human beings, the availability of "experience" is totally confined to the boundaries of a given environment: that is, a particular cultural-linguistic paradigm.

For the "scientific study" of religion (i.e., a theory of religion), the experiential-expressive approach is certainly inadequate. First, it assumes a common human experience and, in this way, a common humanity that is nothing less than the imposition of one cultural-linguistic paradigm onto others. Second, it asserts universal truths applicable to all, from the same limited perspective. When the factors of language, culture, belief, and history—formative elements of real difference—are taken seriously, the experiential-expressive method is revealed for what it is—simply one view among many. Though the experiential-expressive method is inadequate for the scientific study of religion, the opposite question remains: Can the cultural-linguistic approach best serve theology?

THE CULTURAL-LINGUISTIC METHOD APPLIED: THE DOCTRINE OF THE TRINITY

The understanding of doctrine as rules for discourse (a necessary part of a cultural-linguistic approach to religion) can accomplish the goal of doctrinal reconciliation without capitulation because rules "retain an invariant meaning under changing conditions of compatibility and conflict."[56] Specifying their contextual application can sometimes solve opposition between rules. The cultural-linguistic method will approach the specifically doctrinal aspect of theology through a preference for second-order discourse (grammar) over first-order discourse (truth claims). This is necessary to avoid the divisive and crippling debates surrounding various absolute "truth" claims made about objective realities. One can then avoid the confusion with inner relations to outer realities (a "material" point) and instead focus on the "theoretical" aspects of a methodology that works from various cultural and linguistic influences to the individual. Theological questions, in turn, are pursued within an established theoretical construct.

The cultural-linguistic method, or rule theory, can be illustrated by applying it to one divisive ecumenical issue, the traditional doctrine of the Trinity. This application will affirm the original intent of the doctrine of the Trinity while simultaneously bridging ecumenical divisions over it. The goal is to maintain the unconditionality of classic Christological and Trinitarian affirmations while allowing for new understandings and formulations of the doctrine that can better serve the needs of contemporary ecumenism.

One must first differentiate between "doctrines" and "the terminology and conceptuality in which they are formulated."[57] Church doctrines are "communally authoritative teachings regarding beliefs and practices that are considered essential to the identity or welfare of the group in question."[58] "For a rule theory, in short, doctrines *qua* doctrines are not first-order propositions but are to be construed as second-order ones; they make, as was said in the closing of the previous chapter, intrasystematic rather than ontological truth claims."[59]

Terms in doctrine such as *substance* (*ousia*), *person* (*hypostasis*), and *in two natures* (*en dyo physeis*) are "postbiblical novelties" that describe the content of revelation but are not found in Scripture itself.[60] Additionally, the variety of doctrinal forms in early Christianity points to a plurality evident in "the multiplicity of Christological titles in the New Testament."[61] Therefore, the terms used to construct the doctrine of the Trinity are distinguished from that which the terms designate. "This is easier to do if the doctrines are taken as expressing second-order guidelines for Christian discourse rather than first-order affirmations about the inner being of God or of Jesus Christ."[62] Divisive first-order language and its attendant "truth claims" (material points), those that claim a direct correspondence with some objective reality, are bypassed in favor of second-order discourse that concentrates on the guidelines for discussing material points (truth claims).[63] This approach to doctrinal reformulation is consistent with early Christian attempts to designate doctrine as communities of faith developed. A "grammatical analysis of the data of Scripture" has been prominent from the beginning of Christianity.[64] The emphasis during the early formation of doctrine is on the rules by which one speaks—not on the ontological reality that the words signify. The regulative, not the propositional, approach determined early Church doctrines.

> As a result of this "logical" (or one could say "grammatical") analysis of the data of Scripture and tradition, Athanasius expressed the meaning of, for example, consubstantiality in terms of the rule that whatever is said of the Father is said of the Son, except that the Son is not the Father (*eadem de Filio quae de Patre dicuntur excepto Patris Nomine*). Thus the theologian most responsible for the final triumph of Nicaea thought of it, not as a first-order proposition with ontological reference, but as a second-order rule of speech. For him, to accept the doctrine meant to agree to speak in a certain way.[65]

Three "regulative" principles (or rules) constituted the perimeters for the content of Christological and Trinitarian doctrine in the early Church. The first was the monotheistic principle: "There is only God, the God of Abraham, Isaac, Jacob, and Jesus." The second was the "principle of historical specificity: the stories of Jesus refer to a genuine human being" who lived and died in a particular space and time. The third was the principle of "Christological maximalism": "[E]very possible importance is to be ascribed to Jesus that is not inconsistent with the first rules."[66] These three regulative principles evident in the New Testament period provided the boundaries for the Christological and Trinitarian controversies that followed over the next four centuries. These principles constrained "Christians to use available conceptual and symbolical materials to relate Jesus Christ to God in certain ways and not in others."[67] Therefore, it is absolutely necessary to maintain these three principles, or, taken together, this paradigm, in any reformulation of the doctrine of the Trinity, though the actual terms that constitute the paradigm can and should change.

The terminology and concepts of "one substance and three persons" or "two natures" may be absent, but if the same rules that guided the formation of the original paradigms are operative in the construction of the new formulations, they express one and the same doctrine. There may, on this reading, be complete faithfulness to classical Trinitarianism and Christology even when the imagery and language of Nicaea and Chalcedon have disappeared from the theology and ordinary worship, preaching, and devotion.[68]

The application of a rule theory for reformulating the doctrine of the Trinity first establishes the paradigm that governs the use of particular terms and concepts.[69] This paradigm is the standard by which faithfulness to a particular historical doctrine is measured. Therefore, the discussion of the doctrine of the Trinity most effectively takes place on the level of second-order discourse (descriptive language) as opposed to first-order discourse (material points or truth claims). This is possible as long as these terms and concepts designate a rule or guideline to speak by and not a corresponding ontological reality in the subject matter they reference.[70]

A critical distinction in doctrinal authority is achieved when doctrine is thought of not in terms of an ontological correspondence of language and "truth" claims but in terms of a rule theory of language where doctrines function as a grammar of belief. "Yet though the ancient formulations may have continuing value, they do not on the basis of rule theory have doctrinal authority. That authority belongs rather to the rules they instantiate."[71] The authority for determining doctrine does not lie in magisterial communal authority to propound first-order propositions, nor does it lie in existential needs (experiential-expressive); rather, it lies in the magisterial authority to propound regulative principles operative at the initiation of a given doctrine.[72]

This application of "rule theory" to the doctrine of the Trinity has not suggested specific new terms for framing a contemporary doctrine of the Trinity. It has removed the hurdle of reliance on divisive first-order propositions (dependent on a correspondence theory of language), and it has established the possibility by which a discussion on the second-order level might occur.

The view of language necessary for a rule theory clearly holds that the human subject has no access to ontological truth through language in doctrine. Rather, one is grasped by the rules of grammar or the principles of a paradigm (e.g., monotheism, historical particularity, Christological maximalism).

These rules form and construct belief through doctrines that can change as long as their "principles" remain unchanged. And it is in this intrasystematic or intratextual sense that "truth claims" are maintained.[73] The motive for this shift from human (propositionalist/experiential-expressive) to narrative authority becomes evident when one closely examines the purpose of theology for Lindbeck.

THEORY OF RELIGION VERSUS THEOLOGY, AND THE PURPOSE OF THEOLOGY

The cultural-linguistic theory is one that can be religiously neutral. The theorist examines the data of a religion and its given doctrines and deduces the regulative principles prominent in their communication. The methodological starting point emphasizing the determinacy of language and history, a priori, keeps comfortably to the "facts"—the paradigmatic principles of doctrines and narratives that determine a particular community of faith. One then uses the postmodern linguistic and historical "turn" to analyze religion and doctrine while maintaining a degree of "theoretical neutrality." Because the goal is not to defend some universal truth claim but to analyze second-order discourse and its relation to the regulative principles from which it emerges, rule theory is applicable to any doctrine in any tradition.[74]

A cultural-linguistic starting point for a theory of religion interprets religions as the diverse accumulation of cultural and linguistic factors: thus, "religion" is as varied as the subject matter. The Arabic/Middle Eastern/Quranic paradigm is the structure of reality for Muslims. This may be quite different from the Indonesian/Southeast Asian/Quranic paradigm that also structures the reality of Muslims. The Pacific Rim/Oriental/Buddhist paradigm offers a structure of reality for inhabitants of that area, culture, and language. In like manner, the Roman Catholicism of Kenya differs in many ways from that of Rome. At a theoretical level, every community of belief is a different set of historically bound cultural and linguistic factors structured in ways that produce quite different reality systems and experiences. Thus, in this theory, characterized by a moderate postmodern understanding of history and language, there is no right or wrong, revealed or contrived religion. There are only different structures of reality emerging from diverse regulative paradigms located in the midst of various cultural and linguistic factors.[75]

Lindbeck admits that this kind of neutrality is not possible for a *theological* investigation of religion—and this becomes evident in his discussion of why he chose the cultural-linguistic framework when proposing a *theological* approach to doctrinal reconciliation. The key to this choice of method has more to do with theology than it does with theory, and this becomes evident when one discerns what is authoritative for Lindbeck and why. For example, one could compare aspects of Lindbeck's method to early sections of the *Church Dogmatics* of Karl Barth, a theologian clearly influential upon him.[76] "Further, on the specifically theological side, Karl Barth's exegetical emphasis on narrative has been at second hand a chief source of my notion of intra-textuality as an appropriate way of doing theology in a fashion consistent with a cultural-linguistic understanding of religion and a regulative view of doctrine."[77] Because a given faith narrative is determinative of a particular cultural-linguistic construct, Karl Barth's "Word of God" theology is appropriated by Lindbeck. Christianity, through Scripture, provides the cultural-linguistic construct for a Christian believer.[78]

SUMMARY AND EVALUATION

Given the strict boundaries for accessing meaning, the prominence of narrative, and the noncorrespondence of language to ontological reality, the choice of the cultural-linguistic approach points to a deeper issue. The human subject is not capable of extracultural or linguistic "truth." This results in a suspicion of human authorship for theology that is anything more than secondary to a particular faith narrative. This suspicion initially becomes evident in the descriptions of propositionalism and experiential-expressivism. In the former, traditionalists seize upon absolute truth and falsity as a form of control. In the latter, existential orientation selfishly determines what is of value in both religion and doctrine. But the full flowering of a suspicion for human authorship, with more of its implications, stems from the thought of Karl Barth. Language, especially biblical language (the Word of God), becomes *the* cultural-linguistic narrative that determines and ultimately transforms a believer through the analogy of faith.

For this reason, *The Nature of Doctrine* is a theological effort couched in a theoretical construct. A cultural-linguistic approach to Christian theology essentially supports a "Word of God" theology, in which the biblical narrative becomes determinative of the experience of believers. Once the theoretical, cultural-linguistic construct is established, former first-order propositions can be discussed freely in terms of second-order "grammar." A rule theory of language puts competing first-order propositions on a level playing field: that is, discussion of "truths" or "meanings" are best accomplished intra-textually with reference to the principles of a particular paradigm. This is preferable both to a propositional approach to religion and doctrine that stresses the direct intelligibility of absolute truth claims and to an experiential-expressive approach that emphasizes existential orientations as the bench-mark for doctrine and truth.

By including "theology" as a subset of a cultural-linguistic "theory," Lindbeck has accomplished two things. First, any common (Lindbeck adds "nontheological") designations for universal experiences or truth claims become problematic due to the conceptual dependence of experience on formative linguistic and cultural factors. Thus, human experience is effec-tively removed for grounding theology. Instead of competing "experiences" grounding religion and doctrine, the corresponding dominant faith narra-tive becomes determinative of each. Second, because theory is concerned with regulative principles, the authoritative narratives and their attendant truth claims (within a given theology—i.e., intrasystematically) become immune to theoretical criticism (Lindbeck adds, "except on intra-systematic grounds and lack of assimilative power").[79] Theory becomes agnostic because it never engages in first-order discourse.

For a cultural-linguistic approach to Christianity, narrative authority of the Barthian type amounts to a perfect fit. Clearing away obstacles for the formative power of the biblical narrative becomes the goal of theology. The theologian simply comments on the intrasystematic meaning(s) of a given narrative to a particular community. What remains questionable is the ability of this approach to engage those *outside* the particular narrative—in this case, the scriptural narrative.

Lindbeck speaks at length of theology as having an internal mission, specifically for those who share the "grammar." But if Scripture, understood in Lindbeck's postmodern theological sense, is the authoritative point of ref-erence for Christians in general, it seems that those outside a particular Christian cultural-linguistic reality construct are simply cut off. There is no access to the claims of Christianity, for these are contained solely in the bib-lical narrative. John Thiel, in *Imagination and Authority,* sums up this point:[80]

Lindbeck sees the crisis of Christian faith in the modern world as nothing less than the threat of its extinction. His notion of constrained authorship addresses that threat through the theologian's efforts to describe the meaning of the biblical text not for the culture at large but for the community of faith and in so doing to instruct the community in authentic speaking and acting. One might say that Lindbeck's alternative to the "modern" theologian very much resembles the ancient Christian catechist living in a pagan world.[81]

A cultural-linguistic theological approach to religion and doctrine has profound consequences for how one defines the role of theology in contemporary society. If there is some degree of interpenetration between the faith community and society at large, that reality will affect the theological approach (e.g., perhaps by appealing to principles that transcend a particular community). If, conversely, no real communication is feasible, or if such communication is viewed as the importation of alien values, the theological task will remain an "internal" mission. "Foundational theologies seek theoretical grounding in a nonscriptural anthropology, epistemology, or method because they assume the need to engage culture in and through theological reflection and they find the possibility of rapprochement in an appropriate secular theory. For Lindbeck the possibility of such rapprochement has evaporated."[82]

If one begins from an antifoundationalist (postmodern) interpretation of Wittgenstein's understanding of language and applies this to religion, one can effectively remove human agency from theological authorship (i.e., the affirmation of first-order truth claims). In its place one can then insert the biblical Word as *the* narrative for defining (second-order discourse) the language of a community. Language and culture determine reality. Within languages and cultures, narratives of belief determine reality. Within dominant narratives, meaning is accessible. Meaning, in turn, is grounded on the regulative principles upon which the narrative is built. Thus, the Bible is used as *the* narrative for Christian theology. "A scriptural world is thus able to absorb the universe. It supplies the interpretive framework within which believers seek to live their lives and understand reality."[83] For the strictly theological and the strictly inner-Church teaching enterprise, one relies, not on propositional truth claims or an unspecifiable experience, but on Scripture. A particular interpretation of scriptural authority conforms easily to a cultural-linguistic approach to religion and doctrine.

It is important to note the direction of interpretation. Typology does not make scriptural contents into metaphors for extrascriptural realities, but the other way around. It does not suggest, as is often said in our day, that believers find their stories in the Bible, but rather that they make the story of the Bible their story. The cross is not viewed as a figurative representation of suffering nor the messianic kingdom as a symbol for hope in the future; rather, suffering should be cruciform, and hopes for the future messianic. More generally stated, it is the religion instantiated in Scripture which defines being, truth, goodness, and beauty, and the nonscriptural exemplifications of these realities need to be transformed into figures (or types or antitypes) of the scriptural ones. Intratextual theology redescribes reality within the scriptural framework rather than translating Scripture into extrascriptural categories. It is the text, so to speak, which absorbs the world, rather than the world the text.[84]

This interpretive framework emphasizes how life is to be lived in light of what the Bible says about God in stories concerning the nation of Israel and ultimately in Jesus Christ. If extrascriptural categories are made controlling in the reading of Scripture, the real meaning within it is corrupted.[85]

The believer, so an intratextual approach would maintain, is not told primarily to be conformed to a reconstructed Jesus of history (as Hans Küng maintains), nor to a metaphysical Christ of faith (as in much of the propositionalist tradition), nor to an *abba* experience of God (as for Schillebeeckx), nor to an *agapeic* way of being in the world (as for David Tracy), but he or she is rather to be conformed to the Jesus Christ depicted in the narrative. An intratextual reading tries to derive the interpretive framework that designates the theologically controlling sense from the literary structure of the text itself.[86]

One remaining concern for the feasibility of a cultural-linguistic theological approach is realized in the hermeneutic question. How can human beings, who are formed so totally by the culture and language into which they are born, access the meaning of Scripture through time and space? The question of whether written words or recorded deeds in one culture and time can simply be understood *in themselves* (i.e., unmediated), when transposed into another culture and time, becomes critical here. This problem of history is not a problem for a theology that maintains that revelation, of itself, creates the possibility for its own understanding. Because this is an intratextual (or intrasemiotic) truth claim, it is immune from the critique of theory—hermeneutic, pragmatic, or otherwise. Meaning is accessible only within a particular narrative that is situated within a particular cultural-linguistic context. Thus, the intrasemiotic presupposition that the biblical narrative constructs reality and determines belief bypasses the hermeneutic problem of historical understanding or the fragility of human reason to receive revelation. If historical occurrences can be understood in themselves through the proper narrative (i.e., ahistorically, or without context), then disclosing the correct interpretation (i.e., the regulative principles contained in it) becomes the job of the theologian. But whose interpretation and which interpretation of regulative principles will prevail in such a task becomes the question—especially among and between traditions of Christianity that differ widely on this topic.

The Nature of Doctrine and similarly *Religious Experience* put heavy emphasis on the brokenness of the human condition, the inability of human language to correspond to an intelligible reality (external reference), and the rejection of positive characteristics that may suggest elements of a common human subjectivity. The decentered ego is no longer in control of language or history but is rather the product of both. It is possible that these presuppositions represent a greater cause for denominational division than any disagreement over doctrine. Unless one can approximate some agreement on the foundational issues of theological authorship, both human and divine, and the relationship (implying a mutuality) between the two, the possibility of real ecumenical dialogue remains questionable.

It is now necessary to step back for a moment from this close textual analysis to clarify the contradictions thus far, especially as they concern "experience," "language," and "theology." What exactly is the contemporary problem? Precisely how does moderate postmodernism challenge Schleiermacher's project? The next chapter will attempt to clarify this situation and then to question the core assertions upon which the postmodern approach is grounded.

George Steiner's *Real Presences:* The Framing of the Contemporary Problem

A problem represents the partial transformation by inquiry of a problematic situation into a determinate situation. It is a familiar and significant saying that a problem well put is but half-solved. To find out what the problem and problems are which a problematic situation presents to be inquired into, is to be well along in inquiry.

—John Dewey, *Logic: The Theory of Inquiry*

A word should be stated on the development of our story thus far. This inquiry has been largely descriptive. Two distinct and contradictory approaches to language, experience, and the purpose of theology have been described and systematically analyzed. Now, in this third moment of inquiry, one that follows the *thesis* of Schleiermacher and the *antithesis* of postmodernism, both the movement from descriptive to constructive inquiry and some form of *synthesis* must take place. The three topics through which the previous story has been charted continue to situate the critical areas of difference and the problematic situation that this book seeks to address. Before the actual work of this chapter, then, it is necessary to briefly recall the critical issues that constitute the problem at the basis of this inquiry.

George Lindbeck and Wayne Proudfoot have argued from specific moderate postmodern presuppositions that directly contradict the appeal to religious experience and the theological project of Friedrich Schleiermacher.

These contradictions, broadly conceived, constitute the contemporary problematic as dialectical. Lindbeck and Proudfoot negate Schleiermacher's assumptions in three ways. Language is essentially descriptive and unlimited for Schleiermacher; it is culture bound and essentially constructive or formative for moderate postmodernists. A "common humanity" to whom a universal "experience" is accessible is assumed by Schleiermacher; the postmodern approach to language argues from factors of difference and so rejects this assumption. Finally, the purpose of theology for Schleiermacher is a greater understanding of the Evangelical faith. Proudfoot argues, conversely, that the purpose of theology from "religious experience" is an attempt to control limit situations. While Lindbeck is more nuanced, he also points to such psychosocial benefits of experiential-expressivism as increased psychic gratification and theological marketability.

For all three topics analyzed—experience, language, and theology—a particular theory of language and its corollary understanding of "experience" are determinate. A particular theory of language embodies an operative philosophical anthropology: that is, a particular conception of language bespeaks a particular understanding of human *being*. In turn, the understanding of experience informs a particular conception of language: that is, an understanding of experience and its limits demarcates a corresponding function of language. Thus, for example, an anthropology that insists upon insurmountable human limitations corresponds to a constructive conception of language. Ultimately, the critical issue becomes how the *mutual relationship* of language and "experience" is decided. This will directly determine the evidence or ground for theology. Thus, because Schleiermacher and Proudfoot/Lindbeck have differed so radically on the nature and relation of language and "experience," they have proposed diametrically opposite positions on the character of theology.

Lindbeck and Proudfoot both employ, via certain moderate postmodern presuppositions, an understanding of language that presumes two realities. Human beings can comprehensively designate the nature and scope of language acts as well as the relation of these acts to the personal consciousness that produced them. This particular conception of language and its consequences for "experience" have not gone unnoticed. In *Real Presences*, George Steiner argues for a very different understanding of language, one that will have direct bearing upon any approach to "religious experience."[1] Steiner found that most arguments on the nature and foundation of language seem to posit a specific understanding of human "experience." "Experience" is either capable of meaning and transcendence or irrevocably trapped in the contingency of its own space and time and a "meaning" accessible only in that contingency. For Steiner, language can be both a barrier and a catalyst for "experience." "Experience" can ultimately be an encounter, through language or art, with an "other."

Steiner proposes, then, a critique and alternative to postmodern linguistic theory and its consequences for "experience." He does so in two stages. First, the hidden sources of postmodernity's approach to language must be isolated and analyzed in both their epistemological and anthropological presuppositions.[2] Second, the presumption that a comprehensive theory can enclose language must be questioned. Is it possible to definitively assert the nature and function of language in a "theory"?[3]

As this chapter moves from descriptive to constructive inquiry, the function of "experience" and its relation to language will be summarized and evaluated for each of the works analyzed thus far. This comparison and evaluation of "experience" will ultimately reconfirm that legitimate theological inquiry can proceed from a particular understanding of "experience."

Language and "experience"—the mutual conditioning of these two critical realities—becomes the focus of this evolving story. It is a relationship that ultimately determines the kind of theology one finds possible. As understood and developed in particular ways by Proudfoot and Lindbeck, the relationship of language to experience ultimately serves as a valuable counterbalance to the optimism of Schleiermacher's thought. But can one move beyond these contradictory moments while taking seriously the concerns of both? Such a possibility can be explored through the work of George Steiner.

The Annihilation of the Object and the Subject

Neither Proudfoot nor Lindbeck pushes his claims to the extremes of postmodernity, but to understand Steiner and the confrontation that he mounts against postmodernity, one must understand postmodernity in its most radical form. Recent scholarship in the arts and humanities (as well as religious studies) has questioned the possibility "of any significant relations between word and world."[4] This intertextual turn has led some postmodernists to assert that *our* "word" is *the* "world." Before addressing the consequences of this method, one must first understand the origination of such a turn.

There is in any meaningful human interaction a correspondence between language and that which it signifies. Language not only refers to other words but can correspond in some way to external reality as well. This correspondence is made possible through a trust in the reality of such reference—the same unthematic trust that is the condition of possibility for communicating anything to anyone. Unfortunately, such correspondence can no longer be assumed. "Skepticism has queried the deed of semantic trust."[5] The very nature of the language act as something that can correspond to a real referent—an "external" reality, such as an object, an idea, or a person—has in some circles been entirely rejected. This break of semantic trust, according to Steiner, occurred in Europe and Russia in the latter part of the nineteenth century. Before this break, even the most radical skeptics never questioned the ability of language to function as a vehicle for the real, as a vehicle for meaningful argument: "even the most astringent skepticism, even the most subversive of anti-rhetorics, remained committed to language. It knew itself to be 'in trust' to language."[6]

What precipitated the challenge to the possibility of real reference in language?[7] Steiner implies that radical, though futile, philosophical efforts aimed at totalizing visions were, in part, responsible for the deconstructive response.[8] These developments instantiated "a terminal lunge towards totality, towards a controlled in-gathering of all cultural-historical values and legacies."[9] The *reaction* to such an all-encompassing "fundamentalism" (as David Tracy would identify it) was to sever the covenant "between word and world." The result was a totalizing vision of another kind. "A fully consequent skepticism will make language a primarily internalized, conventional shadow-system whose autistic rules and figurations have nothing verifiable to do with what is 'out there' (itself a childish, meaningless phrase)."[10]

The origin of the rupture between "word and world" emerged from the thought of Stephané Mallarmé and Arthur Rimbaud.[11] It occurred specifically with "Mallarmé's disjunction of language from external reference and in Rimbaud's deconstruction of the first person singular."[12] Both reject a correspondence theory of language—that for language to cohere with any reality "out there" is not only illusory but actually deceptive. A "correspondence" of language to reality makes language a lie. "Mallarmé's repudiation of the covenant of reference, and his insistence that non-reference constitutes the true genius and purity of language, entail a central supposition of 'real absence.'"[13] Consequently, all language becomes only an internal word game. Words refer to other words and signify no reference to any determined reality. Steiner exhibits this approach with the following:

> The word *rose* has neither stem nor leaf nor thorn. It is neither pink nor red nor yellow. It exudes no odour. It is *per se,* a wholly arbitrary phonetic marker, an empty sign. Nothing whatever in its (minimal) sonority, in its graphic appearance, in its phonemic components, etymological history or grammatical functions, has any correspondence whatever to what we believe or imagine to be the object of its purely conventional reference.[14]

Language has been abused through "lies, imprecisions, and utilitarian dross."[15] To free the real capacity of language to be language, we must totally divest it of any correspondence to a reference (and its attendant meaning) outside of itself. Steiner elaborates on this assertion:

> Made to stand for inaccessible phenomenalities, words have been reduced to corrupt servitude. They are no longer fit for poets or rigorous thinkers (poetry being thought at its most rigorous). Only when we realize that what words refer to are other words, that any speech-act in reference to experience is always a "saying in other words," can we return to a true freedom. It is within the language system alone that we possess liberties of construction and of deconstruction, of remembrance and of futurity, so boundless, so dynamic, so proper to the evident uniqueness of human thought and imagining that, in comparison, external reality, whatever that might or might not be, is little more than brute intractability and deprivation.[16]

This conception of linguistic reference severs a correspondence to external reference by interpreting the actual matter of the object as self-signifying. "Neither the poem nor the metaphysical system is made of 'ideas,' of verbalized external data. They are made of words. Paintings are, insisted Degas, made of pigments and internally relational spaces. Music is made of conventionally organized sounds. It signifies only itself."[17]

Mallarmé's linguistic epistemological alteration combined with Rimbaud's anthropological deconstruction of the first person results in a chasm dividing language from external reference: the dissolution of the self knows only real *absence*.[18] First comes a break in the trust of semantic correspondence; second comes the denial of an "I" and an affirmation, instead, of many selves. This effectively severs any possibility for receiving or maintaining a "meaning" that is capable of being "shared." Neither the nature of language nor the nature of human subjectivity admits the kind of stability necessary for the reception of externally given meaning through an externally accessible referent. "We do not, via language, transcend the real towards the more real. Words neither say or un-say the realm of matter, of contingent mundanity, of 'the other.'"[19]

Similar treatment is given to human subjectivity: "Where 'I' is not 'I' but a Magellanic cloud of momentary energies always in process of fission, there can be no authorship in any single, stable sense."[20] This dissolution of the self grounds the impossibility of any reference to a "common humanity": that is, to an appeal to any "meaning" that might transcend space and time and be accessible to all. And though many authors use language to critique language, "it is not what is said that is being queried: it is the nature, formal and substantive, of the ascription of meaning, of intelligible signification, to the act and medium of the saying."[21]

Two concepts are critical for understanding a "deconstructionist and post-structuralist counter-theology of absence": difference and deferral.[22] "Saussure taught of 'difference': signs are made recognizable and significant by sole virtue of their differences, called 'diacritical' from other signs."[23] "Difference" is also "the act of differing: signs are not 'like' the objects to which they refer or are conventionally taken to refer."[24] Concomitantly, one emphasizes "deferral, that postponement of settled signification, that keeping in flickering motion which adjourns the illusion, the sterile fixity of definition."[25] The deconstructionist view of language is one that stresses absence, fluidity, indefiniteness, breaks of meaning and meaningfulness. Difference and deferral have radical consequences for any universal claim:

> Any truth-claim, philosophical, ethical, political, aesthetic and, above all (where the very use of "above" should alert us to the unfounded pretenses involved), theological, will always be dissolved by the textuality in which it inheres. This is to say that language inevitably undoes the figures of possible, momentary sense which emerge, like ephemeral and mendacious bubbles, from the process of articulation.[26]

Deconstruction proposes a *relative* (i.e., intertextual) meaningfulness that is different from "meaning" traditionally understood. "In the post-structuralist and deconstructive model, it is the reader who produces the text, the viewer who generates the painting."[27] "Meaning" is only possible internally—that is, within language—because there exists no correspondence to an external reference. Thus, "meaning" is as varied as the reader. This freeing of language from external reference liberates specific language acts from the narrow suffocation of any single, totalizing externally imposed definition. Words signify other words and are meaningful to "selves" of "limitless plurality." For Steiner this approach is exemplified by Freudian psychoanalysis.

> When psychoanalysis decomposes intentionality, when it dissolves declared motive into an iceberg mass of hidden evasions, suppressions, fictions which mask the self and mask it from itself, it is developing Rimbaud's intuition and Nietzsche's rebellion against any naive view of human discourse as a vehicle and transmitter of intended verities. The concept, the hermeneutic and therapeutic treatment of utterance and of text as a palimpsest of superposed possibilities, in which each cryptic level subverts that which lies above it and alters that which lies below, is crucial to the Freudian reading of the relations, always both true and false or true in their falsehood, between word and the self. It is not only, in Rimbaud's sense, that the "I" is another. The tongues spoken by the two (or more) parties may differ to the point of mutual incomprehension. Thus psychoanalytic interpretation does not define: it translates into other, momentary, translations.[28]

Such an approach rejects a level of human stability necessary for receiving externally given "meaning"—a "meaning" that might, for example, transcend the language, culture, and social context of a particular subject.[29] If you annihilate the subject of discourse and the object of discourse, what is left? Discourse—and all reference becomes intertextual. This break from external reference and the exclusive affirmation of internal meaning (i.e., intertextuality) is a central presupposition affirmed in the presumption concerning language operative in the arguments of both Lindbeck and Proudfoot. How this is evident in both their works now becomes the focus.

This brief introduction to Steiner's problematic is not, therefore, a direct critique of Lindbeck or Proudfoot—but it does furnish the devices with which one can critique the more benign application of the deconstruction of language.[30] Thus, for example, while Proudfoot and Lindbeck do not develop or outline a "theory" of language, they do presume an intertextual understanding of both the meaning and reference for language: that is, an intertextual understanding of language grounds both the conceptual theory of emotion for Proudfoot and the rule theory of doctrine for Lindbeck.[31] Words refer to other words, and meaning is accessible and referential only within a particular linguistic construct. Such an understanding, closed as it is to the possibility that language may not be the only a priori, can function as their "theory" of language. Such an approach represents precisely what Steiner seeks to refute:

> The incapacity of a "scientific" view and anatomy of language to tell us persuasively of the origin of human speech, of the utter centrality of language-acts within the humanness of what is human, or to elucidate for us the experience we have of the poetic; the necessary insistence of the scientific view that such questions are either otiose or unanswerable—hence not to be asked—are of the very first importance. They suggest that the notion of language as a purely interrelational play of differences, and the notion of man's life in speech as one of diverse language-games with *no imperative of reference except to the pragmatic* [italics added], are radically inadequate.[32]

THEORY AND LANGUAGE

The classical view of "theory" changed radically in the mid-seventeenth century.

> The word "theory" has lost its birthright. At the source, it draws on meanings and connotations both secular and ritual. It tells of concentrated insight, of an act of contemplation focused patiently on its object. But it pertains also to the deed of witness performed by legates sent, in solemn embassy, to observe the oracles spoken or the rites performed at the sacred Attic games. A "theorist" or "theoretician" is one who is disciplined in observance, a term itself with a twofold significance of intellectual-sensory perception and religious or ritual conduct.[33]

Initially, *theory* designated the contemplative grasping of an object. "Thus theory is inhabited by truth when it contemplates its object unwaveringly and when, in the observant process of such contemplation, it beholds, it takes grasp of the often confused and contingent ('vulgar') images, associations, suggestions, possibly erroneous, to which the object gives rise."[34] It is only later that "theory" gives way to its "modern guise" as a subjective speculative impulse exemplified by the theories characteristic of Descartes and Newton.[35] This new understanding of theory is different from the earlier insofar as its "validation" is "located in the outside world, in the realm of the objective."[36] Combined with the positivism of the nineteenth century—a positivism still alive in the contemporary age of applied sciences—the "theoretical," as "experiment and predictive application," becomes associated with "objective" fact.[37]

Initially, two elements were required for theory as utilized in the applied sciences—personal consciousness and empirical reality. A private hypothesis became theory when tested and validated by the "facts": that is, by the "mirroring evidence in empirical reality."[38] When applied to the "hard" sciences, those sciences that depend upon observable and recordable data, "objective" results were not seriously questioned until recently.

Two factors have intensified the debate on the relationship between scientific systems and the world they purport to explain. First, indeterminacy "has put in critical doubt the deterministic classical conditions of proof, of experimental verification." Second, the "principle of complementarity" has illustrated that "identical phenomena are susceptible of alternative theoretical explanations and alternative theory-bound descriptions."[39] Considered together, "indeterminacy and complementarity presume an interference by the observer, by the process of observation, with the phenomenal material."[40] Even so, theory applies. Somehow the external world coheres with the postulates and expectations of investigative rationalism. Airplanes fly.

When "theory" is employed for the humanities, the same two elements (personal consciousness and empirical reality) continue to be necessary. But when an "applied" science methodology or theory is employed for analysis and critique in the humanities and arts, an "error of categories" has occurred. Any attempt to utilize this methodology and maintain this category error in this realm is doomed to failure. Consequently, those who have claimed "the triumph of the theoretical" "are, in truth, either deceiving themselves or purloining from the immense prestige and confidence of science and technology an instrument ontologically inapplicable to their own material. They would enclose water in a sieve."[41]

This is so because two additional criteria must be met for theory to be justified. First, verifiability or falsifiability must be accessible by means of "experiment and predictive application."[42] Second, what is ultimately verifiable must replace that which it supersedes to become the dominant theory—until it is also later disproven and displaced. Both criteria are necessary for applied sciences, but neither is applicable to the humanities or arts. "The Copernican theory did correct and supersede that of Ptolemy. The chemistry of Lavoisier makes untenable the earlier phlogiston theory. Aristotle on mimesis and pathos is not superseded by Lessing or by Bergson. The Surrealist manifestos of Breton do not cancel out Pope's *Essay on Criticism* though they may well be antithetical to it."[43] There is a significant difference between the development of "theory" in the applied sciences and the use of such an approach to analyze works in the humanities. This is so because all "constructs of supposition" (i.e., a controlled and finite area of experiment and observation) are, by the nature of experiment and observation, confined to a particular language circle. Conversely, works in the humanities and arts, by their very nature, transcend that boundary. In *No Passion Spent*, Steiner says:

> *Anything can be said about anything.* The assertion that Shakespeare's *King Lear* "is beneath serious criticism" (Tolstoy), the finding that Mozart composes mere trivia, are *totally irrefutable.* They can be falsified neither on formal (logical) grounds, nor in existential substance. Aesthetic philosophies, critical theories, constructs of the "classic" or the "canonic" can never be anything but more or less persuasive, more or less comprehensive, more or less consequent descriptions of this or that process of preference.[44]

It is not that in the arts or humanities nothing is verifiable or falsifiable but "there can be no verifiable or falsifiable deductions entailing predictable consequences in the very concrete sense in which a scientific theory carries predictive force."[45] Aesthetic and, one could argue by extension, religious experiences, are not irrational, but they are irreducible to another use and set of criteria for reason or *pragmatic* rationalization.[46] As the humanities continue to adopt the methodologies of the "applied" sci-

ences in a striving for greater academic respectability, the ability to interpret *by participation* has sufficiently decreased.[47]

"Theoretical" approaches to the humanities and arts have actually created
distance between a subject and these works in the form of intermediaries—
those who interpret, codify, organize, and identify the "meaning" of various
works. Others, in turn, interpret, codify, organize, and identify these intermediaries, and "interpretive" literature grows exponentially.[48] Because participating in a work is not quantifiable (it fails to satisfy the demands of
theory), the "encounter approach" long dominant in the humanities has
largely given way to secondary literature on primary texts.[49] For Steiner,
works in the arts and humanities are not fully appropriated by just being seen,
read, or heard about. They must be *lived* in a real encounter or experience—
an experience that is a "real presence."[50]

> Virgil reads, guides our reading of, Homer as no external critic can. The
> *Divine Comedy* is a reading of the *Aeneid,* technically and spiritually "at
> home," "authorized" in the several and interactive senses of that word,
> as no extrinsic commentary by one who is himself not a poet can be.
> The presence, visibly solicited or exorcised, of Homer, Virgil and Dante
> in Milton's *Paradise Lost,* in the epic satire of Pope and in the pilgrim-
> age upstream of Ezra Pound's *Cantos,* is a "real presence," a critique in
> action.[51]

In the contemporary American academic scene, the influx of massive
funding and attention given to the applied sciences certainly tempts the for-
gotten humanities and arts away from nontheoretical "encounters" and
toward methodologies that may actually inhibit the understanding of their
own subject matter. "What looks to be certain is that the criteria and practices of quantification, of symbolic coding and formalization which are the
life and breath of the theoretical do not, cannot pertain to the interpretation
and assessment of either literature or the arts."[52]

Steiner's attack on the adequacy of "theory" carries obvious implications
for the question of the legitimacy of "theoretical" analysis of religious experience. While a phenomenology of religious experience is not identical with a
phenomenology of art or literature, religious experience is distinct from the
applied sciences *in the same way* as art and literature. Judgments of religious
experience, art, or literature are not verifiable or falsifiable by experiment

and predictive application, nor are they confined to "constructs of supposition." Religious experience is not quantifiable through empirical theoretical analysis of the kind employed by Proudfoot through a theory of emotion or by Lindbeck through a rule theory of doctrine—for both presume a fixed and closed definition of language as a whole.

Those who have undertaken "theoretical" investigations of religious experience correctly realize the necessity of an empirical component to satisfy the demands of "theory." The "empirical data"—the only given measurable element with which a theorist can do work on this topic—are language, both sacred and secular. But this use of language as evidence in the analysis of religious experience presumes a particular and determinate relation between language and experience. Through its identifying function, language *constitutes* an experience for Proudfoot through emotions, thoughts, and beliefs, and it *shapes, molds,* and "in a sense" *constitutes* experience for Lindbeck.[53] Lindbeck's regulative view of doctrine presumes a fixed (a priori) understanding between experience and language, while Proudfoot's conceptual attribution theory of emotion is derivative of a similar understanding of experience as constituted by language.[54] The regulative view of doctrine and the conceptual theory of emotion are directly determinative upon their respective interpretations of religious experience.

Precisely this limited, confined use of language presumed in their respective theories of emotion and doctrine, one that finally designates the nature of language as predominately or purely constructive (or descriptive), is impossible for Steiner. Linguistic data (e.g., the phonetic, lexical, grammatical, and semantic aspects of language) do not translate directly into meaning.[55] No final or definitive relationship can be ascertained between language and experience (and therefore emotion, doctrine, etc.). The polyvalent relation between a personal consciousness and the reference/meaning of a given language act is inaccessible to universal theoretical formalization. "No interpretive method has bridged the gap between linguistic analysis and linguistic theory properly defined on the one hand and the process of understanding on the other."[56] And while certain aspects of language are quantifiable and rule bound, "the absolutely decisive failing occurs when such approaches seek to formalize *meaning,* when they proceed upward from the phonetic, the lexical and the grammatic to the semantic and aesthetic."[57]

Because the whole of a given language is inaccessible to a single subject, so also is the possibility of enclosing language in a final and fixed definition. A subject's interpretation of a text emerges from multiple factors (a particular language, dialect, history, culture), and the lexical, grammatical, and semantic context of language is infinite. Context includes the whole language through history and, contemporarily, its society and structures throughout history, and, finally, "the history and life-forms of analogous and contrasting aesthetic genres."[58] This, in turn, affects any analysis and its corresponding universal claims concerning language (i.e., whether it is constructive, evocative, descriptive, etc.). Thus, the meaning of language, or even how it functions, cannot be definitively reduced and universalized accordingly. "The circles of informing context spread concentrically to the unbounded."[59] While much can be and should be said about the nature of language, one certainty is our *inability* to definitely enclose it. "No formalization is of an order adequate to the semantic mass and motion of a culture, to the wealth of denotation, connotation, implicit reference, elision and tonal register which envelop saying what one means, meaning what one says, or neither."[60]

The postmodern approach to religious experience and theological inquiry presumes an understanding of language, evident in a regulative view of doctrine and a conceptual theory of emotion, finally as historically, culturally bound—formative—and finite in possibility. If this view is taken to its conclusion, "reference" that is external, prior to, or beyond a particular linguistic paradigm becomes inaccessible. This, of course, becomes the critical issue for any analysis of "religious" experience.

What is needed is an approach to language and its relation to experience that is located somewhere between a "systematic exhaustive hermeneutic" and a "gratuitous, arbitrary play of nonsense."[61] This determination of how language functions is correspondingly informed by the understanding of the limit and function of "experience." The relation between "experience" and language determines much of the possibilities for theological inquiry. So it is to the unique character of "experience" emerging from and conditioning each particular author's understanding of language that this inquiry now turns.

LANGUAGE AND EXPERIENCE

There is language, there is art, because there is "the other." We do address ourselves in constant soliloquy. But the medium of that soliloquy is that of public speech—foreshortened, perhaps made private and cryptic through

covert reference and association, but grounded, nevertheless, and to the
uncertain verge of consciousness, in an inherited, historically and socially
determined vocabulary and grammar.

—Steiner, *Real Presences*[62]

Before any suggestion can be made to in any way resolve or move beyond the
problem delineated thus far, a review of the relation between language and
experience must be included. In this way, the relation of language and experience, as such, can be recognized as the critical factor for specific understandings of theology.

Experience is an endlessly ambiguous term, yet it must be specifically
defined in the works taken up thus far. The relationship of language to experience has been central to the issues analyzed through each author's work.
The constructive nature of this chapter will narrow the inquiry about "experience" into a concrete reflection on the meaning of the term itself as it is
used by Schleiermacher, Proudfoot, Lindbeck, and Steiner. The inquiry will
then ask, What is the relation of "experience" to language?

It is ironic that the theologian held responsible for the turn to "experience" used the term *experience* (*das Erlebnis, die Erfahrung, empfinden*)
so seldom. In the *Speeches*, experience is the combination of "intuition"
(*Anschauung/anschauung*), the immediate perception of the *action* of some
reality, and "feeling" (*Gefühl*), the result of this action of the universe upon
oneself, that grounds Schleiermacher's description of "religion." Considered
together, though split into two terms for descriptive purposes, intuition and
feeling ultimately allow the subject to encounter and acknowledge a causality
beyond the action of the object and the self. This experience of the self as
receptive of wholeness or completion (i.e., of infinity) results in the feeling of
"dependence" (*Abhängigkeit*)—the sense that one lacks what only the universe offers. It is by undergoing interaction with the universe that one comes
to a greater knowledge of the self and experiences the infinite.[63]

The basis of ecclesial life in *The Christian Faith* is "piety" (*Frömmigkeit*),
a particular determination of feeling (*eine Bestimmtheit des Gefühls oder des
unmittelbaren Selbstbewußtseins*). Two contrasting elements determine
human existence—a self-caused element and a nonself-caused element.[64]
This distinction is possible only when the reality of *change* is recognized.
Being changed (i.e., the recognition of being subjected to a causality external to oneself) is the acknowledgment of dependence, one's "co-existence

with an Other." The "other" may be society, a nation, nature, even the universe. But at one level the other is absolute. It is absolute at the level of immediate self-consciousness: one recognizes always and absolutely a dependence on an other that determines feeling. Feeling is that "non-objective" sense of immediate self-consciousness that grounds all knowing and doing.[65] The recognition that any state of consciousness is always subject to a changing determination from more than simply the Ego yields the truth that "the whole of our spontaneous activity comes from a source outside of us."[66] The feeling of absolute dependence is human experience encountering and acknowledging an external causality, an "Other," that is absolute. Schleiermacher designates this "Other" with the name *God* and the "feeling of absolute dependence" as *being in relation to God* (*als in Beziehung mit Gott Bewußt sind*).[67] The character of "experience," variously framed as intuition/feeling (religion) or the feeling of absolute dependence (piety), is a recollection of an encounter. The experience that grounds Schleiermacher's appeal to piety is one of being in relation to an other. It is absolute, though generally passive (i.e., in the mode of receptivity) in nature.

Schleiermacher grants a priority to the givenness of experience over its description in language. A description never quite returns one totally to the wellspring of that experience of (or encounter with) *causality* in its original moment. In his hermeneutics, for example, language is descriptive and capable of transcending itself back to the thoughts and experiences of historical authors. One can ride the river of language back into the minds (thoughts, intentions, experience) of great thinkers. And even though it can never recapture the original, language can even take us, approximately, into the experience of existence itself. Though Schleiermacher has a very nuanced understanding of both the possibilities and limitations of language, his emphasis leans toward the unlimited possibilities of and through language.

This enthusiasm for the transcendent possibilities in language is negated by the postmodern view of "experience" and language. Wayne Proudfoot acknowledges the ambiguous nature of the term *experience* but still attempts to narrow it down to two senses. The ambiguity of this term is evident "in our ordinary talk about perception."[68] An optical metaphor is central to Proudfoot's interpretation of experience, for the relation of perception and judgment, conscious or not, in identifying "experience" is central.

It [*experience*] can be used to refer to how something seems or appears to a person, without regard to the accuracy of that seeming or appearing. In the example we have repeatedly considered, the woodsman who momentarily takes the fallen log on the trail to be a bear experiences a bear in the first sense of *experience.* It (experience) can also be employed as an achievement word like see or perceive, where the judgment that someone has perceived something assumes the belief that the object is there to be perceived and has entered into the cause of the perceptual experience in an appropriate way. In this second sense, but not in the first, the statement that Albert had an experience of God assumes that there is a God to be experienced. This second sense includes a judgment on the part of the observer about the accuracy of the subject's understanding of his or her experience. This ambiguity has been exploited for apologetic purposes in the literature on religious experience.[69]

Experience, for Proudfoot, carries two possible meanings. The first is an immediate perception on the part of the subject—one that may or may not correspond to any reality. This perception can therefore be correct or incorrect. The second sense *moves to the perspective of the observer,* who identifies an "experience" through the concepts or beliefs operative for the subject. A prior belief that something real is "there" determines the perception either wrongly or rightly. In the first, the act of reception *by the subject,* whether it corresponds to reality or not, is primary. In the second, it is the recognition on the part *of the observer* of particular beliefs, concepts, language, and culture that determines accessibility to the subject's experience. Note that an observer is built into Proudfoot's definition of *experience* itself.

"Experience" functions as perception for Proudfoot. In the first sense, it is the immediate perception of the subject. In the second, it is the perception of the observer. Whether such perception coheres with any reality is determined by concepts that accompany and inform every perception. "Reality" is constructed through these concepts of the subject; thus, "experiences" of a subject become accessible to the observer insofar as there is an awareness of the subject's conceptual references. Any universal appeal to one single reality is unjustified, for such an appeal is always derived from prior *beliefs* that may or may not reference reality—and may or may not be shared by others, or by other cultures. "Experience," for Proudfoot, denotes the process of perception and judgment by a subject and an observer—a level of knowing—with a reality that may or may not exist.

Proudfoot argues for a priority of concepts in identifying experience. Concepts, in turn, emerge from a particular vocabulary constitutive of a particular language. Therefore, language via concept is the possibility for experience. When a subject asserts the indescribability of an experience, it is not the vocabulary that is insufficient but the presumption of direct acquaintance that requires evocative placeholders to render an experience indeterminate.

> Such terms as numinous, holy, and sacred are sometimes employed as if they were descriptive. Reference is made to various manifestations of the sacred, and the term is treated as if it were a theoretical concept. The resultant "theories" of religion are, like the concept of the numinous, designed to evoke that which they are supposed to describe or explain. We have seen, however, that direct acquaintance is neither necessary nor sufficient for understanding religious experience. Such experience includes a cognitive component that can be analyzed and rendered intelligible even in the absence of direct acquaintance with the experience.[70]

Language—concepts—judgment—experience. Experience is the final component of a knowing that evolves from language through concepts.

For all of Lindbeck's countering of the adequacy of "experience," and his insistence that experience is formed by language, he does not present an articulated understanding of experience. "Human experience" for Lindbeck "is shaped, molded, and in a sense constituted by cultural and linguistic forms."[71] "Experience" consists of "thoughts," "sentiments," and "realities" derivative of a culture or language.[72] The subject is the point of interaction for various cultural and linguistic factors of formation. These internalized factors are realized in "experience": that is, in thoughts, sentiments, and realities. The ability to absorb various cultural and linguistic influences is a quasi-a priori, resulting in differing acquired skills for different people.

> This is a complex thesis, and its full discussion lies beyond the scope of this essay. A crude illustration of what is involved may, however, be helpful. There are reported to be tribal languages that do not discriminate between, e.g., green and blue, and the members of these tribes are reported (erroneously, according to some observers) to have difficulty

recognizing the difference between the two colors. They are not color-blind. On the physiological level, their retinas and optic nerves respond differentially to light waves of varying lengths just as ours do, but they lack the verbal categories for experiencing these differences in stimuli. Or, in order to avoid cultural provincialism, one can put the case conversely: *we lack the linguistic a priori for having the visual experiences that they have* [italics added].[73]

Cultures and languages, and by extension "religions," constitute and shape a priori: that is, they cause dispositively and limit all "human experience." "Experience" is the enclosed product of external environmental conditioning. "On this view, the means of communication and expression are a precondition, a kind of quasi-transcendental (i.e., culturally formed) *a priori* for the possibility of experience."[74] Language shapes and confines the possibility of "experience," the range of feelings, sentiments, and realities—the various forms of knowledge used to relate to the world and self.

The character and function of "experience" are quite different for George Steiner and figures prominently in that encounter with meaning in art or literature that is an experience of the "aesthetic," of "selective interactions between the constraints of the observed and the boundless possibilities of the imagined."[75] Experience is not simply a coming into contact with something that exists; rather, it is a meeting, an acknowledgment of the claims and demands of an "other." Aesthetic experience can be the experience of "real presence": "the encounter with the aesthetic" can reveal the "other" through a work of art. "Whatever its stature, the poem speaks; it speaks out; it speaks to. The meaning, the existential modes of art, music and literature are functional within the experience of our meeting with the other. All aesthetics, all critical and hermeneutic discourse, is an attempt to clarify the paradox and opaqueness of that meeting as well as its felicities."[76] "There is language, there is art, because there is 'the other.'"[77] There is something that is not language, and not art, to which language and art respond. "Why there should be the other and our relations to that otherness, be they theological, moral, social, erotic, be they those of intimate participation or irreconcilable difference, is a mystery both harsh and consoling. Goethe's question, 'How can I be when there is another?', Nietzsche's, 'How can I exist if God does?', stand unanswered."[78]

The "other," consequently, is the reason and possibility for communicating. "It is out of the fact of confrontation, of affront in the literal sense of the term, that we communicate in words, that we externalize shapes and colors, that we emit organized sounds in the forms of music."[79] First is the experience of the other, the "confrontation"; second is the communication or recollection of that encounter in art, music, language, and so on. "The meaning, the existential modes of art, music, and literature are functional within the experience of our meeting with the other."[80] Aesthetic experience, for Steiner, is therefore understood dialectically. "All representations, even the most abstract, infer a rendezvous with intelligibility or, at the least, with a strangeness attenuated, qualified by observance and willed form."[81] Rendezvous and representation, "the continuum between both, the modulation from one to the other, lie at the source of poetry and the arts."[82] Encounter with the "other" and the embodiment of this encounter in language, art, or music lead to a third moment—the recognition that such embodiment of encounter bespeaks and ultimately leads one both to a deeper understanding of the "self" and to an approximate experience of the original encounter.

Notice the aboriginal nature of self-transcendence; there is a knowledge of self that comes from the movement toward that which is not the self. "Beyond the strength of any other act of witness, literature and the arts *tell* of the obstinacies of the impenetrable, of the absolutely alien which we come up against in the labyrinth of intimacy."[83] When artists or thinkers give their "findings" (encounters) the "persuasion of form" (art, music, literature), they tell us both about "us" and about that original meeting, "of the irreducible weight of otherness, of enclosedness, in the texture of and phenomenality of the material world."[84] While the meaning of this encounter may be intertextual (i.e., intelligible through other terms used in language), the reference is a separate and external reality not constructed from the subject's worldview. Literature, art, and music allow one to transcend such boundaries and encounter the "other."

This encounter, this acceptance of the demands of an "other," affects both the senses and the intellect: that is, it extends to all aspects of being. There is necessary in this meeting a prior ethics of reception, a courtesy of mind that allows a work of art to speak itself, to be heard, to be received.[85] But there is also the a posteriori effect of this encounter—demands are made by a work of art, music, or literature.

> The archaic torso in Rilke's famous poem says to us: "change your life." So do any poem, novel, play, painting, musical composition worth meeting. The voice of intelligible form, of the needs of direct address from

which such form springs, asks: "What do you feel, what do you think of the possibilities of life, of the alternative shapes of being which are implicit in your experience of me, in our encounter?"[86]

This encounter occurs in a context but is not reducible to any or all factors of that context. "Context is at all times dialectical. Our reading modifies, is in turn modified by, the communicative presence of its object."[87] Causality is mutual. The subject and the work of art are mutually dependent on each other's freedom. The work of art could have *not* been. The subject *can* say "no." Where "freedoms meet," when a work is freely given and freely received in the context of our own liberty, an encounter, an "experience" of real presence, has occurred.[88] One can accept or reject the work of art, and it is such a possibility of real absence, of rejection, that gives presence to the force of any work. While this encounter never results in a complete knowledge, this does not mean "that intelligibility is either wholly arbitrary or self-erasing. Such deduction is nihilistic sophistry."[89]

For Steiner, the infinite reach and context of language prohibit us from turning it into merely a constraint. There is an experience of the transcendent in language. At the same time, we must accept elements of the deconstructionist critique. Passage on the river of language is not as uncluttered as Schleiermacher would have it.

> Schleiermacher's famous postulate whereby the reader can make out more of the authentic intent and significance of the text than could its author is fundamental to modern hermeneutics. It sets a wary transgression at the heart of interpretation.
>
> Deconstruction has, in logical turn, undermined Schleiermacher's confident paradox. It has shown its circularity. Neither the expression of an author's or artist's putative intentions nor the re-interpretation, the possible refutation of these by his readers or viewers, [has] any stable, evidential status.[90]

The relationship between experience and language is more complex, with an emphasis on the dialectics of encounter. Both the deconstructionist and psychoanalytic critiques "remind us of the circularities, of the processes of infinite regression implicit in any invocation of a writer's or artist's motives and stated intentions. The structures of language, the formalizations of art and of music, are those of indeterminacy."[91] This indeterminacy militates against a fixed meaning, a striving for theoretical respectability, and instead entails approximation.

> I have said before: a good reading falls short of the text or art object by a distance, by a perimeter of inadequacy which are themselves luminous as is the corona around the darkened sun. The falling-short is a guarantor of the experienced "otherness"—the freedom to be or not to be, to enter into or abstain from a commerce of spirit with us—in the poem, the painting, the piece of music.[92]

It is crucial to recognize the term *experience* here. Experience, for Steiner, is encounter and response. Encounters, if offered and received in freedom, are a coming up against a real presence, to being. Language, in its infinite context, does set the initial boundary for any encounter, but it always functions as more than simply restraint. "All good art and literature begin in immanence. But they do not stop there. Which is to say, very plainly, that it is the enterprise and privilege of the aesthetic to quicken into lit presence the continuum between temporality and eternity, between matter and spirit, between man and 'the other.'"[93] Language is a catalyst for transcending both the work and the personal subjectivity to encounter real presence—being—being-in-relation-to. Transcendence, for Steiner, is the movement beyond the self, or anything constructed by the self, toward that which is truly Other. "This essay argues a wager on transcendence. It argues that there is in the art-act and its reception, that there is in the experience of meaningful form, a presumption of presence."[94]

The relation of language to experience ultimately leads to theology because for Steiner the guarantee of a correspondence between "word" and "world" ultimately must be God. This guarantee, this reinsurance of correspondence between language and external reality, is inspired by Descartes and Kant. "Descartes wagers on the unprovable assumption that God has not devised a phenomenal universe such as to deceive human reason or such as to make impossible the recurrent application of natural laws. . . . Kant postulates a fundamental disposition of accord between the fabric of human understanding and our perception of things."[95] Steiner will continue this "verification transcendence," as he terms it, *with a wager on meaning in language.* God, consequently, is necessary to reinsure sense, the presumption of meaningfulness in our encounter, our recollection of the "other" through intelligible form.

> It is a theology, explicit or suppressed, masked or avowed, substantive or imaged, which underwrites the presumption of creativity, of signification in our encounters with text, with music, with art. The meaning of meaning is a transcendent postulate. To read the poem responsibly ("respondingly"), to be answerable to form, is to wager on a reinsurance of sense. It is to wager on a relationship—tragic, turbulent, incommensurable, even sardonic—between word and world, but on a relationship precisely bounded by that which reinsures it.[96]

A CRITICAL EVALUATION

The radical questioning of the linguistic act embodied by the severance of external reference from language represents a "fundamental break in the history of human perception."[97] History, available as anything other than private recollection, has been discourse. This discourse presumes a real relation between the world and language. Language predicates, nominates, and adjectivally qualifies our understanding of reality. It does not create reality, though it does contain the possibility of communicating meaning. Language embodies the correspondence, the meaning, between the subject and the linguistic reference. For Steiner, meaning and reference can be intertextual, but reference can also be ontological. For Proudfoot and Lindbeck, all reference is intertextual. Though historically bound, language for Steiner can transcend time and space to read and communicate such ontological reality, such meaning to others. What was possible through language was presumed self-evident when the foundation of communication was a correspondence between "word and world." In the everyday of common sense it still is.

But any appeal to religious experience as a basis for theological inquiry is rejected by Proudfoot and Lindbeck largely due to their implicit acceptance of a constructive (noncorrespondence or intertextual) theory of language that undergirds both a conceptual theory of emotion and a rule theory of doctrine. This results in an understanding of "experience" that functions as perception. There is no primordial direct or immediate experience because experience is produced by and confined to preexperiential concepts, beliefs, and attitudes—that is, culturally bound products of language. The only "immediate" (quasi a priori) is the innate ability to learn language. From this understanding of language emerges a theory of religion confined to the data (i.e., the language) of religious experience.

Steiner argues three theses that serve to counter the arguments of Proudfoot and Lindbeck. First, language cannot be comprehended by and then confined to a single "theory." Theory and language as understood by Proudfoot and Lindbeck embody an error of categories, one in which an applied science methodology has been misappropriated for inquiry into an area (i.e., religious experience, religion) that lacks quantification. Second, such an understanding of language neglects the aboriginal nature of human "experience" as self-transcendent. To understand either language or "experience," a mutuality in the relation between them and not a priority in conditioning must be emphasized. Finally, what appears to be a rejection of a common humanity by Proudfoot and Lindbeck (and postmodernism in general) is, in fact, an affirmation of a particular kind of common anthropology—one in which "word and world" fail to cohere due to the brokenness of the self. "Experience," as a limited level of knowing, is simply made universal. Each of these three theses need explanation.

The ability to analyze and "fit" language into a single definite function is never seriously questioned by either Proudfoot or Lindbeck, but this forms the critical assumption that language principally constructs experience— belief for emotion and language for doctrine. Lindbeck cites Wittgenstein prior to the introduction of his regulative theory of doctrine, while Proudfoot does the same prior to the development of a conceptual theory of emotion. Appeals to Wittgenstein by both Proudfoot and Lindbeck offer *one interpretation* of his thought; Steiner offers another. Ultimately it is the reality *beyond* language that *is* accessible and most vital to being human.

> The close of the *Tractatus* diacritically situates outside speech, outside demonstrable conventions of intelligibility and falsification, the domains of religious, of moral, of aesthetic experience and response. In drastic *ethical* contrariety to the logical positivists, for whom such domains are of the order of non-sense, but in *technical* concurrence with them, Wittgenstein severely contracts the bounds of that which can meaningfully (in "an adult code") be said. In the vision of the early Wittgenstein—and "vision" is the least inaccurate term—the

existential realm "on the other side of language," the categories of felt being to which only silence (or music) give[s] access, are neither fictitious nor trivial. On the contrary. They are, indeed, the most important, life-transforming categories conceivable to man (but how?). They define his humanity.[98]

The categories of "felt being," those located outside language, are critical for humanity—and this realm transcends language. This is quite different from the deterministic and finite language theories that the early Wittgenstein is cited to support. Language for Wittgenstein is very limited, but what is, is not confined to language. Thus, although Wittgenstein severely limits how one ascertains or ascribes "meaning" to language, one cannot simply assert that he "wanted his supposition to be extended to its nihilistic finality."[99] Consequently, both Lindbeck and Proudfoot are drawn to a particular interpretation of Wittgenstein's theory of language not only for what it says about language *qua* language but also for its affirmation of a certain conception of human nature. Steiner offers another anthropology as well.

Aesthetic experience, that encounter with and response to an "other," bespeaks the self-transcendent nature of both experience and language. Awareness of self, knowledge of self, and in some cases love of self occur as a result of an encounter and response in freedom to that which is not the self. Art, literature, and music function as media of self-transcendence. These modes of access, these "means to dialogue with God," bespeak the movement from self to other and back to self that characterizes the human spirit.[100] Language is finite insofar as it is culturally and historically determined but unbounded in the possibilities for encountering the "other."

The character of the highest level of "experience" for Schleiermacher has been designated a "being-affected-by" that "Other" absolutely. This experience is one of passive reception. Conversely, "experience" is understood (vaguely) as a level of perception or knowing in this sense in Proudfoot and Lindbeck. Because a priority is given to language in the formation of this perception or knowing, little more than the "self" becomes the object of Proudfoot's "religious experience," while meaning outside the cultural-linguistic community remains inaccessible in Lindbeck's understanding of doctrine. Experience for Proudfoot and Lindbeck is a level of perception, an active function of human being resulting from language and concepts. Finally, Steiner understands "experience" as a reciprocal encounter with an

"other" that is subsequently recollected through language. "Aesthetic experience," as a *living* encounter with art, music, and literature and the "real
presence" of the "otherness" therein, embodies such an encounter. This
understanding of aesthetic experience is the most inclusive conception of
experience analyzed thus far: it is not just a knowing, or a passive being-in-
relation-to but a reciprocal encounter.[101]

> As the act of the poet is met—and it is the full tenor and rites of this
> meeting which I would explore—as it enters the precincts, spatial and
> temporal, mental and physical, of our being, it brings with it a radical
> calling towards change. The waking, the enrichment, the complication,
> the darkening, the unsettling of sensibility and understanding which
> follow on our experience of art are incipient with action. Form is the
> root of performance. In a wholly fundamental, pragmatic sense, the
> poem, the statue, the sonata are not so much read, viewed or heard as
> they are *lived*. The encounter with the aesthetic is, together with certain
> modes of religious and of metaphysical experience, the most "ingres-
> sive," transformative summons available to human experiencing.[102]

Consequently, while it may seem that Proudfoot and Lindbeck reject any
notion of a common human experience, they do not reject such a claim; they
simply frame such commonality in terms of different, universal anthropological assumptions. At the root of their limiting anthropology is an understanding of language that rejects a correspondence between language and
external reference. A "Truth" or set of truths does exist for Lindbeck and
Proudfoot. But this "Truth" or set of truths is mediated by and *confined* to
particular historical and linguistic contexts. Intertextual truth, in conjunction with the brokenness of the "self" (in its inability to access external
reference), is common to humanity. Conversely, a correspondence understanding of language—one in which sign and signified communicate real
presence—is, according to Steiner, "strictly inseparable from the postulate
of theological-metaphysical transcendence."[103] "A Logos-order entails, as I
want to show, a central supposition of 'real presence.'"[104]

> Western theology and the metaphysics, epistemology and aesthetics
> which have been its major footnotes, are "logocentric." This is to say
> that they axiomatize as fundamental and pre-eminent the concept of a

"presence." It can be that of God (ultimately it *must* be); of Platonic "Ideas"; of Aristotelian and Thomistic essence. It can be that of Cartesian self-consciousness; of Kant's transcendent logic or of Heidegger's "Being." It is to these pivots that the spokes of meaning finally lead. They insure its plenitude. That presence, theological, ontological or metaphysical, makes credible the assertion that there "is something *in* what we say."[105]

And again: "The issue is, quite simply, that of the meaning of meaning as it is re-insured by the postulate of the existence of God. 'In the beginning was the Word.' There was no such beginning, says deconstruction; only the play of sounds and markers amid the mutations of time."[106]

As I have argued, Steiner's understanding of the polyvalence of human experience can contribute substantially to a Christian theology emerging from human experience: that is, a Christian reflection on human experience as self-transcendent. Yet while Steiner is helpful in addressing some errors in postmodern philosophical anthropology, problems arise with his position on "verification transcendence," that is, God as guarantor. To make such an approach to God fundamental is ultimately insufficient for a Christian theology.[107] God as the guarantor of a correspondence of language to external reality instantiates a theological functionalism reminiscent of Descartes and Kant.[108]

Real Presences explicitly refers to Descartes, who, in the *Third Meditation*, maintains that God guarantees the correspondence between "articulate consciousness and the matters of our perceptions and intellection, a correspondence indispensable to the very possibilities of rational thought and of social modes."[109] It further draws upon Kant, who "postulates a fundamental disposition of accord between the fabric of human understanding and our perception of things."[110] Steiner, in turn, introduces the guarantor God to undergird a correspondence in language between words and external reference. God reinsures the "received" meaning correspondent to external reference. But an approach to God that harnesses God to a system of thought as insurance for certitude—moral, epistemological, linguistic—is fraught with problems of its own. James Collins, in *God in Modern Philosophy*, comments on such a theological functionalism:

The functionalist notion of using the conception of God to develop or shore up one's philosophical system has exercised a profound and steady attraction over the modern rationalists. As the analysis of pre-Kantian philosophy shows in classical outline, God must be invoked in a functional role as soon as one takes a certain view of philosophy itself. This role is required for the theory of God when philosophy is treated primarily as a deductive system aiming at a complete body of truths, obtained in an *a priori* and purely intellectual fashion. Such a view of philosophy provides an emergency answer to the disturbing challenge of the skeptics. God must then be called in to guarantee the objectivity of ideal constructs, the continuity of deduction, the comprehensiveness of the results, and their necessary generation of human happiness.[111]

The consequences of such a functional theology are problematic for Christian theology, for they "ten[d] to compromise the transcendence and freedom of this guarantor-God."[112] God may ensure epistemological certitude for Descartes and Kant and linguistic certitude for Steiner, but this alone is insufficient for Christian theology. The guarantor-God supports a secular mode of reasoning by expanding God's power and perfection "into primary deductive principles in philosophy," so that God is subordinated "to the demands of a rationalist system and hence given a functionalist treatment."[113] This can result in a vague pantheistic monism that can rationally, though not necessarily, undergird and reensure meaning in language— a wager is, after all, only a wager, not an affirmation.[114] This approach of course leads to the following inevitable question by Steiner: "How can 'the totally Other' act on us, let alone give any signal of its utterly inaccessible existence?"[115]

It is to such a contemporary question that Christian theology must respond. And if such a response, such a theology, is to give an honest account of itself, it must emerge from the lived reality of God as personal and historical, that is, as realized in relation to humanity in history. While Steiner responds significantly to some of the linguistic and anthropological challenges of postmodern theology, the guarantor-God is simply insufficient for grounding a Christian theology. For such a response to the contemporary problems regarding experience, language, and theology, it is now necessary to turn to an explicitly Christian systematic theologian.

Karl Rahner explores the Christian faith from an inclusive understanding of human experience, that is, from a careful reflection upon human existence. His theology is directly pertinent to the contemporary problem charted by the topics analyzed thus far. Steiner's "experience" as encounter, one that includes a person's existence in its entirety, can be employed for the formulation of theology, for it affirms the aboriginal reality of human self-transcendence. One can begin from Steiner's claim of that "irreducible weight of otherness" toward which works of art, music, and literature point. So it is toward the mystery of the self and the mystery of the "other" that this story now turns.

CHAPTER FIVE

Karl Rahner's Theology of Mystery: One Response to the Void

What has surely emerged from our study of a half-dozen recent philosophers is how important theological motifs and considerations are in the development and articulation of their projects. Besides that, they are all engaged, in no doubt very different ways, in recreating, rediscovering, something like the religio-metaphysical conception of human life into which Christianity erupted. Also, they all believe, and argue, that as moral agents, as subjects, we are indebted to something other than ourselves. In one way or another, they believe that human life as a moral and spiritual enterprise is essentially *responsive*. However tentative, provisional, off centre and misguided they may be, their projects cannot be dismissed as posturings against the void.

—Fergus Kerr, *Immortal Longings*

It would be too simplistic to assert that Karl Rahner's theology resolves all the points of contention outlined thus far—to do so would trivialize the very real problems and contradictions inherent in theological reflection today. But one might inquire how Rahner, arguably the most prominent Catholic theologian of the twentieth century, responds, whether consciously or not, to the issues outlined previously.

Steiner has provided solid justification for rejecting the postmodern understanding of experience and language—at least in its extreme manifestations. But as noted, the theological consequences of "verification transcendence" are unacceptable or inadequate for a Christian theological response.

For such a response, one must look to a theologian especially concerned with Christian theological reflection upon contemporary intellectual challenges.

Rahner's *Foundations of Christian Faith* is an inquiry that engages, at a foundational level, "the fact of Christian existence," one that is admittedly "very different today in individual Christians."[1] The starting point for such theological reflection is determined by the operative question for Rahner: "What is a Christian, and why can one live this Christian existence today with intellectual honesty?"[2] For Rahner, two things are given. We exist, and we have received Christianity. The question then becomes, In what way is our existence prepared to receive this gift? "Given that this self-revelation of God has occurred, Rahner wants to discover what must be true about the structure of human knowledge and loving for such a revelation to be recognized and received."[3] For the purpose of the present inquiry, how would Rahner frame the variables at issue?

Rahner first deals with questions of theological method, especially those that center upon experience, language, and the character of theology, from the perspective of one "who is a Christian and wants to be a Christian."[4] But if the Christian is to respond, and respond adequately, he or she must do so in terms of the problem itself. This was very important for Rahner. Where the problem leads, the Christian theologian must venture—into competing and contradictory understandings of language, experience, and conceptions of human existence that seriously challenge an intellectually defensible faith. "Theology is a theology that can be genuinely preached only to the extent that it succeeds in establishing contact with the total secular self-understanding which man has in a particular epoch, succeeds in engaging in conversation with it, in catching onto it, and in allowing itself to be enriched by it in its language and even more so in the very matter of theology itself."[5]

The Christian theologian must engage in a sustained and ongoing dialogue with modes of thought outside itself in a unique way that has little theological precedent. "[A]s theologians today we must enter into dialogue with a pluralism of historical, sociological, and natural sciences, a dialogue no longer mediated by philosophy."[6] This engagement of theology with other disciplines allows it to enter into a dialogue mediated by differing and contradictory interpretations of the topics traced through the authors thus far. Issues related to language, "experience," and the purpose of theology are central. This is especially true for Rahner because it is the contemporary *situation* that "provides current theology with its starting-point."[7] The challenges faced by contemporary theologians are unique in Rahner's view. The plurality of sciences, including and especially philosophical pluralism, and historical consciousness constitute a radical departure from past epochs.

> Rahner, then, wants to present a version of Christianity which shows how deeply connected it is to other aspects of life. In effect, he is out to free people from the extrinsicist conception of grace. In this respect he is an apologist: he wants to remove one of the principal obstacles to religious belief, for Christians as well as non-believers: the fear that Christianity as a system of belief is fundamentally alien to our every-day lives. He wants to show that, on the contrary, it is the articulation of something very deep in us.[8]

Theology always mediates the truths of faith to a particular historical context. To do so adequately, it must acknowledge the inevitability of its own historicity. When a given historical situation is grasped, even provisionally, the content of faith can be presented within it. Thus, it is within the dialogue on varying conceptions of language, experience, and theological inquiry, a dialogue that is critical for contemporary theology, that Rahner's thought must make a response. Here a note ought to be made about the pluralism that Rahner embraces. At root it is a pluralism that takes seriously the historicity of theological inquiry. By this I mean that all theology is contextual but not utterly reducible to such a context. Some, like Fergus Kerr, who have recognized this pluralism even go so far as to identify Rahner's method as nonfoundationalist: "On the other hand, if one takes his remarks about the inescapability of pluralism with the seriousness with which he makes them, and assumes that he himself understood his transcendental theology as one approach among others, we open up a way of reading his work which we might (with Kilby) call modest, postmodern—in a word: 'non-foundationalist.'"[9] This is not to say that Rahner is not indebted to very specific philosophical movements; rather, it is to say that all theology must respond to the historical context in which it occurs. And because that context is always changing, theology and theological method must continually change as well. Second, Rahner's theology, as a theology of mystery, will always remain "unsettled" if it is taken seriously. God is not provisional mystery but absolute mystery, with all that this implies.[10] As Kerr so clearly states: "Instead of conceiving ourselves in terms of the self-conscious autonomous subject who is striving to ascend to the absolute, we should think of ourselves rather as the gift of the mystery."[11]

Given this, the dialogue with what has been termed moderate postmodernism can be constructively advanced through an analysis of Rahner's foundational theology. By entering into the mutuality of three dialectical moments that makes up his method and confirms his affirmation of a unity of philosophy and theology, one can concretely address the critical variables that have driven this inquiry.[12] This unity of philosophy and theology is critical to a *foundational* level of inquiry that "summons man before the real truth of his being. It summons him before the truth in which he remains inescapably caught, although this prison is ultimately the infinite expanse of the incomprehensible mystery of God."[13]

First, there must be reflection upon human experience, "upon man as the universal question which he is for himself, and hence we must philosophize in the most proper sense."[14] Second, one must take up (among other topics) history and language: "the transcendental and the historical conditions which make revelation possible must be reflected upon."[15] Finally, one must reflect on Christian doctrine and its informing relation to experience, "the fundamental assertion of Christianity as the answer to the question that man is, and hence we must do theology."[16] These three moments "mutually condition one another and therefore form a unity, a unity that is of course differentiated." These moments can also be utilized to address the topics analyzed thus far.[17]

The first of these three moments, the reflection upon human experience, is critical, for current problems in theological reflection have arisen through fundamentally different conceptions of human experience. Arguments on the nature of human experience have already been put forth by Schleiermacher, Proudfoot, Lindbeck, and Steiner. It is toward these, and other conceptions of human experience, that Rahner responds.

> Thus the task of theology must precisely be to appeal in all the various conceptual forms in which it is objectified, to this basic experience of grace, to bring man again and again to a fresh recognition of that fact that all this immense sum of distinct statements of the Christian faith basically speaking expresses nothing else than an immense truth, even though one that has been explicated throughout all the levels of man's being: the truth, namely, that the absolute mystery that is, that permeates all things,

upholds all things, and endures eternally, has bestowed itself as itself in an act of forgiving love upon man, and is experienced in faith in that ineffable experience of grace as the ultimate freedom of man.[18]

Human experience must finally be understood as grounded by and drawn toward *holy mystery*. This should not be understood in the sense of a "placeholder." It should not be so distant as to force a "*sacrificium intellectus.*"[19] And it is not something senseless and unintelligible; rather, it is infinitely intelligible (and thus always beyond our comprehension) and immanent. Thus, human being should be understood as irrevocably oriented toward absolute mystery: that is, to God. This approach to theology through the mystery of and acceptance of Christian personhood makes accessible the notion of salvation that grounds Rahner's theology.

Reflection upon human experience necessarily moves into the second topic developed throughout this work: the relationship of "experience" to its communication, to language, to reflection, or, as Rahner designates it, to its "objectification." Thus, in the introduction to *Foundations*, he states: "It is precisely this permanent and insurmountable difference between the original Christian actualization of existence and reflection upon it which will occupy us throughout. The insight into this difference is a key insight which represents a necessary presupposition for an introduction to the idea of Christianity."[20]

This "original actualization" immediately enters into the domain of language upon reflection. It shapes language and is shaped by language. Ultimately, such mutuality allows for a deeper understanding of both the objectification of "original experience" and the originality of experience. This relationship of experience and language directly influences a corresponding understanding of the nature and function of doctrine and theology. For Rahner, a progressive reflection upon Christian existence, mediated by language and culminating in doctrine, reveals, incrementally, a greater depth to such original actualization through the very language used to express it and the doctrine used to preserve and nourish it.

This understanding of doctrine as both expressive and constructive will reveal the plurality of theologies and methods operative for Rahner—a plurality that allows his theology to be legitimately in dialogue with the postmodern critique. In particular, it can lead to a grasp of the nature and purpose of his dogmatic theology. The unity of foundational and dogmatic theology will contain all three differentiated moments—a reflection on Christian actualization of existence as self-transcendent, language as both descriptive and constructive, and doctrine as informative of the "original actualization." These, of course, mutually condition each other.[21] This dogmatic theological exercise can be illustrated by Rahner's dogmatic treatment of the doctrine of the Trinity.

HUMAN EXPERIENCE AND HOLY MYSTERY

> There is no need to explain in any great detail that a notion of person and subject is of fundamental importance for the possibility of Christian revelation and the self-understanding of Christianity. A personal relationship to God, a genuinely dialogical history of salvation between God and man, the acceptance of one's own unique, eternal salvation, the notion of responsibility before God and his judgment, all of these assertions of Christianity, however they are to be explained more precisely, imply that man is what we want to say here: person and subject.
>
> —Rahner, *Foundations*[22]

The concepts of person and subject "point to a basic experience which indeed does not simply take place in an absolutely wordless and unreflexive experience, but neither is it something which can be expressed in words and indoctrinated from without."[23] Such an experience is irreducible to words, yet it is dependent upon language for its objectification. Thus, language is the a posteriori condition through which one can point toward a basic and original experience that is designated as personhood and subjectivity.

Every person can come to an awareness of his or her being as a product of something else—of history, of culture, of language. Empirical, or regional anthropologies—those that posit humanity solely as the product of the world—are legitimate insofar as they seek to understand and analyze the human being "whose origins lie within the world, that is, who has his roots in empirical realities."[24] And precisely this experience of being at the disposal of something other than the self enters into the understanding of person and subject. "Man experiences himself precisely as subject and person insofar as he becomes conscious of himself as the product of what is radically foreign to him."[25] The fact that the human being can engage such analysis is revelatory of something beyond any deterministic origin. "In the fact that man raises analytical questions about himself and opens himself to the unlimited horizons of such questioning, he has already transcended himself and every conceivable element of such an analysis or of an empirical reconstruction of himself. In doing this he is affirming himself as more than the sum of such analyzable components of his reality."[26]

Thus, such efforts at regional anthropology will never, can never, capture all that being human *is*.[27] The person is always more than the sum of regional anthropologies. This is so because "the experience of radical questioning and man's ability to place himself in question are things which a finite system cannot accomplish."[28]

Insofar as human beings experience a standpoint "outside of and above the system of empirical, individual and specifiable data," they also experience "a question which has already gone beyond every possible empirical and partial answer, has gone beyond it not in its positive content but in the radical nature of the question."[29] It is through such awareness of our own irreducibility that we experience ourselves as subjects. The experience of subjectivity, of recognizing the irreducibility of human being to empirical criteria used to analyze it, bespeaks an awareness of the person in his or her totality: that is, as "person." Being a person means that one takes responsibility for the self as one and whole even as it brings itself before the empirical sciences in the pursuit of greater knowledge and understanding.

The human being experiences himself or herself as person and subject. Yet the determination contained in such an assertion will always elude categorization as "a regional element in man." This is so because the subjectivity and personhood in every human being is "copresent in every individual experience as its *a priori* condition."[30] The designation of such elements of transcendental experience "does not appear in its own reality when man is dealing with something individual and definable in an objective way, but when in such a process he is *being* subject and not dealing with a 'subject' in an objective way."[31] This awareness of ourselves in the act of knowledge, this subjectivity and its corresponding "personhood" (one that is exercised even when rejected) bespeaks a level of knowing or experiencing—of actualizing—that transcends empirically verifiable reality.

To say that man is person and subject, therefore, means first of all that man is someone who cannot be derived, who cannot be produced completely from other elements at our disposal. He is that being who is responsible for himself. When he explains himself, analyzes himself, reduces himself back to the plurality of his origins, he is affirming himself as the subject who is doing this, and in so doing he experiences himself as something necessarily prior to and more original in this plurality.[32]

Once knowledge or experience has been designated finite (i.e., reducible to a plurality of components), such a designation bespeaks the infinite—for to designate something as closed and final, one must transcend that very boundary in order to posit such a claim.[33]

This spirit is in the world: that is, the world is the necessary condition for the actualization as spirit. This spirit, this subjectivity and personhood, can never be isolated and analyzed as such; rather, it becomes evident only through reflection upon the encounter with categorical reality. For this reason, the human person for Rahner is always in history—in fact, that history is the possibility for movement toward that which transcends it. For example, the fact that everything and anything can be questioned bespeaks a movement beyond the finite. "The infinite horizon of human questioning is experienced as an horizon which recedes further and further the more answers man can discover."[34] This horizon is never grasped but is perhaps touched as it recedes ever further.[35] Ultimately, the human being questions and will continue to question because the movement of the mind constantly transcends the answers already discovered. The finite necessitates a movement toward the infinite.

Rahner identifies this unthematic knowledge of the infinity of reality, an experience necessary and prior to categorical finite experience, as "*Vorgriff*, or the pre-apprehension of 'being.'"[36] There is a preapprehension of being rather than nothing because while the "absurdity of what confronts him" is an element of human existence, so is the experience of hope and the movement toward "liberating freedom."[37] Thus, "what grounds man's openness and his reaching out in the unlimited expanse of his transcendence cannot be nothingness, an absolutely empty void. For to assert that of a void would make absolutely no sense."[38] This openness of human existence is real, though "not self-explanatory"; it is given, not created by the subject; and it reveals a movement to the more real as horizon, constantly out of reach, but ever present.

It is self-evident that this transcendental experience of human transcendence is not the experience of some definite, particular objective thing which is experienced alongside other objects. It is rather a basic mode of being which is prior to and permeates every objective experience. We must emphasize again and again that the transcendence meant here is not the thematically conceptualized "concept" of transcendence in which transcendence is reflected upon objectively. It is rather the *a priori* openness of the subject to being as such, which is present precisely when a person experiences himself as involved in the multiplicity of cares and concerns and fears and hopes of his everyday world. Real transcendence is always in the background, so to speak, in those origins of human life and human knowledge over which we have no control.[39]

When that horizon toward which human openness tends, an openness *not* constructed or controlled by the subject, moves in upon the human being, he or she experiences "grace."[40] Instead of being ever distant, the horizon now becomes inexpressibly close. God communicates God's self to that which is not God. Such communication can be appropriated personally as Father, as Son, as Holy Spirit. This "infinite horizon of being making itself manifest" is never captured adequately by reflection and should not be confused with it.[41]

Transcendental experience is often easily overlooked because it becomes explicitly present only through the "mediation of the categorical objectivity of man or of the world around him," for example, through language.[42] Neither language nor transcendental experience is derivative of the other, but language can be an aspect of categorical objectivity that makes transcendental experience explicitly present. Underlying all categorical activity is the "silent and uncontrollable infinity of reality . . . always present as mystery. This makes man totally open to this mystery and precisely in this way he becomes conscious of himself as person and subject."[43] The decision related to the whole of one's being to accept or reject such mystery upon its movement toward us in grace, is also integral to transcendental experience. For this reason Rahner includes responsibility and freedom when arguing that we are "person" and "subject."[44]

There is freedom and responsibility constitutive of human existence whenever human beings accept or reject anything pertaining to the whole of their existence—even when they choose to deny their own ability to do so.[45] "When freedom is really understood, it is not the power to be able to do this or that, but the power to decide about oneself and to actualize oneself."[46] This self-determination, of course, suggests an alternative to the essential claims of postmodern anthropology.

> If someone says that man always experiences himself as determined and controlled from without, as functional and dependent, as able to be analyzed and reduced into antecedents and consequences, the reply must be: the subject who knows this is always at the same time a responsible subject who is challenged to say something and to do something with man's absolute dependence and self-alienation and determination, challenged to take a position on it by either cursing it or accepting it, by being skeptical or by despairing, or whatever. So even when a person would abandon himself into the hands of the empirical anthropologies, he still remains in his own hands. He does not escape from his freedom, and the only question can be how he interprets himself, and freely interprets himself.[47]

Salvation occurs within and through historical reality (as do the actualization of personhood, subjectivity, responsibility, and freedom). This history is not an element beside these transcendental elements. Rather, such aspects of human existence are denied or affirmed in and through history, through living in space and time, and through language. There is no transcendentality outside the categorical. Consequently, "it is in history that the subject must work out his salvation by finding it there as offered to him and accepting it."[48] Such a possibility occurs when the transcendental orientation of the human being accepts the offer of the horizon to the self: that is, when he or she accepts grace, the self-communication of God to that which is not God, while remaining God.

> In this sense we can say without hesitation: a person who opens himself to his transcendental experience of the holy mystery at all has the experience that this mystery is not only an infinitely distant horizon, a remote judgment which judges from a distance his consciousness and his world of persons and things, it is not only something mysterious which frightens him away and back into the narrow confines of his

everyday world. He experiences rather that his holy mystery is also a hidden closeness, a forgiving intimacy, his real home, that it is a love which shares itself, something familiar which he can approach and turn to from the estrangement of his own perilous and empty life. It is the person who in the forlornness of his guilt still turns in trust to the mystery of his existence which is quietly present, and surrenders himself as one who even in his guilt no longer wants to understand himself in a self-centered and self-sufficient way, it is this person who experiences himself as one who does not forgive himself, but who is forgiven, and experiences this forgiveness which he receives as the hidden, forgiving and liberating love of God himself, who forgives in that he gives himself, because only in this way can there really be forgiveness once and for all.[49]

The acceptance of the self as transcendent is found in an acceptance of the forgiving mystery of the term of such transcendence. Thus, when one accepts the communication of that term, without ever controlling it, there is really an acceptance of the self-communication of absolute mystery and the realization that we exist for such self-communication.[50] In salvation, the grace of God becomes a constitutive principle of the self.[51]

In the experience of self, the infinity of existence is clearly not at our disposal. There is the experience of a constantly revealing and receding horizon of being, a horizon that constitutes and evokes the self. Human beings never master or control what grounds and surrounds them and what they move toward, though they can freely accept or reject such movement. This acknowledgment and free acceptance of dependence, of not being at one's own disposal, bespeaks human existence. By its very nature it is incomplete but always oriented toward absolute mystery.

The knowledge of God is, nevertheless, a *transcendental* knowledge because man's basic and original orientation towards absolute mystery, which constitutes his fundamental experience of God, is a permanent existential of man as a spiritual subject. This means that the explicit conceptual and thematic knowledge, which we usually think of when we speak of the knowledge of God or of proofs for God's existence, is a reflection upon man's transcendental orientation towards mystery, and some degree of reflection is always necessary.[52]

To be oriented toward absolute mystery means that in the depth of human *being* there is a movement toward that which has bestowed such being. This original transcendental experience always issues from out of a subjectivity "[which] listens, which does not control, which is overwhelmed by mystery and opened up by mystery."[53] It does not recognize itself as independently transcendent; rather, it realizes transcendence as a gift. For this reason, transcendence is not something to grasp but something to be grasped by, to accept as the horizon offering itself as grace. Where and how an individual lives the acceptance of such grace takes place will vary greatly with the individual person.[54] Ultimately, the term and source of this transcendence, this gift to human existence, "can be called God," though the term *holy mystery*, one deliberately more personal than *absolute mystery*, is preferable.[55]

> If we use a less familiar and less well-defined phrase like "holy mystery," in order to express the term of transcendence and the source from which it comes, then the danger of misunderstanding is somewhat less than when we say: "The term of transcendence is God." We must first describe the experience and the term of the experience together before what is experienced can be called "God."[56]

The term of transcendence, like the experience itself, is indefinable because it cannot be grasped, encircled, or controlled. Finite human experience can never completely grasp the infinite term of its transcendence. "The infinite horizon, which is the term of transcendence and which opens us to unlimited possibilities of encountering this or that particular thing, cannot itself be given a name."[57] No conceptualization is adequate, for it is not the sum of many individual factors, nor can it be defined within the horizon of knowledge that it gives to us.

> The term of transcendence admits of no control over itself because then we would be reaching beyond it and incorporating it within another, higher and broader horizon. This contradicts the very nature of this transcendence and of the real term of this transcendence. The infinite and silent term is what disposes of us. It presents itself to us in the mode of withdrawal, of silence, of distance, of being always inexpressible, so that speaking of it, if it is to make sense, always requires listening to its silence.[58]

There is also no objective experience of the term itself because it can only be known and freely accepted subjectively, by the individual in the context of his or her own life.[59] For this reason, "the term of this transcendence is the presence of this transcendence, which is only present as the condition of possibility for categorical knowledge, and not by itself."[60]

Mystery designates the reality of existence that is so near that it is the condition for the possibility of any thought or action, while remaining a horizon, elusive to direct definition or immediate objectification.[61] Indirectly, one can and does "know" mystery unthematically through the original transcendental experience of human existence. Such mystery becomes "holy" in God's answer to the question we are.

Transcendental experience is not just the condition for the possibility of knowledge as such but also the "possibility for a subject being present to himself and just as basically and originally being present to another subject."[62] For a subject to possess this self-presence and to give and accept another subject freely "means ultimately to love."[63] Thus, while one can *begin* reflection upon the source of transcendental experience as knowledge, where it is *fulfilled* is something more.[64]

> The incomprehensibility of God in the vision must not be understood merely as an indication of the finiteness of created knowledge, as the "end" to which it comes. *Rather it must be understood as precisely that which it wants to reach. If this is correct, then indeed the essence of knowledge itself changes, it becomes something else, for which the incomprehensibility of God is no longer a forbidding boundary but is that which is sought* [italics added].[65]

Note the critical distinction between an impersonal end to which knowledge arrives (the aboriginal movement of every human being) and the desire inherent in the movement to reach such an end (the acceptance of the self-communication of God). The movement from transcendental knowledge into transcendental love occurs not by "knowing" the unknowable as such but by surrendering the self to the term that has drawn it. "Hence man must let himself fall into this incomprehensibility as into his true fulfillment and happiness, let himself be taken up by this unanswered question. This unintelligible risk, which sweeps away all questions, is usually called worshipful love of God. It alone allows the darkness to be light."[66]

This love, this salvation, is actualized through a freely accepted dependence on the term of transcendence. And note the particular definition of love that is operative here: "Take as the definition of love precisely this description of letting oneself fall into the incomprehensible (whereby this 'letting' is destiny and deed in one, hence free and voluntary)."[67] The mystery that is absolute has opened and drawn us irrevocably toward itself, has offered itself as our end, and has done so through our very possibility for freedom and love.[68]

To summarize, human experience is self-transcendent in the presence of holy mystery. Human beings actualize their existence in history. Personhood and subjectivity are actualized through questioning and knowledge, through responsibility, and thus through freedom to decide for the whole of the self. This actualization occurs through the historical: that is, through the categorical reality (including language) confronted on a daily and sometimes monotonous basis. The acceptance of the self as the question for which there is no finite categorical answer is nothing less than the acceptance of the term of human transcendence lovingly offered as grace, the horizon of being, that moves in upon the person in love.

The condition for the possibility of self-actualization is both distant as the ever-receding horizon of possibility and immanent in the nearness of its free offer of itself as the end toward which human knowledge moves. The striving for knowledge reaches its completion in the self-surrender of love, a love intimately connected to love of self and neighbor—that is, in history. Then the human can truly be understood as spirit in world.

> [T]he categorized explicit love of neighbor is the primary act of the love of God. The love of God unreflectedly but really and always intends God in the supernatural transcendentality in the love of neighbor as such, and even the explicit love of God is still borne by that opening in trusting love to the whole of reality which takes place in the love of neighbor. It is radically true, i.e., by an ontological and not merely "moral" or psychological necessity, that whoever does not love the brother whom he "sees," also cannot love God whom he does not see, and that one can love God whom one does not see only *by* loving one's visible brother lovingly.[69]

This entire prior exercise in theological objectification bespeaks a deeper level of actualization, an original experience that can be only inadequately described. Such a distinction between an original experience and its objectification is made explicit at the close of the first chapter of *Foundations:*

> All of the ideas which we have used here on that level of reflection which we have consciously chosen should be seen only as an attempt to evoke an understanding of existence in the light of which every individual, in the concrete experience of his own existence, must himself experience that this self-understanding is basically inescapable, whether one chooses to accept it or protest against it. This is so however little the concepts, words and statements we have used can really and adequately recapture, or were intended to recapture, the real and original experience of personhood and freedom, of subjectivity, of history and historicity, and of dependence.[70]

The original experience of human actualization, one designated as self-transcendent, has been partially recaptured. "Concepts, words and statements" attempt to describe the object of reflection—a prior original experience of transcendental actualization in history and the term of such transcendental actualization as coterminous with such an experience. Rahner's explicit understanding of the relationship between original experience as self-transcendent—and its actualization through language—is now necessary to evaluate.

The Originality of Human Experience and the Necessity of Language

> There is in man an inescapable unity in difference between one's original self-possession and reflection. This is disputed in different ways by theological rationalism on the one hand, and on the other by the philosophy of religion of so-called classical "modernism." For basically every rationalism is based upon the conviction that a reality is present for man in spiritual and free self-possession only through the objectifying concept, and this becomes genuinely and fully real in scientific knowledge. Conversely, what is called "modernism" in the classical understanding lives by the conviction that the concept or reflection is something *absolutely* secondary in relation to the original self-possession of existence in self-consciousness and freedom, so that reflection could also be dispensed with.
>
> —Rahner, *Foundations* [71]

Theological rationalism and classical modernism are varieties of interpreta-tion that have been evident in the framing of the problematic thus far.[72] The first presumes an objective knowledge of a thing "in itself," with no admixture of subjective contribution to this knowledge.[73] This persuasion grounds a rejection, or at best a deep suspicion, of an appeal to experience for theol-ogy. The second presumes such an "absolute" priority of experience over its objectification that reflection becomes superfluous. Instead of positing a unity between a reality and the concept that objectifies it, Rahner argues for a deeper unity of a "reality and its 'self-presence' which is more, and is more original."[74]

> When I love, when I am tormented by questions, when I am sad, when I am faithful, when I feel longing, this human existentiell reality is a unity, an original unity of reality and its own self-presence which is not *totally* mediated by the concept which objectifies it in scientific knowledge. This unity of reality and the original self-presence of this reality in the person is already present in man's free self-realization. That is one side of the question.[75]

There is a moment of reflection that belongs to this original knowledge, though it does not "capture this original knowledge and transpose it inte-grally into objectifying concepts."[76] There is an original self-possession or knowledge and its concept, which "belong together and yet are not one."[77] This preconceptual awareness, "this original unity which we are driving at between reality and its knowledge of itself, always exists in man only with and in and through what we can call language, and thus also reflection and communicability."[78] Through language an original experience becomes accessible to reflection and communicability by the subject. Original experi-ence takes a priority over language, though any actualization of such experi-ence, and any reflection or communication of it, presumes language. Thus, Rahner explicitly rejects both Proudfoot and Lindbeck's understanding of doctrine (or belief) as *solely* constructive of experience. "The experience of God which we are pointing to here is not some subsequent emotional reac-tion to doctrinal instruction about the existence and nature of God which we receive from without and at the theoretical level. *Rather it is prior to any such teaching, underlies it, and has to be there already for it to be made intelligible at all* [italics added]."[79] Not only does language clarify experience, but original experience clarifies language. (There was a glimpse of this in Steiner's assertion that a "real presence" is the recounting of an original encounter, one then communicated through a work of art or literature.) While there is a way in which language clarifies experience for Rahner, the opposite is also true: experience clarifies language. This tension characteristic of human experience is best captured by the idea of analogy.

> And this original relationship is what we are calling analogy: the tension between a categorical starting point and the incomprehensibility of the holy mystery, namely, God. We ourselves, as we can put it, exist analogously in and through our being grounded in this holy mystery which always surpasses us. But it always constitutes us by surpassing us and by pointing us towards the concrete, individual, categorical realities which confront us within the realm of our experience. Conversely, then, these realities are the mediation of the point of departure for our knowledge of God.[80]

This tension between original experience and language—between an "experience" (of longing, for example) and its objectification in concepts—is thus dialectical. First, there is a movement from original "experience" out through actualization to its objectification. "The original self-presence of the subject in the actual realization of his existence strives to translate itself more and more into the conceptual, into the objectified, into language, into communication with another." But the opposite is also true: "One who has been formed by a common language, and educated and indoctrinated from without, experiences clearly perhaps only very slowly what he has been talking about for a long time."[81] It seems that from this particular text, original actualization is made manifest first in conceptualization (*Begrifflichkeit*), which requires language (*die Sprache*), then in communication (*die Mitteilung*), and finally in a theoretical knowledge (*theoretische Wissen*) that points back to the original actualization. Both angles are mutually informing, and while priority is given to original experience, it is, de facto, dependent upon language for its reflection and communication. "To that extent reflection, conceptualization and language have a *necessary* [italics added] orientation to that original knowledge, to that original experience in which what is meant and the experience of what is meant are still one."[82]

The tension is fluid, not static, between an original experience and its objectification through conceptualization and reflection. Speech expresses nonthematic experience, and nonthematic experience, in turn, gives intelligibility to the language used to express it. For example, "It is possible for someone to have authentic experiences of love, and express these experiences in erroneous ways." Conversely, "[i]t is possible to give a very accurate and correct description of an experience, and to have never had such an experience before."[83] For this reason, "Experience as such and subsequent reflection upon this experience, in which its content is conceptually objectified, *are never absolutely separate* [italics added] one from the other."[84] It is the mutual relationship between an original experience and its objectification that is stressed, though undoubtedly a priority is given to experience.[85]

The distinction and relationship between original "experience" (transcendental experience of the self through actualization in knowledge, freedom, and ultimately love), a term that has been explored in some detail already, and its objectification in language (reflection, conceptualization) are critical.[86] They emerge directly from a particular understanding of language.

> When I ask why it is that language expresses something meaningful, then of course I can put what I am now thinking into language, but the fact remains that I am expressing something that is not simply identical with language as such. I would like to put it this way: Language is always simultaneously the language of something distinct from the language itself and is not contained in it.[87]

Language is always there, it is always the expression of something distinct from itself, and the focus of language is not simply contained in the language. Such an assertion absolutely contradicts postmodern linguistic theory. Similarly, experience is never simply and totally contained within language, though language may very well be the possibility for and actuality through which an experience is made explicit.

Thus, enclosing language in a comprehensive understanding of its meaning and content is not possible. "Ultimately, that is simply not within the control of persons speaking, even if they believe that for themselves and in their reflection nothing more is to be found in their language than what they reflectively regard as, and accept as, content."[88] Language is incommensurable but necessary for any actualization of the self.

Perhaps another way to frame the relationship of original experience to language is to say that language is the a posteriori that really opens up our a priori transcendentality. Because all questions, including the question of the self, occur in the actualization of existence, and such questions presuppose a framing by language, one could argue "that our transcendentality is only actualized when we begin to learn our language, because we only ask questions through this language."[89] Such language, as the vehicle for such actualization, would contain the possibility for reflection and communication.

The relationship between original experience, its actualization, and its objectification is critical for Rahner, and it leads directly into the third moment of his method—how Christianity can be "the answer to the question which man is." The precise question now becomes: How can the explicit objectification of Christian truth in doctrine inform our human existence and likewise be formed and re-formed by it? Reflection upon such a question will call for a precise understanding of the role of doctrine as an interpretation of God's absolute self-communication and the purpose of such self-communication—salvation.

THE FUNCTION OF THEOLOGICAL DOCTRINE

> First of all, a dogmatic statement is meant to be a true statement by the very fact that a human statement has this intention and makes this claim. It intends a definite objective content which has its own existence opposite the speaker— it is not merely the publication of a subjective state of the speaker; it does not ultimately wish to objectify the subjectivity of the speaker but rather to bring the objectivity of the matter referred to nearer to the listener and thus to subjectify in this sense. In as far as these dogmatic statements to a great extent do not refer simply to objects of direct sense experience and are also not concerned simply with one's own spiritual experience, such statements can only be analogous, i.e., they point to the meant object with the help of positive representations and point the way to surpassing those representations by transcendence and negation.
>
> —Rahner, "What Is a Dogmatic Statement?"[90]

A dogmatic statement mediates the truths of faith to a specific time and place. Thus, the formulation of such statements will emerge from a tension between the received "truths of the faith" as they unfold through history—and the situation of the believer in space and time. A dogmatic statement, whatever its specific characteristics, mediates and communicates the intelligibility of the content of faith so as to allow for its appropriation by the believer in a particular history. But these truths are not totally extrinsic either, for they also speak to the reality actualized by believers in their struggle to live in faith as Christians.

> Christian teaching, which becomes conceptual in reflexive, human words in the Church's profession of faith, does not simply inform man of the content of this profession from without and only in concepts. Rather it appeals to reality, which is not only said, but also given and really experienced in man's transcendental experience. Hence it expresses to man his own self-understanding, one which he already has, although unreflexively.[91]

Dogmatic statements, those distinct from statements in Scripture, possess five general characteristics: they claim to be true in an ordinary sense, they are statements of faith, they possess an explicitly ecclesiological character, they lead one into "the mysterium," and, finally, they are not identical "with the original Word of revelation and the original statement of faith."[92] The role of theological doctrine and its relation to experience and language emerge from a closer analysis of each characteristic.

Dogmatic statements possess the same possibilities of "ordinary statements" insofar as they also contain the difference between what is meant and what is said.[93] There is also the same possibility for the unthematic preconceptual knowledge to be true even if the "conceptual-objective" expression is false. Thus, dogmatic statements possess varying degrees of truth as bespeaking the very natural human inability to conceptualize perfectly the truths of faith.[94] And because dogmatic statements do not merely emerge subjectively from reflection upon human experience but also are received objectively in the unfolding of the history of dogma, a dogmatic statement is also a statement of faith.

> Because and insofar as faith is always the listening by a concrete human being to the Word of God, the real fact of having heard, the success of the listening to the Word of God which is actually present only when it is heard and understood, can always happen solely in a simultaneous understanding of faith, i.e., in a confrontation (which naturally admits

of many degrees) of God's message with what man already is, with man in so far as he is a spiritual being and with the man as he is listening to this message.[95]

A dogmatic statement is received in the living faith of the hearer; thus, it not only is "about some theological object" but is the *appropriation* of such an object, "an exercise of faith."[96] Such an exercise of faith is a human activity "in which man's own subjectivity together with its logic, its experience, native concepts and perspectives, already enters into play."[97] Some degree of reflection is inherent to the hearing, and for this reason a dogmatic statement is "merely a further development, an unfolding of that basic subjective reflection which already takes place in the mere obedient listening to the Word of God, i.e., in faith as such."[98] Dogmatic reflection and a dogmatic statement can never be totally separate from the faith that makes both possible. Thus, a dogmatic statement refers to the object of faith (*fides quae creditur*) as well as the exercise of faith (*fides qua creditur*).

Whenever these two aspects are separated—for example, if a nonbeliever seems to understand a dogmatic statement as well as a believer but does not exercise faith—there can be a "science of religion" but no theology as such. Rahner emphasizes this elsewhere: "Hence, all theology is 'kerygmatic.' Otherwise it is merely speculative philosophy of religion."[99] This is so because the exercise of faith, the actual existential acceptance of faith, "opens up . . . a whole view of reality, even though it seems that the profane theoretician of religion can know and say just as much or as little about Christianity as the believing theologian."[100] A dogmatic statement is a statement of faith not only because of its object but also because of the subjective act of believing—and in being this it can effect three critical functions. First, it "participates in its own way in the expressed profession and praise of the message Christ has given us about himself and which leads us to him—in the expression of that message listened to and accepted." Second, it "leads towards the historical event of salvation" by accomplishing the first. Finally, it embodies an existential and not just theoretical relationship to "the historical event of salvation" and in so doing is "*ex fide ad fidem*" even in its theoretical character.

The manifestation of faith that doctrine serves is not just an individual faith, but a communal manifestation of faith, namely the faith of the Church. And so it is necessary to delineate the ecclesiological character of a dogmatic statement:

This means that here the Church reflects on the message—given by and received from Jesus Christ and transmitted in belief of the primitive Church—in relation to each particular, historically conditioned situation and based on her consciousness of faith and its original source. She reflects on this message and proclaims the one permanent faith anew in the form of this new theological reflection, in such a way that this faith retains and acquires once more as inevitable a presence as possible for the one who hears the message of the Church to make a decision.[101]

A dogmatic statement is an ecclesiological statement insofar as it accomplishes its purpose "of being the concrete form of faith in a new spiritual situation."[102] While individual theological reflection is valuable, and should be ecclesiological, "superior to it is the theology of the Church in which the Church as a whole engages in theological activity through the bearers of her established *magisterium*."[103] Such theology emerging from the Church, one that always retains its reference to the "message of the first witnesses of the Lord, the faith of the primitive Church in the normative concrete form in which it is found in Holy Scripture," demands obedience from the believer and is labeled dogma.[104] Such a designation by the magisterium occurs when the Church claims in her magisterium "that this her message constituted this way (i.e., become theology) *is* (and does not merely speak about) the here and now valid form of the Word in which God has spoken to us in our heart."[105] While this always includes a "communal linguistic ruling on terminology," that should not be confused with "the thing itself."[106] Thus, it is necessary to acknowledge that though the reality referred to is infinite and incomprehensible, the terminology at our disposal is finite and limited.[107] Dogmatic statements are, therefore, historical, limited, and open both to further unfolding and new terminology as necessary to mediate the truths of faith to particular historical situations. This tension and difference between the reality signified and the terms used to signify reveals another important function of the dogmatic statement—to lead one beyond the concepts to the reality signified.

The dogmatic statement—like the kerygmatic one—is basically possessed of an element which (in the case of intramundane categorical statements) is not identical with the represented conceptual content. Without injuring its own meaning, *the represented conceptual content is in this case merely the means of experiencing a being referred beyond itself and everything imaginable* [italics added]. That this reference is no mere empty, frustrated desire to transcend, that it is not simply the formal horizon for the possibility of objective conceptualization, but the way in which man really moves towards the self-communication of God as he is in himself—is brought about by what we call grace, and is grasped and accepted in what we call faith. We do not refer here to the concept of transcendence or the concept of grace, but to these realities themselves.[108]

A dogmatic statement can be what it must be only if it does not reduce its reference to the finite and manageable. Rather, through the finite and manageable, it should affirm and reconfirm the permanent mystery and the permanent incomprehensibility to that which it refers. The terminology, the signs, the language of dogmatic statements ought to "silently refer the believing man beyond themselves into the impenetrable light of God himself."[109] Note the self-transcendence of language employed for doctrine. "[T]heological discourse does not only speak about the mystery, but . . . it only speaks properly if it is also a kind of instruction showing us how to come into the presence of the mystery itself."[110] The reality signified and the means to signify such reality are different. Thus, it is erroneous to believe that "one has already arrived at the reality in theological dogmatic discourse when one possesses its conceptual term."[111] "This term is mystagogical quite apart from its function of substituting for the reality and of being its image. Over and above this, it invokes the experience granted by grace of the absolute mystery itself, to the extent in which this mystery communicates itself to us in that grace which is the grace of Christ."[112]

The discussion of concepts, language, terminology, and so forth has occurred in the context of a faith statement and a faith act oriented toward an object of faith. Such faith is existentially relevant: that is, it informs the whole of a subject's reality and the possibilities for all aspects of such reality. But such reflection in faith upon the truths of the faith should not be confused with or made identical to the "Word of revelation" or the "original statement of faith," though it may well be empowered by both.

The difference between the original kerygma and a dogmatic statement, therefore, does not lie in the fact that in the former there is as it were the pure Word of God alone and in the latter only human reflection. If this were the case, then there could be indeed merely non-binding theological discourse talking round about this Word of God, but not a statement of faith which though different from the original Word of God, as announced originally, receives its real binding presence in the course of history. There could only be a history of theology in this case and not a history of dogmas. The fact that the latter exists can be explained only because the original statement of faith already includes that moment of genuine human reflection which makes it legitimate and necessary and which continues to be effective and to unfold itself in later theology.[113]

Scripture owns a peculiar and unique position in salvation history because revelation has a history: that is, "quite definite events fixed in place and time in which this revelation (which is determined for all later ages) takes place in such a way that later ages remain permanently bound by this historical event."[114] This revelation is accessible only through its historical manifestation. For this reason, "there are certain events and statements for future ages which form the enduring and unsurpassable *norma normans, non normata* for all later dogmatic statements." What is handed down is thus distinguished from "the unfolding tradition of what has been handed down."[115]

If this constitutes the specific task of doctrine, the question arises: What kind of theology issues from such an understanding of experience and language? The initial moment in a response has already been suggested in the description of Karl Rahner's foundational theology. This response can be augmented further through an understanding of his dogmatic theology. The nature and scope of dogmatic theology will culminate in a brief illustration of Rahner's treatment of the doctrine of the Trinity.

Dogmatic Theology

Dogmatic theology is "the conscious and methodical explanation and explication of the divine revelation received and grasped in faith."[116] It is not simply a reflection upon God, nor is it simply a reflection upon the transcendental conditions for the possibility of encountering God; rather, dogmatic theology is an explanation of how divine revelation encounters the human and is "grasped in faith." Because of this principle of intersubjectivity—a principle that always understands faith and truth as intersubjective—the proper work of theology is in "history," as concerned with the actualizing of one's existence as one encounters divine revelation through *living* a Christian existence and not in isolated propositions as such.[117]

> For the whole point of the message of Christianity is that God, in his own unrelated sovereignty and glory, can be the content and centre of human existence, and in the liberty of his grace actually desires to do so. We, therefore, by no means have to do with a God who "really" has nothing to do with us. So theocentrism, rightly understood, is therefore transformed into anthropocentrism through the grace which God himself communicates. And conversely, man can find himself only when he gives himself up in adoration and love into the free incomprehensibility of God, i.e., when he himself transforms his anthropocentrism into theocentrism.[118]

But there is an indispensable propositional element. It is in the unity of what Rahner identifies as "theoretical" and "practical" reason that man's faculty of knowledge is comprised and through which theology is accomplished. Theoretical reason is that "which grasps 'metaphysically' the transcendental necessities and tries 'scientifically' to systematize empirical experiences and bring them into definable functional combinations." Practical reason is that knowledge "which is ultimately immanent to the free—and hence not arbitrary—decision by which man always lives, one way or the other, and which can be gained only in such decision."[119] When these two forms of reason are combined, the totality is based on a necessary connection, not an opposition, between the theoretical and the practical—a connection translated directly into doing theology.

Theology is the science (i.e., the "methodical reflection along lines appropriate to the subject-matter") of the Christian faith, a faith in terms of both act and content (*fides qua and quae*) that is presupposed in "the Church and in the student of theology."[120] If faith as both act and content were not presupposed, one would have a science of religion but not theology proper. The kerygmatic element must always be in theology. Kerygma is the proclamation of Jesus Christ, accepted, appropriated, and continually active and effective in communicating itself as the salvific word.[121] It is a meeting between believer and believed that empowers "those who are convinced of and filled by this word of the Lord to speak in turn in the same way, so that their mission is summed up in the words: 'He who hears you hears me' (Luke 10:16)."[122]

> Thus kerygma, in its fullest sense, is the actual and historically determined proclamation of the word of God in the Church by the proclaimer, authorized by God, who bears witness. This word, spoken by the proclaimer in the power of the Spirit and in faith, hope, and charity, *brings into being and makes present what is proclaimed* [italics added] (the promise of God to man) as an evangelical message of salvation and as a committing and judging power; it does this in such a way, moreover, that salvation history, both beginning and end, becomes present "now" in Jesus Christ, and that this word, which has become an event in what is said and heard, can be received by the listener in faith and love.[123]

Insofar as the theology of the Church, and the theologian, emerges from both the act and content of faith, such a kerygmatic element grounding any critical reflection upon the reception of divine revelation will always distinguish theology from a science of religion.

Thus, theology is essentially "practical," not because it disdains the theoretical, but because "it is orientated to the *acts* [italics added] of hope and of love, which contain an element of knowledge which is unattainable outside them."[124] Once again the principle of intersubjectivity is critical here, for it is not sufficient for something to be simply "known"; it must be realized in one's existence as well. "Orthodoxy and orthopraxis combine to influence one another in a basic inexpressible unity which can only come to light in practice, because knowledge is only sound when it has surpassed itself and become love—which is its way of surviving as contemplation."[125]

The nature of dogmatic theology as intersubjective requires more than simply the subjective impulse of a theologian, and for this reason it is necessarily ecclesiastical, social, and historical.[126] The faith of the Church is thus seen as connected to the historical word of divine revelation: "Church theology is necessarily dependent on Scripture and tradition."[127] And since the Church, the community of faith, "is an institutional society, Church theology is essentially related to the magisterium in the Church," though it does not lose its critical function by being so related. There is a social aspect to theology because the human is both individual and social. Theology, as a "reflection on the faith in which anthropocentrism and theocentrism combine, by virtue of the self-communication of God to man," cannot and must not be restricted to the private and individual.

Theology as essentially intersubjective in the dimensions of Church, society, and history has God in God's self for its formal object. All things are considered in theology in terms of both their beginning and their end in God. But Rahner insists that this stipulation must extend beyond the meaning it has been given traditionally. There is no possibility of, or purpose for, considering God in God's self as somehow separate from history. God's saving action in history allows one some entrance into the nature of God.[128] Thus, the formal object of theology is God in God's self-communication: that is, God as active and salvific in human history.

> If this is correctly understood as at once the central saving event and word of revelation, and as the inner principle of the faith which inspires theology, the mysteries of the Trinity and incarnation and of justifying, divinizing grace are already comprised in it and hence the fundamental mysteries of salvation are considered together. And since salvation and revelation are the history of this divine self-communication—creation being merely the constitution of its recipients—theology as critical reflection on salvation can also be comprised within this formal object.[129]

God communicating God's self as the formal object of theology offers advantages for a transcendental understanding of theology, "since the formal object and the subjective principle of theology (God as the uncreated grace of faith) would clearly be the same."[130] Thus, there is an essential unity between theology and anthropology. It is not enough simply to communicate a knowledge about God; dogmatic theology must articulate how God who communicates himself is accepted in faith by the human subject.

Dogmatic theology is the *intellectus fidei* that necessarily mediates and is informed by the *auditus fidei* (historical theology) and *praxis fidei* (practical theology).[131] Dogmatic theology is in service to the Church and society and has as its formal object God in his self-communication. This encompasses

God both in his internal self-communication, which is his Trinitarian reality, and in his self-communication to humanity in the Incarnation and grace. Therefore, there is a real unity between Rahner's foundational theology and his dogmatic theology because in every tractate in theology one is, finally, dealing with God in his self-communication. This formal object of theology affects not only the structure but also the content of dogmatic treatises. This can be illustrated through the doctrine of the Trinity, in which God in God's self-communication "immanently" is understood to be that reality communicated "economically."[132] Self-communication becomes the governing concept that grounds Rahner's understanding of the Trinity, both in itself and in the Incarnation and grace.

DOGMATIC THEOLOGY APPLIED: THE TRINITY

Traditional Trinitarian theology has reflected so much on inner-Trinitarian life that the doctrine has come to lack any real connection to humanity, and specifically to Christian piety. A question on the Trinity to any average Christian believer will confirm this. It is fascinating that Rahner is now the third theologian in this work to acknowledge this real separation between Christian faith and the doctrine of the Trinity. Schleiermacher sought to do away with what he understood to be an injurious doctrine. Lindbeck thought the problem to be simply in how one spoke about it. Rahner will perform some regulative tasks with regard to the language of the Trinity, but only to bring the ontological reality of the Trinity as *the* mystery of salvation more fully into contemporary Christian piety.[133] This is the key to all dogmatic theology—the real relation between God's gift of self in the Incarnation and in uncreated grace and one's acceptance of such in faith.

> We must point out that in every dogmatic treatise what it says about salvation does not make sense without referring to this primordial mystery of Christianity. Wherever this permanent perichoresis between treatises is overlooked, we have a clear indication that either the treatise on the Trinity or the other treatises have not clearly explained the connections which show how the mystery of the Trinity is for us the mystery of salvation, and why we meet it wherever our salvation is considered, even in the other dogmatic treatises.[134]

The self-communication of God as the formal object of theology makes possible the connection of various treatises to the doctrine of the Trinity through a fundamental theological principle: "The 'economic' Trinity is the 'immanent' Trinity and the 'immanent' Trinity is the 'economic' Trinity."[135] Essentially, this says that the way God communicates is the way God is.

This axiom can accomplish three things. First, it communicates effectively the "really binding data" presented by the magisterium on the doctrine of the Trinity. Second, it remains consistent with biblical statements concerning salvation history and its threefold structure. Finally, it effectively communicates the reality of the Trinity present in every Christian act of faith. All of this presupposes grace understood as the self-communication of God in Christ and his Spirit, as opposed to "created grace."[136]

Presuming these goals and presuppositions, the doctrine of the Trinity can only be understood as relational. "And we are sure that the following statement is true: that no adequate distinction can be made between the doctrine of the Trinity and the doctrine of the economy of salvation."[137] This is true given the particular view of human nature to which God communicates himself.

> Human nature in general is a possible object of the creative knowledge and power of God, because and insofar as the Logos is by nature the one who is "utterable" (even into that which is not God); because he is the Father's Word, in which the Father can express himself, and, freely, empty himself into the non-divine; because, when this happens, that precisely is born which we call human nature.[138]

With this understanding of human nature, one can then posit that "what Jesus is and does as man reveals the Logos himself; it is the reality of the Logos as our salvation amidst us."[139] Given this connection of the person Logos in human nature through Jesus Christ, one can say, "The Logos with God and the Logos with us, the immanent and economic Logos, are strictly the same."[140]

Because the Logos "posits human nature as his way of positing and expressing himself," this person communicates himself to humanity in "his own personal particularity and diversity."[141] The same can be said of the Father, who gives himself to us as Father through the Son, resulting in a mutual love that is the Holy Spirit.

[T]hese three self-communications are the self-communication of the one God in three relative ways in which God subsists. The Father gives himself to us, too, as *Father,* that is, precisely because and insofar as he himself, being essentially with *himself,* utters himself and *in this way* communicates the Son as his own, personal self-manifestation; and because and insofar as the Father and the Son (receiving from the Father), welcoming each other in love, drawn and returning to each other, communicate themselves in this way, as received in mutual love, that is, as Holy Spirit.[142]

This self-communication of God is a free, personal act of self, given from person to person. It is in this way that the "three-fold, free, and gratuitous relation to us" is the Trinity itself and not merely a copy of it. This is the mystery revealed to us only by Christ.

This reflection upon the self-communication of the Trinity reveals that what is given remains incomprehensible and continues in its originality. God "is there" as freely, historically, self-uttered truth. This self-communication causes an act of loving welcome that does not reduce this communication to a created level. Thus, the Trinity can be understood in terms of salvation history through God's self-communication in the Incarnation and grace.

But if it is true that we can really grasp the content of the doctrine of the Trinity only by going back to the history of salvation and of grace, to our experience of Jesus and of the Spirit of God, who operates in us, because in them we really possess the Trinity itself as such, then there never should be a treatise on the Trinity in which the doctrine of the "missions" is at best only appended as a relatively unimportant and additional scholion.[143]

The mystery of the Trinity is connected to the mystery of ourselves and goes well beyond the logical difficulties encountered in Trinitarian theology. The human "understands himself only when he has realized that he is the one to whom God communicates himself."[144] Acceptance of this mystery as mystery is important, for often, subtle concepts can function as anesthesia to worshiping with a lack of total understanding. The Trinity is beyond the control of all concepts, yet for the Christian, it is as close as the question of ourselves. It is a reality to be embraced in the way that we embrace the mystery of our own existence.

SUMMARY

Rahner's work thus intellectually argues Christianity "as the answer to the question which man is" through an interplay of three mutual moments that culminates in the free acceptance of human existence as that which is made for holy mystery.[145] The living, unfolding faith of the historical event of God's absolute self-communication in Jesus Christ is carried forward, made intelligible, and communicated to generations through the gifts of grace and faith. Such reflection concentrates on human existence, the historical possibilities for revelation, and the informing role of doctrine as bespeaking the answer to the question that humanity is.

Theological doctrine allows the believer to subjectively appropriate the objective events and statements of salvation history while also allowing the subjective experience of Christian personhood to become objectified in theological doctrine. The doctrine of the Trinity accomplishes this through a reflection upon the Incarnation "through a mode of conceptualizing reality through basic categories or paradigms drawn from the personal world of conscious and free human existence," that is, ontologically.[146] In this way the doctrine of the Trinity, the most central doctrine to Christianity, is brought out of its "splendid isolation" and made real for Christian piety.

The mutually informing relation between received teaching and the existential actualization of faith realized in history and handed down through theological doctrine is embodied in the three moments of Rahner's method. These three moments of *foundational theological* reflection form a differentiated unity whose purpose is to "give people confidence from the very *content* of Christian dogma itself that they can believe with intellectual honesty."[147] This unity is also the preliminary step in any specifically dogmatic theology that has as its goal a transcendental anthropological understanding of received doctrine: that is, a method that "examines an issue according to the necessary conditions given by the possibility of knowledge and action on the part of the subject himself."[148]

Throughout this exposition of Rahner's thought, various aspects of the postmodern critique have been definitively addressed. These can be explicitly situated, along with a review of the relevant moments of the dialectic of this story (Schleiermacher, postmodern critique, transcendental response) in the next chapter.

The Retrieval of Experience

In the final chapter of this work, I will synthesize the dialectical moments of the inquiry, and in this synthesis there is a story. This story is critical for the contemporary discussion of God as it navigates competing and sometimes contradictory metaphysical anthropologies. The first moment of this inquiry, Friedrich Schleiermacher's turn to the subject, will be utterly rejected by postmodernism, the second moment. In the third moment, a theology will emerge that recognizes, though it does not reduce human experience to, the world that is worded. The result is a limited retrieval of aspects of the first two moments in a manner that can enrich contemporary theological inquiry.

Friedrich Schleiermacher's theological project sought to reorient and ground the essence of religion, the Christian faith, and the nature of dogmatic theology in a particular conception of human subjectivity as intrinsically related to God. The goal of this "turn to the subject" was to rescue an essentially relational faith from one that had become externalized in the "objective" dictates of metaphysics, morals, and outdated dogma. This rescue was accomplished through an understanding of human experience as intrinsically, though passively, connected to divine causality. Such being-in-relation to God is universal to humanity.

Language attempts to capture such relationality in order to share such piety with others, and through such sharing to be Church. This expression of Christian affections is secondary to the original and prior relationship and, as such, is primarily descriptive. Interior piety, being-in-relation to God, is never fully recaptured by language.

Dogmatic theology is the practical science that transposes the essential aspects of historical doctrine for the piety of a particular Christian community through a both technical and divinatory grasp of original Christian teachings. Historically received doctrine can then be interpreted in a manner that accesses the original intention of the author, an intention that has a priority of quality over its expression. The goal of such dogmatic theology is to increase the piety of a particular community at a given time. The human being who is essentially in relation to God (religion) can accept the certainty of the feeling of absolute dependence (faith) that is awakened and continually sustained through correct presentation of Christian doctrine (dogmatic theology).

A particular piety, one intrinsically grounded in human subjectivity, is both the essence of religion and faith and the criterion for doctrinal evaluation. Because language is essentially descriptive, doctrines can be understood as religious affections set forth in speech. Thus, doctrine must be evaluated by how much it resonates with, and increases the piety of, a given time. The difficulty with such an approach, at least for a historical faith, is revealed when one must determine how to attend to a historical reality that may not coalesce with a particular piety at a given time. If one must err in such a choice, says such a method, one must err on the side of the primacy of piety. Hence, doctrine must continually change, possibly even becoming extinct. This has been illustrated by Schleiermacher's treatment of the doctrine of the Trinity.

Measuring the value of a doctrine by its service to piety may preserve piety at a particular place and time—but what happens to the *original and historical* reference that gave rise to the doctrine? And if doctrine performs such an indispensable function for the maintenance and increase of piety, what will ultimately become of piety? Eventually, piety can simply come to reflect piety—to the dissolution of doctrine altogether.

Schleiermacher appropriates the Anselmian quest of faith seeking understanding through the topics or themes of experience, language, and the nature of theology. Thus, through a reframing of faith as *certainty* in the redemptive efficacy of the feeling of absolute dependence (experience), expressed effectively in Christian doctrine (language), a greater understanding of the Evangelical faith can result (theology of piety). In the recasting of these topics, Schleiermacher opens up the problem this work addresses. Both the topics introduced by Schleiermacher and the presuppositions upon which they depend are severely critiqued through the "turn to language" characteristic of the contemporary postmodern critique of religious experience. Postmodernism will reject Schleiermacher's understanding of human interiority, the nature of language, and the purpose of theology as he frames them. The competing claims of both methods characterize a significant contemporary problem in systematic theology.

Wayne Proudfoot accepts the evocative function of doctrine clearly articulated by Schleiermacher's dogmatic theology, but he does not understand it to be expressive of an interior relationship to an external being in any way. Proudfoot transposes the evocative function of dogmatic theology that Schleiermacher describes to Schleiermacher's philosophical theology, the starting point of his entire defense of religion and Christian faith. Due to a radically different understanding of human subjectivity, one that does not allow for an interiority of any kind, not only does theological doctrine become evocative, but also the very appeal to the "experience" of absolute dependence itself becomes constructive. Consequently, Schleiermacher's appeal to the feeling of absolute dependence is not one of description but one of creation. Philosophical theology does not make descriptive claims about any existing universal reality in human subjectivity. The "appeal to experience" constructs the very reality it presumes to describe. It has been employed by theologians as an apologetic defense for religion. What is often purported to be simple description of an experience of God is discovered to be an elaborate attempt to evoke the same.

Any appeal to experience is constructive rather than descriptive because all "experience" is derived from concepts that ultimately emerge from one's given language. Employing Wittgenstein, via Kant, Proudfoot asserts the a priori nature of language and concept in relation to "experience." As a result, the critical relations in Schleiermacher's project become inverted.

Language is the a priori, and experience emerges from particular interpretations of received concepts and beliefs. Faith is a construction born of human anxiety with no external reference beyond the concept. Theology is the account, the explanation constructed to support a response to limit experiences characteristic of human existence (e.g., death). Because "experiences" are constituted extrinsically by "concepts" that may or may not reference reality as it is (if there is such a thing), any appeal to "experience" as intrinsic, such as Schleiermacher frames, is actually an appeal to a prior belief system. This can be illustrated effectively through an analysis of mysticism. The key to understanding the origin of mystical experience is to understand the belief system of the mystic. The latter will be found, ultimately, to constitute the former.

Finally, Proudfoot opts for a theoretical analysis of religious experience over a theological one because the theorist, as an outside observer, is free of the particular belief system being evaluated. A theorist is better positioned to evaluate neutrally a "religious experience" through a conceptual attribution theory because no personal belief is at stake.

The core of Proudfoot's critique embodies absolute contradictions to Schleiermacher's project in the areas already designated as controlling for this inquiry. First, there is no immediacy between the "self" and the external world—all reality is mediated through language, concepts, and only then experience as a level of perception. Thus, experience is a kind of knowing, and one never transcends one's linguistic-conceptual constraints. Language is constructive, so "experience" can never be universal because language systems and cultures differ significantly. If there is no universal experience, there can be no universal religion and no universal truth.

George Lindbeck's concern is more substantively theological. He wishes to engage in ecumenical dialogue that can accomplish "doctrinal reconciliation without capitulation." Schleiermacher's project does not allow for such a possibility because it is primarily concerned with piety, even when it specifically concerns the doctrine of a particular community. Such an understanding of doctrine is unsatisfactory due to its inability to ensure doctrinal continuity. Since the nature of any doctrine is directly connected to a given nature of "religion," Schleiermacher's understanding of both religion and doctrine becomes inadequate for Lindbeck's goal. What becomes necessary is a new approach, one adopted by other academic sciences: the cultural-linguistic method.

The cultural-linguistic method appropriates an interpretation of Wittgenstein and applies it to the nature of religion. Thus, religion for Lindbeck becomes an idiom through which certain attitudes, beliefs, and experiences, including any particularly religious ones, become possible. Whereas doctrine for Schleiermacher is understood as derivative of a specific piety, for Lindbeck it is the piety that is derivative of specific doctrines. This is so because religions, like languages, structure comprehensive interpretations of reality. *Religion* is exclusively an external word.

This understanding of the primacy of external narrative allows the theologian to approach doctrinal disputes in terms of rule theory. Second-order discourse, the grammar of belief, and not first-order discourse, the truth claim itself (i.e., "an inner relation to an outer reality"), becomes the focus of dialogue. This preference for intrasystematic truth claims over ontological truth claims allows doctrines to change "while remaining the same." Thus, intrasystematic discourse and its attendant truth claims are preferable to discourse that claims to correspond to external reality. The traditional doctrine of the Trinity is a case in point. The early Church fathers were not concerned with designating the inner being of God in Godself (a first-order claim); rather, they were concerned with the rules of speech through which the Christian speaks within regulative principles that ground a given doctrine (a second-order claim).

Finally, Lindbeck posits the possibility of a neutral theory of religion in which one can examine the data of religion and doctrine by deducing the regulative principles prominent in their communication. Such an approach gives one a comprehensive view into the interpretations of reality (attitudes, beliefs, experiences) particular to a specific religion. For a theory of religion, the principles themselves (first-order truth claims) never become the subject of inquiry—only the second-order discourse that instantiates them. Theory is essentially agnostic.

Lindbeck admits that a theological theory of religion and doctrine cannot remain neutral. The preference for an external Word of God theology is one type of Christian theology consistent with the formative emphasis of the cultural-linguistic approach. For the strictly inner-Church mission of Christianity—and in the cultural-linguistic method this is the only kind of mission possible—it is the Christian narrative that is formative. One does not rely on propositional truth claims that supposedly and directly reference ontological truth, nor does one rely on doctrines derivative of a particular existential state; rather, one realizes that the biblical Word constitutes and defines the language, the beliefs, the attitudes, and the experiences of the Christian believer.

In a manner strikingly similar to Proudfoot, Lindbeck has moved the discussion of "religious experience" away from any interior/relational/ontological categories of direct correspondence to an externally given or even "revealed" phenomenon emerging from a particular cultural-linguistic construct. Unlike the "pure" theorist who is content to view all religions as defenses against the void, Lindbeck frames Christianity in terms of this formative external theory. Either way, Schleiermacher's project has been definitively contradicted.

George Steiner understands the essence of language to be not only that which moves in upon the human and forms it but also that through which the human moves out beyond the self and experiences the "other." Language always transcends itself. And with Steiner, this story moves into its final, synthetic stage. Through the deconstruction of the first-person singular and the disjunction posited between language and external reference, radical postmodernism has annihilated both subjectivity and objectivity and canonized the view that one's *word* is one's *world*. Moderate postmodernism has simply made this radical view more palatable.

Such an approach to language presumes the ability to finally designate the nature and scope of language and its correlative influence on human subjectivity. It is precisely this approach that Steiner views as a major category error. Modern "theorists" of language have utilized, inappropriately, an applied science methodology for analysis in the arts and humanities. One could argue by extension that the same has been done in terms of religion.

Aesthetic experience, for Steiner, emerges from that rendezvous with otherness captured in the forms of art, literature, and especially music. The critical aspect of this "real presence" is the mutual causality between human subjectivity and "language." There is first an encounter that is real and with an "other." It is recollected, i.e., re-presented, through art, literature, and music. Finally, one can be moved to an approximate experience of the original through the very language (form) used to capture it. The paradoxical power of language is its function as both barrier and catalyst. Thus, while an "encounter" may occur through language, it corresponds to more than the projected self—it can reference an external reality. The relationship between language and subjectivity is essentially dialectical. It is through language that self-transcendence is realized.

While Steiner is helpful in responding to the postmodern annihilation of subjectivity and external linguistic reference, problems arise with the theological implications of "verification transcendence." What ultimately ensures the "meaning of meaning" in language for Steiner is God. Theology is essentially functional. The problem with this theological functionalism is the invocation or employment of God simply to support a kind of certitude: that is, the reduction of God to the fulfillment of a function in a particular philosophical system. Whether this "other" can act upon us, or encounter us, is questionable if its only role is to shore up a system that cannot be decisively proven.

Karl Rahner's theology explicitly explores the problems inherent to the themes of "experience," "language," and the nature of theology through the three mutually conditioning moments that constitute his foundational theology. A reflection upon human experience, a reflection upon the transcendental and historical conditions that make revelation possible, and a reflection upon Christian doctrine offer one response to the contemporary problematic.

What emerges is a metaphysical anthropology that understands the human person as fundamentally oriented to God.

> [I]f man is a being of transcendence towards the holy and absolutely real mystery, and if the term and the source of transcendence in and through which man as such exists, and which constitutes his original essence as subject and as person, is this absolute and holy mystery, then strangely enough we can and must say: mystery in its incomprehensibility is what is *self-evident* in human life. If transcendence is not something which we practice on the side as a metaphysical luxury of our intellectual existence, but if this transcendence is rather the plainest, most obvious and most necessary condition of possibility for all spiritual understanding and comprehension, then the holy mystery is the one thing that is self-evident, the one thing which is grounded in itself even from our point of view.[1]

Thus, through Rahner's thought, an understanding of "experience" is retrieved that directly addresses the issues at the heart of this work. Human experience is aboriginally self-transcendent and actualized through the historical reality of language. This contrasts with the absolute interiority of Schleiermacher's subjectivity, in which reflection is superfluous to the experience of absolute dependence itself. It also challenges the absolute exteriority of postmodern subjectivity, in which language through concept is formative of all experience. For Rahner, the orientation of human subjectivity and personhood to mystery, absolute and holy, is actualized in and through the language one learns and the history one inhabits. A qualified turn to language must be accepted, but the scope of such acceptance should be carefully designated.

Through language one not only transcends the self but forms and informs the self through doctrine as well. There is a real subjective interiority complemented by truly formative external forces. While a particular language cannot be universal, the movement of the person as subject in freedom, responsibility, and dependence toward the horizon of being can be. There are concrete ways of rejecting this movement, but on the level of possibility it is universal to human personhood.

In grace, the horizon of being toward which all persons can strive in nature, through language and in history, moves in lovingly upon humanity in God's absolute self-communication—the Incarnation. Jesus Christ is the definitive answer in history to the transcendental yearning of human being. In Christ, the answer is freely and definitively given to the question that the human person is. For this reason, Christian theology is always anthropocentrically theocentric: every Christian statement about God is also a statement about humanity. Human beings are made for three-personal holy mystery—Father, Son, and Holy Spirit.

Christian doctrine performs both constructive and descriptive functions and clarifies the relationship between "experience" and "language" as dialectical. Doctrine refers to the reality of God in human history, the economy, and in Godself, the immanent God, because in grace, God acts in human history as Father, Son, and Holy Spirit, in self-communication, giving and revealing himself as he is immanently. "The 'economic' Trinity is the 'immanent' Trinity and the 'immanent' Trinity is the 'economic' Trinity."[2] Such reference presupposes a life of faith in that hope and in that promise. Christianity claims the historical event of Jesus Christ to be a definitive, ontological statement about God and humanity. While there is a regulative element to all doctrine, its main concern is to communicate effectively the truth about humanity and God manifest in Jesus Christ and the Spirit. But Christian doctrine can be intelligible only insofar as it responds to the graced self-transcendent yearning of Christian personhood, in which the term of such transcendence is already experienced. In this way, the infinite is the possibility for the very actualization of finite human existence freely embraced in Christian discipleship. When this question that is human hope is met by the moment of God's answer and *effectively* communicated in faith as such, Christian doctrine, as kerygmatic, ecclesiastical, and leading into holy mystery, has fulfilled its function.

The narrowness and limitedness posited by postmodernity concerning the closed nature of human experience, language and theology are both a real challenge to, and paradoxically a resource for, Christian theology. By tempering the optimism of Schleiermacher's hermeneutics, one can and should accept a limited turn to language in order to attend to doctrine as both constructive and descriptive of Christian discipleship. This can speak not only to the individual believer for whom the doctrine is efficacious but also for the continuity of the tradition that communicates such historical kerygmatic truth. As for the first two moments of the dialectic in this inquiry, the choice is not an either/or but a careful and nuanced both/and.

Of the three ways one can evade transcendental experience, according to Rahner, the postmodern critiques evaluated thus far waver somewhere between skepticism and despair. While they embody certain concrete realities in human life that must be taken seriously, the "void" is not and cannot be the final word for the Christian.

Christianity, as the answer to the question humanity is, believes that God has communicated God's self absolutely, concretely, and *effectively* in history. In Jesus Christ, despair and skepticism do not have the final word—for the highest possibility and reality of human existence has been actualized for our benefit. Graced by the perfect actualization that has been revealed as Incarnation, the Christian attempts to freely give the self to God in loving self-surrender through a life lived for others as exemplified by Jesus Christ.

In an age when the human being is often considered only within the confines of its own language and culture, contemporary Christian systematic theology has a unique opportunity to retrieve what real human existence could be and in fact has been. Its best response to the contemporary problematic in theology, consequently, is not to think about thinking, or to talk about talking, but to remind the contemporary person that the core of our being yearns in spirit and freedom for a fulfillment of being that only God can give.

Notes

INTRODUCTION

1. More precise developments in the history and rise of what has been termed postmodernism will be presented, with the help of George Steiner, in the summary of the contemporary problematic in chapter 4.

2. Carl A. Raschke, "The Deconstruction of God," in *Deconstruction and Theology*, ed. Thomas J. Altizer et al. (Crossroad, 1982), 4.

3. Ibid.

4. Ibid.

5. Fred Lawrence, "The Fragility of Consciousness: Lonergan and the Postmodern Concern for the Other," *Theological Studies* 54 (March 1993): 60.

6. Raschke, "The Deconstruction of God," 3.

7. Ibid.

8. Thomas Guarino, "Between Foundations and Nihilism: Is Phronesis the Via Media for Theology?" *Theological Studies* 54 (March 1993): 37.

9. Ibid.

10. Ibid., 38.

11. Ibid., 39.

12. Ibid., 40.

13. Ibid.

14. Ibid., 40–41, including n. 16.

15. Fredric Jameson, *Postmodernism* (Duke University Press, 1990), 12, 342.

16. Raschke, "The Deconstruction of God," 6, 9. This is a Derridean strain of deconstruction.

17. Ibid., 7.

18. Ibid.

19. Ibid., 9.

20. Ibid., 7.

21. Ibid., 8.

22. Ibid., 9.

23. Guarino, "Between Foundations and Nihilism," 42–44.

24. Guarino makes this statement when describing what Habermas does *not* do.

25. Guarino, "Between Foundations and Nihilism," 52.

26. Ibid., 54.

27. David Tracy, "The Uneasy Alliance Reconceived: Catholic Theological Method, Modernity, and Postmodernity," *Theological Studies* 50 (September 1989): 560. Tracy further suggests Paul Ricoeur, "Hermeneutics and the Critique of Ideology," in *Hermeneutics and the Human Sciences* (Cambridge University Press, 1981).

28. David Tracy, "Theology and the Many Faces of Postmodernity," *Theology Today* 51 (April 1994): 108.

29. David Tracy, *Plurality and Ambiguity* (SCM Press, 1987), 49. For a very helpful discussion on language and the postmodern concern for plurality, see chapter 3, "Radical Plurality: The Question of Language," 47–65.

30. Ibid., 49.

31. As noted, *deconstruction* and *postmodernism* will be used interchangeably when referring to the negation with which both begin their critiques.

32. Tracy, *Plurality and Ambiguity*, 62–63.

33. Ibid.

34. Ibid.

35. Tracy, "The Uneasy Alliance Reconceived," 560.

1. Schleiermacher and the Turn to the Subject

1. "Neque enim quaero intelligere ut credam, sed credo ut intelligam.—Nam qui non crediderit, non experietur, et qui expertus non fuerit, non intelliget." Anselm of Canterbury, *Proslogion*. I. De Fide Trin. 2, quoted in Friedrich Schleiermacher, *Der Christliche Glaube*, title page. For the importance of this statement, see Richard R. Niebuhr, introduction to *The Christian Faith*, by Friedrich Schleiermacher, ed. H. R. Mackintosh and J. S. Stewart, vol. 1 (Harper Torchbooks, 1963).

2. See Richard E. Palmer, *Hermeneutics* (Northwestern University Press, 1969), 40, for Schleiermacher's contribution.

3. Friedrich Schleiermacher, *On Religion: Speeches to Its Cultured Despisers*, trans. Richard Crouter (Cambridge University Press, 1993). Henceforth referred to as the *Speeches.*

4. Friedrich Schleiermacher, *The Christian Faith*, 2nd ed., ed. H. R. Macintosh and J. S. Stewart (T. & T. Clark, 1989).

5. Friedrich Schleiermacher, *Hermeneutics: The Handwritten Manuscripts*, ed. Heinz Kimmerle, trans. James Duke and Jack Forstman (Scholars Press, 1977).

6. Various authors attribute the beginning of hermeneutics, as well as the beginning of the appeal to human subjectivity *for theological grounding,* to Schleiermacher.

7. The audience for the *Speeches* is a debated point among Schleiermacher scholars. I concur with Crouter, who maintains that the original audience "held all positive, historically manifest religion in contempt" (Schleiermacher, *Speeches*, 67).

8. Schleiermacher, "First Speech: Apology," in *Speeches*, 77.

9. Schleiermacher, "Second Speech: On the Essence of Religion," in *Speeches*, 120.

10. The role of community for access to religion will be discussed in greater depth later. "Fourth Speech: On the Social Element in Religion; or, On Church and Priesthood" emphasizes this point. "Once there is religion, it must necessarily be social" (Schleiermacher, *Speeches*, 163).

11. Schleiermacher, *Speeches*, 88.

12. All his subsequent works emphasize that direct ministry is paramount for theological acuity. This point was repeatedly stressed in Schleiermacher's *Brief Outline on the Study of Theology*, trans. Terrence N. Tice (John Knox Press, 1966).

13. Friedrich Schleiermacher, *The Life of Schleiermacher as Unfolded in His Autobiography and Letters*, trans. Frederica Rowan (Smith, Elder, 1859), 206, letter CV, dated April 4, 1799.

14. Religion was clearly demarcated from the Kantian constructions of pure reason (metaphysics) or practical reason (morality).

15. Schleiermacher will accomplish this same goal later, in terms of dogmatic theology (*The Christian Faith*) and criteria for determining the relevancy of historically received doctrines for dogmatic theology (*Hermeneutics*).

16. Schleiermacher, *Speeches*, 95.

17. This interiority is crucial to understanding Schleiermacher's view of the human subject. See Schleiermacher, *Life of Schleiermacher*.

18. Richard Crouter states in the translator's introduction to Schleiermacher's *Speeches* that "Schleiermacher is concerned less with telling his readers 'what to believe' than he is showing 'what it is to believe'" (*Speeches*, 40). I disagree. I believe that the content of belief itself is altered when an "experience" of God is made the starting point for theological reflection.

19. Schleiermacher, *Speeches*, 91.

20. Ibid., 92. The "mediators" as exemplars of "religion," exemplars of a particular balanced existence within the anthropology given, are the real source of knowledge of religion.

21. Ibid., 88.

22. Crouter describes this approach from the second series of Schleiermacher's letters, letter no. 88 in the German; see also letter no. 153. Schleiermacher continues this line of argument; see Schleiermacher, *Speeches*, 94, n. 32.

23. Schleiermacher had Kant in mind, especially with his remark that "to recommend it [religion] merely as an aside is too insignificant." This is probably a reference to the *Critique of Practical Reason*.

24. Schleiermacher, *Speeches,* 97–98.

25. Ibid., 101–2. In his glossary to the *Speeches,* Crouter translates *Anschauung/anschauen* as "intuition" and both *Empfindung/empfinden* and *Gefühl* as "feeling" (ibid., x, xi, glossary).

26. Ibid., 102.

27. Ibid., 103.

28. Ibid., 80.

29. Ibid. Crouter notes in the introduction that this "fundamental polarity was widely shared in eighteenth-century literary theory, philosophy, and physics." For examples, see ibid., 79–80, n. 6.

30. Ibid., 80.

31. Ibid.

32. Ibid., 81.

33. Ibid., 82.

34. Ibid., 82–83.

35. Ibid., 83. Later, George Steiner will have a similar view of art, and especially music, in *Real Presences* (University of Chicago Press, 1989).

36. Ibid., 103.

37. Ibid.

38. Ibid., 105. The German for this term is *Anschauung/anschauen.*

39. Ibid., 104.

40. Ibid.

41. Ibid.

42. Ibid., 109.

43. Ibid., 107.

44. Ibid., 109. The German term for "feeling" is *Gefühl.*

45. Niebuhr comments extensively on Schleiermacher's understanding of language. See Richard R. Niebuhr, *Schleiermacher on Christ and Religion* (SCM Press, 1964), 83–84.

46. Schleiermacher, *Speeches,* 111–12.

47. Ibid., 112.

48. Ibid.

49. The text states this clearly (ibid., 112).

50. Ibid.

51. Ibid.; see also pp. 118–19.

52. Ibid., 112.

53. Ibid.

54. Ibid., 119.

55. Ibid., 129. The only use of this term *dependence* (*Abhängigkeit*) foreshadows, for Crouter, the mature definition of religion as "the feeling of absolute dependence" in Schleiermacher's *The Christian Faith.*

56. Schleiermacher, *Speeches*, 120.

57. This was later developed in "Fifth Speech: On the Religions." The term *revelational* is appropriate here, for later Schleiermacher asks: "What is revelation? Every original and new intuition of the universe is one, and yet all individuals must know best what is original and new for them" (ibid., 133).

58. Ibid., 124. Schleiermacher makes this more explicit later (127).

59. Ibid., 130.

60. Ibid., 135.

61. In the case of Christianity, the mediator would place a central role in the determination of intuition/feeling.

62. Schleiermacher defines apologetics and polemics in *Brief Outline*, 31.

63. Authority conceived specifically as an appeal to the magisterium or an appeal to a particular interpretation of Scripture.

64. At issue is the absolute nature of any phenomenological starting point for theological inquiry, as well as certain historical ambiguities surrounding Christ and the Church he founded. Schleiermacher, in his correspondence, agreed with one critic's reading that the fifth speech actually annihilates itself, but he thought it necessary to make his point. See C. W. Christian, *Friedrich Schleiermacher* (Word Books, 1979), 74–75; see also pp. 66–69 for discussion of the same topic.

65. Schleiermacher states this in a postscript to proposition 14. Proposition 14 states: "There is no other way of obtaining participation in the Christian communion than through faith in Jesus as the Redeemer" (Schleiermacher, *The Christian Faith* [1989 ed.], 68).

66. Ibid.

67. Ibid.

68. Ibid.

69. Anselm of Canterbury, *The Prayers and Meditations of St. Anselm with the Proslogion*, trans. Benedicta Ward (Penguin Books, 1973), 244.

70. Freidrich Schleiermacher, *On the Glaubenslehre: Two Letters to Dr. Lücke*, trans. James Duke and Francis Fiorenza (Scholars Press, 1981), 78.

71. Schleiermacher specifically states, "Do I not have good cause, then, to believe that even here Sack has not taken seriously enough the distinction between Introduction and the work of Dogmatics itself?" (ibid., 79).

72. Schleiermacher, *Brief Outline*, 19.

73. Ibid., 27. For a clear treatment of historical theology, see pp. 25–26; for the tripartite structure of philosophical theology, see pp. 25, 91; for practical theology, see p. 91.

74. Ibid., 31. These tasks are taken up in propositions 11 through 19, though propositions 2 through 10 are preparatory for a specifically Christian designation.

75. Schleiermacher, *The Christian Faith*, 3, proposition 2.

76. Ibid.

77. Ibid. For a definition of ethics, see Schleiermacher, *Brief Outline*, 27.

78. Schleiermacher, *The Christian Faith* (1989), 5. The definitions of *ethics* and *philosophy of religion* are crucial for understanding his method.

79. Ibid., 5. See also Schleiermacher, *Brief Outline*, 31. Apologetics is explained in section 39 of the *Brief Outline*.

80. Schleiermacher, *The Christian Faith*, 5.

81. Ibid., proposition 3 (Schleiermacher, *Der Christliche Glaube*, ed. Hermann Peiter, 14).

82. Ibid., 8.

83. Ibid. *Insichbleiben* is the German for "abiding-in-oneself." *Aussichheraustreten* is the German for "passing-beyond-self."

84. The similarity to the understanding of the human subject in Schleiermacher's *Speeches* is clearly evident.

85. Schleiermacher, *The Christian Faith*, 8.

86. Ibid., 6.

87. Ibid., 7. Note the critical assumption that one can speak about "everybody's experience."

88. Ibid., 13.

89. Ibid., 28.

90. Ibid., 30.

91. Ibid., 47. This, of course, will be problematic for postmodernity.

92. Ibid., 7. "The immediate presence of the whole undivided Being, etc." The German for "determination" is *Bestimmtheit*.

93. Ibid., 9.

94. Ibid., 10–11.

95. Schleiermacher adds, "Of course we reject it if it means that the Feeling is derived from the Knowing and the Doing from the Feeling. But if no subordination is intended, then the assertion might just as well be the description of any other quite clear and living moment as of a religious one" (ibid., 11).

96. Ibid., 8.

97. Ibid., 9.

98. Ibid., 12, proposition 4 (Schleiermacher, *Der Christliche Glaube*, ed. Peiter, 23).

99. Schleiermacher, *The Christian Faith*, 17. This precise aspect of Schleiermacher's approach receives strong emphasis from the postmodern critique. The debate over the priority of experience or language is, therefore, central. For more on how Schleiermacher understands this distinction, see p. 30. This is further reinforced in the discussion on doctrines as religious affections set forth in speech (77).

100. Ibid., 12.

101. Ibid.

102. Ibid., 13.

103. Ibid., 13–14.

104. Ibid.

105. Ibid., 13.

106. Ibid., 14.

107. Ibid., 15.

108. Ibid.

109. Schleiermacher, *The Christian Faith*, 16.

110. Ibid. How he actually comes to identify this "other" has become a most important issue—an issue that will specifically concern the postmodern critique. See Nicholas Lash, *Easter in Ordinary* (University of Notre Dame Press, 1986), 127–28.

111. Schleiermacher, *The Christian Faith*, 17.

112. Ibid.

113. See also the first sentence of proposition 6, *The Christian Faith*, 26.

114. Ibid., 26, proposition 6.

115. Ibid., 27.

116. Ibid.

117. Ibid. Note the evocative role of language here.

118. Ibid., 28.

119. Ibid., 29.

120. It is not clear whether interiority has two levels, one prelinguistic and the other preconceptual, or simply one level that is prereflexive. This ambiguity is only heightened when it is viewed in the context of the development of Schleiermacher's hermeneutics. It seems that at one point Schleiermacher considered thought and its expression to be identical, whereas later he separated them. This will be discussed more fully in the next section, which deals with the turn to the subject in hermeneutics.

121. Ibid. The appeal to human relationality and community in any serious approach to faith is crucial, but theology has more than simply an internal mission. The same preface to *The Christian Faith* notes that the first edition is composed "with special reference to the Union of the two Protestant communions—the Lutheran and the Reformed" (ibid., viii).

122. Schleiermacher identifies it as the "Art of Interpretation." Schleiermacher, *Hermeneutics*, 101.

123. Some material on hermeneutics can be found in Schleiermacher's short responses to other scholars who debate the veracity of his approach.

124. For an interesting commentary on Schleiermacher's conception of hermeneutics, see Palmer, *Hermeneutics*, 40.

125. Schleiermacher, *Brief Outline*, 56–68.

126. Ibid., 50.

127. Ibid.

128. In *The Christian Faith,* this consists of both exegetical theology and dogmatic theology. This is further reinforced in *The Christian Faith* on p. 116, paragraph 3.

129. This ecclesiastical value of propositions, its "reference to the religious emotions themselves," is vital to the purpose of *The Christian Faith,* as is the scientific value, or "the definiteness of concepts which appear in it, and their connection with each other" (Schleiermacher, *Brief Outline,* 83–84).

130. See also Schleiermacher, *The Christian Faith,* 76–78, 88–93, and 125–27.

131. Schleiermacher states: "No matter can thus be introduced except in so far as it has a demonstrable and definite connection with the religious affections which are found within the antithesis (expressed in the concept of redemption)" (ibid., 125).

132. For how Schleiermacher defines *redemption,* see p. 54.

133. It would follow from the priority of human interiority to its expression in both the *Speeches* and *The Christian Faith* that the original intention of an author would have both a priority and a qualitative superiority over any expression of that intention in a particular doctrine.

134. Schleiermacher, "Manuscript 1: The Aphorisms of 1805 and 1809–1810," in Schleiermacher, *Hermeneutics,* 42.

135. Schleiermacher, "Manuscript 3: The Compendium of 1819 and the Marginal Notes of 1828," in Schleiermacher, *Hermeneutics,* 97–98.

136. Schleiermacher, "Manuscript 2: The First Draft of 1809–1810," in Schleiermacher, *Hermeneutics,* 70.

137. Ibid.

138. Schleiermacher, "Manuscript 5: The Academy Addresses of 1829: On the Concept of Hermeneutics, with Reference to F. A. Wolf's Instructions and AST's Textbook," in Schleiermacher, *Hermeneutics,* 182.

139. Palmer comments on this divinatory component; see Palmer, *Hermeneutics,* 89.

140. Schleiermacher, *Hermeneutics,* 185.

141. Ibid., 184.

142. Schleiermacher, "Manuscript 3," 100 (parentheses mine for clarification). This view of language, which affirms the infinity of language and its irreducibility to space and time, sets Schleiermacher's hermeneutics in opposition to postmodern linguistic theory. This will be explored later in more detail.

143. Palmer, *Hermeneutics,* 21. For how Palmer views Schleiermacher's later thinking, see pp. 88–89, on which Palmer makes reference to Schleiermacher's *Hermeneutics.*

144. Palmer, *Hermeneutics,* 92–94. This further reinforces Schleiermacher's view of language as essentially descriptive and his view of "experience" as inaccessible to linguistic or reflective operations.

145. Ibid., 92–93.

146. For Schleiermacher, occasionally these two are the same.

147. Schleiermacher, *The Christian Faith*, 54.

148. These sections have been chosen to illustrate Schleiermacher's hermeneutics for the sake of brevity. For a more detailed argument and informative illustration of Schleiermacher's hermeneutic principles, see Friedrich Schleiermacher, "On the Discrepancy between the Sabellian and Athanasian Method of Representing the Doctrine of the Trinity," trans. M. Stuart, *Biblical Repository and Quarterly Observer* 19 (July 1835): 1–80. This article is now out of print, but both aspects of his hermeneutical theory are evident throughout.

149. Schleiermacher, *The Christian Faith*, 738.

150. This is evident throughout the Christology and specifically on pp. 144, 395, and 399 of *The Christian Faith*.

151. Ibid., 738.

152. Ibid., 742.

153. Ibid., 747.

154. See p. 396 for further support for this argument. Throughout the development of the sections on Christology, Schleiermacher emphasizes the understanding of Christ in nature and work (chaps. 92–105) as being independent of the doctrine of the Trinity. This is reemphasized on p. 741 in terms of both Christology and ecclesiology.

155. Ibid., 749.

156. Ibid., 748.

157. Schleiermacher would not use that term per se but would speak of knowing as much as possible through relation in the feeling of absolute dependence. We can "know," then, the effects of the phenomenal but not the essence of the noumenal. *Sensation* here is properly understood in the Kantian sense of that which is necessary for any knowledge.

158. For Palmer's review of Schleiermacher's hermeneutics, see Palmer, *Hermeneutics*, 92–93.

159. The assumption of a common humanity permeates Schleiermacher's project. See Schleiermacher, *The Christian Faith*, 7, 12, 28, 30, 47.

160. The feeling of absolute dependence does depend on being in history, but Schleiermacher scholars seem to stress the ahistorical nature of it on the whole.

161. Niebuhr, *Schleiermacher on Christ and Religion*, 183.

162. In the first endnote to *The Nature of Doctrine*, Lindbeck specifies that "the type of theology I have in mind could also be called 'postmodern'" (135). It should be noted that both works qualify as "moderately" postmodern.

163. The topic of language and experience will inevitably lead to questions concerning the possibility of knowing history and to what degree this is possible. A glimpse of the problem was evident in Schleiermacher's hermeneutics.

2. Wayne Proudfoot's *Religious Experience*

1. Wayne Proudfoot, *Religious Experience* (University of California Press, 1985). *Religious experience* is the favored term used by Proudfoot throughout the work. I have enclosed the term in quotation marks at the beginning of this analysis because it is not certain that Schleiermacher would have found that such a term illumined or captured his own thought.

2. Proudfoot explicated this position further in personal correspondence to me in response to this chapter:

> You say that I deny a common humanity. Nope. But I suppose it depends on what you mean. There are a lot of things that are common. To begin with, we are physically and biologically pretty much the same. This is important, because most of our experience comes through the senses or other relations between the body and environment. The meaning of birth, sex, and death may vary greatly in different cultures, but all cultures have to deal with them, and they are, at base, rooted in biology. Environments differ across cultures, too, but there are many similarities. You may think these trivial. But they enter into our desires, needs, beliefs, and ways of living in the world. I don't deny other common factors as well. Anger, hope, fear, joy, guilt, etc. But, of course, the significance of these, and the conditions under which they are likely to be experienced and expressed, sometimes vary greatly from culture to culture. It is not wrong to speak of them as common, and in some contexts it is quite appropriate. But we ought to be careful about saying they are common and then tacitly reading our own more local understandings into them. Study of language and history is relevant here, not because I am a determinist, but because this is the way one gains access to meanings in other cultures, including those in our own historical tradition.

3. See also Proudfoot, *Religious Experience*, 219.

4. This assertion will be developed more fully later in this chapter, but Proudfoot states it clearly on p. 219. In correspondence on my chapter, Proudfoot expressed a more nuanced view (compared with that expressed on p. 219) on language and experience:

> I am not a determinist. I think people make choices, act, attend selectively, etc. I would not say that they are entirely determined by history and language. One can come to understand the way they conceived their choices, the beliefs they had at their disposal for understanding what was happening to them, and the desires they had, only by a study of language and history. That doesn't mean that we can come to a complete understanding, but we gain access to other persons, communities, and their worlds by the study of language and history.

I am not an idealist either. I don't think language is everything. I often say that an experience is constituted by the way in which a person identifies it or labels it. That does not mean that is caused by language, or entirely made up of language. The point comes rather from reflection on the term "experience."

The constructive section of this work will take up that very task, a reflection on the term "experience."

5. Proudfoot, *Religious Experience,* xiii. It should be noted that from the beginning of *Religious Experience* the origin of "religious experience" is understood and illustrated only in terms of its use as a ground for theological inquiry. No sustained development is given to the topic of religious experience prior to the late eighteenth century, even in the chapter on mysticism. As will be seen toward the end of this work, this is intentional.

6. Ibid., 2.

7. Ibid., xiii.

8. Ibid., xiv. This is critical for understanding not only Proudfoot's critique of Schleiermacher but also Proudfoot's own use of the term *experience.*

9. Proudfoot states that if this sense or feeling precedes and is independent of all thought, it can never conflict with modern science or the "advance of knowledge in any realm" (ibid., 1–2).

10. Ibid., xv. Again, criticism focuses on independence from *extrinsic* influences like language and culture.

11. Ibid., 24.

12. Ibid., xv-xvi.

13. Ibid., 27.

14. This brief exposition of Wittgenstein is Proudfoot's interpretation of his thought.

15. Proudfoot, *Religious Experience,* 29.

16. Proudfoot, *God and the Self: Three Types of Philosophy of Religion* (Bucknell University Press, 1976), 151.

17. Proudfoot, *Religious Experience,* 30.

18. Ibid., 32.

19. Ibid., 78.

20. Ibid., 33.

21. Ibid., 80.

22. Ibid., 81.

23. Ibid.

24. This approach influenced the later "James-Lange" theory of emotions, which claims that emotions are directly perceived: that is, emotions are experienced prior to the language that expresses and conceptualizes them (ibid.).

25. As with other thinkers, such as Wittgenstein, Kant, and Peirce, this is Proud-foot's interpretation of their thought.

26. Proudfoot, *Religious Experience*, 84.

27. Ibid. It should be noted that Proudfoot conflates Aristotle's goal of arousing emotions in a particular audience with Schleiermacher's *Gefühl*. One has the intention of arousing an emotion, while the other is attained through a careful process of self-reflection.

28. Proudfoot, *Religious Experience*, 84.

29. This comparison has direct consequences for how one understands Schleier-macher's experiential grounding of religion in the *Speeches* and is evident when *feeling* and *emotion* are collapsed into identical terms.

30. Proudfoot, *Religious Experience*, 85.

31. Ibid., 87.

32. Ibid.

33. Ibid., 88.

34. Proudfoot states this in explicit reference to Otto, though the last sentence in this chapter ("In this respect Otto is not alone") (ibid., 118) alludes to its application to other thinkers and figures as well.

35. Ibid.

36. Ibid.

37. Ibid., 36.

38. Ibid., 144.

39. Grace Jantzen, in a review of Proudfoot's book, correctly notes that "he moves from the clearly correct claim that the logic of emotion requires conceptual dimen-sions, to the much more doubtful claim that the *origin* of the emotion lies in the inter-pretive structure." Grace Jantzen, "*Religious Experience* [Review]," *Journal of Theological Studies*, n.s., 38 (1987): 593–95.

40. Proudfoot, *Religious Experience*, 36.

41. Ibid.

42. Ibid.

43. Ibid.

44. Ibid., 8.

45. Ibid., 38.

46. Schleiermacher's conception of a common humanity has been referenced throughout chapter 1 and seems to be of a general nature. See also Friedrich Schleiermacher, *The Life of Jesus*, ed. Jack Verheyden, trans. S. Maclean Gilmour (Fortress Press, 1975), 10.

47. This will become evident in Proudfoot's interpretation of the early thought of Charles Sanders Peirce.

48. Proudfoot, *Religious Experience*, 43.

49. Proudfoot introduces this terminology and a distinction of these two traditions on p. 46 and emphasizes Kant's influence on both.

50. Proudfoot, *Religious Experience*, 46.

51. Ibid., 47.

52. Ibid., 47–48.

53. This comes out clearly in Proudfoot's statement on the divinatory aspect of Schleiermacher's hermeneutics (ibid., 50, 51).

54. Ibid., 51.

55. This is consistent with the general character of postmodernism suggested earlier. In this sense, Proudfoot is solidly Jamesian in the individuality that he assumes for the subject matter. The lack of any "common humanity" results in an empirical approach focusing on individual phenomena. For this view of James, see Nicholas Lash, *Easter in Ordinary* (University of Notre Dame Press, 1986).

56. Proudfoot, *Religious Experience*, 51.

57. Proudfoot makes the distinction between the early and late Peirce. See "Peirce on Natural Belief in Religion," in *Faithful Imagining: Essays in Honor of Richard R. Niebuhr*, ed. Sang Hyun Lee et al. (Scholars Press, 1995), 152.

58. Proudfoot, *Religious Experience*, 62.

59. Proudfoot, "Peirce on Natural Belief," 155.

60. Ibid.

61. Proudfoot, *Religious Experience*, 65–66.

62. In contrast, John Dewey states that it is the "*situation* that has these traits." John Dewey, *Logic: The Theory of Inquiry* (Henry Holt, 1938), 106.

63. Proudfoot, *Religious Experience*, 48.

64. Ibid., 67.

65. Ibid., 61.

66. Ibid., 204.

67. Ibid., 179.

68. Ibid., 180.

69. Ibid., 181.

70. Ibid., 182. Note the presumption of conceptual reference as opposed to a causal reference for "religious experience."

71. Ibid., 184.

72. Proudfoot cites Mircea Eliade as an influential critic of reductionism, stating that when Eliade refers to the irreducibility of the sacred, "he is claiming that it is the intentional object of the religious experience which must not be reduced. To do so is to lose the experience, or to attend to something else altogether" (Proudfoot, *Religious Experience*, 192). This approach to religious experience is not satisfactory for the postmodern theorist.

73. Ibid., 193.

74. Ibid., 196–97.

75. In correspondence on this topic, Proudfoot states:

> I don't quite agree with the theory of religion vs. theology distinction. I would use whatever theories are available. But if one is speaking of theories of religion, I would say that theologians have their own, sometimes explicit and sometimes implicit, theories of religion. I was trying to tease those out of Otto and Schleiermacher, for instance, and to bring to the surface what I took to be their implicit assumptions.
>
> For instance, contemporary biblical scholars might believe that the Bible is to be studied like any other book. Textual analyses, epigraphy, attempts to identify different authors and the meanings of particular terms in historical context, are all to be employed much as if one were studying the *Iliad* or other parallel ancient texts. Such a biblical scholar might also believe that, even given all of this, the Spirit of God was, in some sense, present in the authors from which the text comes down to us in a way that differentiates it from the *Iliad* and other books. Her colleague might disagree, thinking that the more secular explanations are sufficient. They might agree on all of the scholarly issues and still have different "theories" of the Bible. The first thinks that the historical and textual factors alone don't fully account for the Bible. In a very similar way, people can differ in the "theories" of religious experience. One could call the first a theologian and the second a theorist of religion, but they are both theorists of religion.

76. Proudfoot cites Katz extensively in this section (see pp. 122–25, 128, 136, and 151). The operative word in describing mystical experience is *constituted*. "The interpretations are themselves constitutive of the experiences" (Proudfoot, *Religious Experience*, 123).

77. Ibid., 155.

78. Ibid., 163.

79. Ibid., 169.

80. Ibid., 119. This defensive or apologetical emphasis put forth by Proudfoot assumes an intimate familiarity with the motivation of the respective authors and restricts their motives in describing religious experience to the purely apologetical. How one can access this motive, especially if Schleiermacher's divinatory aspect of hermeneutics fails, is never clearly specified.

81. Ibid., 121.

82. Ibid.

83. See David Tracy (*Plurality and Ambiguity*, 94) for the opposite conclusion.

84. Proudfoot, *Religious Experience*, 125.

85. Ibid., 125. Proudfoot cites Steven Katz (1978, 54) here. This is a linchpin in Proudfoot's thesis.

86. Ibid., 126.

87. Ibid., 123–24.

88. Ibid., 137.

89. Ibid., 140.

90. Ibid., 139.

91. Ibid., 145.

92. Conversely, "Any experience whose object can be captured in a descriptive phrase or that can be explained in naturalistic terms is, *ipso facto,* not a mystical experience" (ibid., 148).

93. The meaning of *feeling* is different for each.

94. Ibid., 236.

95. Proudfoot, *God and the Self,* 226. Derrida suggests a similar view for the origin of language.

96. Ibid., 227.

97. Ibid.

98. Ibid., 229.

99. Ibid.

3. George Linkbeck's *Nature of Doctrine*

1. Lindbeck states: "The type of theology I have in mind could also be called 'postmodern,' 'postrevisionist,' or 'post-neo-orthodox,' but 'postliberal' seems best because what I have in mind postdates the experiential-expressive approach which is the mark of the liberal method." George Lindbeck, *The Nature of Doctrine: Religion and Theology in a Postliberal Age,* (Westminster Press, 1984), 135, n. 1.

2. Ibid., 9.

3. This concern is framed in terms of halting the ghettoization of theology from nontheological thinking (ibid., 25).

4. Ibid., 10. Paradoxically, Lindbeck points out that "the motivations for this book are ultimately more substantively theological than purely theoretical" (ibid., 18). The issue then becomes whether a "religiously neutral" approach couched in a theoretical construct of the kind that he develops is possible for dealing with theologically substantive problems as he defines them. Lindbeck later adds an important distinction. While religious and theoretical neutrality is desired, theological neutrality is impossible (ibid., 10).

5. Lindbeck extends a particular understanding of language to doctrine in the same way that Proudfoot extends a particular understanding of language to emotion.

6. Lindbeck, *The Nature of Doctrine*, 16.

7. Ibid.

8. Ibid., 16.

9. Ibid.

10. Ibid., 16.

11. Ibid., 17.

12. Ibid., 16.

13. Ibid., 17.

14. Ibid.

15. Ibid.

16. Ibid.

17. Lindbeck gives this third, "hybrid" approach little more than a passing glance (ibid., 16). But the hybrid approach warrants a greater and more exhaustive analysis, for it is quite different from pure experiential-expressivism as defined by Lindbeck.

18. Lindbeck was subsequently criticized on this exposition by Charles C. Hefling and Dennis M. Doyle. See Charles Hefling, "Turning Liberalism Inside-Out," *Method: Journal of Lonergan Studies* 3 (1985): 51–59, and Dennis M. Doyle, "Lindbeck's Appropriation of Lonergan," *Method: Journal of Lonergan Studies* 4 (1986): 18–28.

19. Lindbeck follows this last point with the comment that "in this thesis, Lonergan is obviously speaking as a Christian theologian rather than simply as a theorist of religion" (Lindbeck, *The Nature of Doctrine*, 31). Lindbeck remarked in his comments on my chapter that the above quote "is not meant as a criticism of Lonergan, but simply points to the fact that the aprimordial religious experience can be described in opposition to Lonergan while agreeing with theses 1–5." But is it possible to differentiate a theory of religion from any theological presuppositions? Is there an "objective" corner from which one can evaluate theological methods? Lindbeck answered in correspondence, "Of course not, but theses 1–5 are claimed by many to be independent of theology."

20. Lindbeck, *The Nature of Doctrine*, 32.

21. Ibid.

22. Ibid., 17–18 and 27, n. 10.

23. Ibid., 25. Proudfoot is specifically referenced: "See Wayne Proudfoot, 'Attribution Theory and Psychology of Religion,' *Journal for the Scientific Study of Religion* 14 (1975): 317–330. A forthcoming book by the same author expands on the significance of attribution theory for the understanding of religious experience and, in my view, greatly strengthens the argument of the next chapter" (ibid., 29, n. 31).

24. Ibid., 20.

25. Ibid., 23.

26. Ibid., 25.

27. Ibid., 22.

28. Ibid. Lindbeck remarked in correspondence that such self- expression and self-realization are "not necessarily enjoyable self-expression and realization—[they] can be experienced as difficult but obligatory tasks."

29. Ibid.

30. Ibid., 25.

31. Ibid., 23.

32. Ibid., 38. This was already developed in the previous chapter and will not be repeated. In the summary of the contemporary problematic, a response to this approach characteristic of Wittgenstein will be developed more fully. Lindbeck mentions Wittgenstein on pp. 13, 20, 24, 27–28, 33, 38–39, 43–44, 107, 111, and 130.

33. Ibid., 33.

34. Ibid., 39.

35. Ibid., 40.

36. In remarks on this section, Lindbeck changed this sentence to the following: "While the experiential-expressive approach to religion tends to view itself as a phenomenological description of religious experience, the cultural-linguistic approach tends to view itself as an explanatory description of religious experience." First, note the difference in terminology from Lindbeck, *The Nature of Doctrine*, where terms such as *inner* and *outer* were "derived" from each other; here, Lindbeck draws a distinction between description and explanation. Such terminology, of course, coincides with the two forms of reductionism outlined by Proudfoot; see Wayne Proudfoot, *Religious Experience* (University of California Press, 1985), 196–98.

37. This is clear from Rahner's introduction to *Foundations of Christian Faith* and Bernard Lonergan's two subsections in *Method in Theology* (Seabury Press, 1972) titled "Religious Experience" and "Expressions of Religious Experience." Because reflection is subsequent, experience can be understood as implicitly prior to such reflection.

38. Lindbeck, *The Nature of Doctrine*, 36.

39. Ibid., 34.

40. This, of course, excludes the possibility of an experience of God that totally transcends cultural and linguistic boundaries.

41. "One must be, so to speak, inside the relevant context; and in the case of religion, this means that one must have some skill in how to use its language and practice its way of life before the propositional meaning of its affirmations becomes determinate enough to be rejected" (Lindbeck, *The Nature of Doctrine*, 68). This is self-evident. Meaning is intrasystematic, but the question concerns "experience" as completely confined to such a context or as possibly self-transcendent: Can there be a contextually transcendent reference that is somehow accessible?

42. Ibid., 32.

43. Ibid., 33.

44. Ibid., 34.

45. Ibid., 38. Proudfoot makes an almost identical argument.

46. Ibid., 36.

47. Ibid., 36–37. This is essentially identical to Proudfoot's argument that language is always that "third," the interpreter and possibility of any experience.

48. Lindbeck's extremely brief explication of mental activities attempts to support this position. It precedes a critique of "some professed Thomists such as Lonergan and Rahner" (ibid., 38). According to Lindbeck, Aquinas believed that language actually structured what was otherwise unintelligible reality.

49. Ibid.

50. Ibid.

51. Ibid., 23–24.

52. Ibid., 129. And if there are, they remain inaccessible to human reason.

53. Ibid.

54. This emphasis on *difference* is necessary from a postmodern emphasis on language and history.

55. This was the *only section* of the chapter that according to Lindbeck "required removing." Lindbeck then refers to the following sentence: "The issue is not whether there are universal norms or reasonableness, but whether these can be formulated in some neutral, framework-independent language" (Lindbeck, *The Nature of Doctrine*, 130). It is not clear how this contradicts the point just made: for a truth claim to be asserted, one must know the idiom in which it is formulated.

56. Ibid., 18.

57. Lindbeck, *The Nature of Doctrine*, 92.

58. Ibid., 74. It is not immediately clear how such a self- interested or self-referential definition of doctrine can be of aid in ecumenical endeavors.

59. Ibid., 80.

60. Ibid., 92.

61. Ibid.

62. Ibid., 94.

63. For an interesting statement on first- and second-order discourse, see George Hunsinger's comments in *The Nature of Confession: Evangelicals and Postliberals in Conversation* (Inter-Varsity Press, 1996), 248.

64. Lindbeck, *The Nature of Doctrine*, 94.

65. Ibid. For an excellent critique of Lindbeck's interpretation of the grammatical emphasis by Athanasius, see Alistair E. McGrath, *The Genesis of Doctrine: A Study in the Foundation of Doctrinal Criticism* (W. B. Eerdmans, 1997), 29.

66. Ibid.

67. Ibid., 95.

68. Ibid.

69. Agreement on the principles or rules that determine a particular paradigm is not considered an issue.

70. Lindbeck suggested in correspondence with me that this sentence be phrased as follows: "That is, the use of these terms and concepts describes a rule or guideline *instantiated* and not the corresponding ontological reality in the subject-matter they reference."

71. Lindbeck, *The Nature of Doctrine*, 96.

72. Lindbeck's comments on this section insisted upon the addition of "magisterial" prior to "regulative principles."

73. Lindbeck comments on this section in the following correspondence to me: "The 'principles' involve first-order truth claims, but the doctrinal rule regarding their conjoint assertion is a second-order proposition (i.e., truth claim) about propositions (as Lonergan puts it) which may be instantiated in different and changing formulation of which the Nicene 'consubstantial' and Chalcedonian 'two nature' are examples." This nuance is not evident in the section on the Trinity, but even if it were, the early Christological and Trinitarian controversies were just as concerned with what Lindbeck terms "principles" as they were with the proper language that instantiated such principles.

74. In this sense it could be considered neutral: that is, it makes no particular truth claim for or against the claims of any faith it analyzes, and it can be applied to any and all.

75. I do not deny here that Lindbeck would make truth claims or that he would hold for an epistemological realism. The point is that these claims and this realism are confined (Lindbeck adds here, "from the religiously neutral perspective of the theory of religion") to the *particular historical context.* Universal truth claims made across cultures and history or a transcendental epistemological realism would not be acceptable for Lindbeck. (He adds "unless religiously based" in his comments.) Making such claims would assume some element of a common human experience that would be radically opposed to the claims of postmodernism. (Lindbeck adds "in its secular form.")

76. The purpose of allowing the Barthian influence on Lindbeck to emerge is to reinforce the Barthian view of scriptural narrative as paramount for doing theology. This, I believe, points to an underlying theological anthropology that Lindbeck and Barth share. Also, some crucial aspects of Lindbeck's thought would *not* be acceptable for Barth. First, Barth does not have a regulative view of doctrine; for him, doctrines designate ontological realities. Second, to care about the method of inquiry used by other sciences to the point that one precipitated a radical change in how one did theology would not be acceptable. Third, any diminution of theology as a subset of a theory of religion would be unacceptable.

77. Lindbeck, *The Nature of Doctrine*, 135. For reference to the thought of Karl Barth, see Karl Barth, "The Doctrine of the Word of God," in *Church Dogmatics*, vol. 1, 2d ed., trans. G. W. Bromiley, ed. G. W. Bromiley and T. F. Torrance (T. & T. Clark,

1975). There is little doubt of the influence of Barth on Lindbeck's project as a whole. Lindbeck specifically refers to Barth's thought and influence on pp. 24, 82, 121, 135, 137, and 138.

78. For Karl Barth's understanding of dogmatic theology, see Barth *Church Dogmatics*, vol. 3). The prominence of the biblical narrative for doing dogmatic theology that emerges from Barth's theology could explain how Lindbeck can offer the possibility of a historical document defining a Christian way of life free from extrascriptural categories through space and time. Christian truth is accessible only through the dominant Christian narrative. The task of dogmatic or systematic theology is to give a "normative explication of the meaning of a religion"—a meaning that is accessible *within* the narrative that is formative of that community. "It is in this sense that theological description in the cultural-linguistic mode is intrasemiotic or intratextual" (Lindbeck, *The Nature of Doctrine*, 114).

79. There is a way in which theory can access and evaluate theological claims for Lindbeck (see Lindbeck, *The Nature of Doctrine*, 131). Lindbeck suggests the "reasonableness of religion," which is determined, in part, by a religion's ability to assimilate various factors in an intelligible manner. How this is not simply one epistemology evaluating another, and therefore only relative, is not made clear.

80. John E. Thiel, *Imagination and Authority: Theological Authorship in the Modern Tradition* (Fortress Press, 1991).

81. Thiel, *Imagination and Authority*, 161. For a discussion of the starting point for theology, see ibid. Lindbeck comments on this assertion with the following: "This is our core disagreement, and I grant on p. 134 that you *may* be right, but what are your arguments against the *possibility* that I am the one who is right?"

82. Thiel, *Imagination and Authority*, 161. Lindbeck comments that such rapprochement "cannot be disproved but is, from a cultural-linguistic perspective, unlikely."

83. Lindbeck, *The Nature of Doctrine*, 117.

84. Ibid., 118.

85. This overlooks the fact that Greek thought does exist in the New Testament. Does Lindbeck really mean *extrascriptural,* or does he mean *extracultural?*

86. Lindbeck, *The Nature of Doctrine*, 120.

4. George Steiner's *Real Presences*

1. It is in his critique of a deterministic relationship—for example, a purely constructive relationship—between language and experience that Steiner is most helpful; see George Steiner, *Real Presences* (University of Chicago Press, 1989), 170. Steiner prefers the term *deconstructive* or *poststructuralist* to *postmodern*. He is helpful in the discussion on the nature of language and its relation to experience. This does not imply a

blanket endorsement of Steiner's thought but an endorsement of the general argument presented in *Real Presences*.

2. What Steiner terms *deconstruction* roughly corresponds to what I have characterized as radical postmodernism. Moderate postmodernism would operate from similar foundations, though it would not press the claims of deconstruction as far.

3. Neither Lindbeck nor Proudfoot developed an exhaustive theory of language. But such a theory, one indebted to a particular interpretation of Ludwig Wittgenstein, is explicitly presumed by both and extended to their own particular arguments—emotion for Proudfoot and doctrine/religion for Lindbeck. References have been duly noted.

4. Steiner, *Real Presences*, 86–87.

5. Ibid., 91.

6. Ibid., 92.

7. This focus on "reference" in language is clear in Steiner's development of the problematic in *Real Presences* (94–95).

8. While Steiner implies this (94), it becomes clear that Mallarmé and Rimbaud are freeing language and human subjectivity *from* one or another totalizing vision that they believe stifles the nature of both.

9. Steiner, *Real Presences*, 94. Steiner specifically cites attempts made by Hegel, Schelling, and Comte.

10. Ibid., 91. In the Leslie Stephen Memorial Lecture delivered to the University of Cambridge in 1985 and later published as "Real Presences," Steiner argues that the deconstruction of language occurred through four stages. See George Steiner, *No Passion Spent* (Yale University Press, 1996), 22–24.

11. The following description of the roots of deconstruction adheres in content quite closely to Guarino's description of "radical postmodernism" quoted at length in the introduction to this book.

12. Steiner, *Real Presences*, 94–95.

13. Ibid., 96.

14. Ibid., 95.

15. Ibid., 98.

16. Ibid., 97.

17. Ibid., 98. To employ medieval terminology, such a view reduces a work to its material cause.

18. This is developed in Steiner, *Real Presences*, 100–101.

19. Steiner, *Real Presences*, 97. Steiner continues, "Language speaks itself or, as Heidegger, in direct reprise of Mallarmé, puts it, '*Die Sprache spricht*' (but just this, as we shall see, is Heidegger's initial step out of nihilism and towards a counter-Mallarméan ontology of presence)."

20. Ibid., 100. Steiner elaborates on this point in *No Passion Spent*, 22.

21. Steiner, *Real Presences*, 102.

22. Ibid., 122.

23. Ibid.

24. Ibid.

25. Ibid. Steiner gives the example of Mallarmé's rose (121–22).

26. Ibid., 123.

27. Ibid., 126.

28. Ibid., 99, 109–10. Steiner further supports this argument in *No Passion Spent*, 22.

29. The consequences for theology are readily apparent. If external reference for "meaning" is to be rejected and if meaning is, instead, accessible only from within a given language, the conditions for the possibility of accessing a "revelation" outside one's language or culture context becomes problematic. One answer to such a problem is Lindbeck's resort, via Barth, to a "Word of God" theology that creates of itself its own possibility for understanding.

30. Therefore, while one cannot attribute to Proudfoot and Lindbeck the claims of radical deconstruction, the logical, albeit less extreme, consequences of such an approach become apparent in both their works.

31. In short, this is why all emotions are attributed to concepts and not to any ontological or existential immediacy for Proudfoot and why, for Lindbeck, doctrine refers to other doctrine and never to an ontological truth.

32. Steiner, *Real Presences*, 84–85.

33. Ibid., 69.

34. Steiner specifically refers to a quote by Sir Thomas Browne: "I have true Theory of death when I contemplate a skull, or behold a skeleton with those vulgar imaginations it casts upon us" (ibid., 69).

35. Ibid., 69–70.

36. Ibid., 70.

37. Ibid., 75.

38. Ibid., 70.

39. Ibid., 70–71.

40. Ibid.

41. Ibid., 75.

42. Ibid.

43. Ibid., 76.

44. Steiner, *No Passion Spent*, 25.

45. Steiner, *Real Presences*, 75. This, of course, introduces the paradox of arguing for something that a priori is admittedly incapable of being proven in the applied science sense of *proven*.

46. Steiner defines the term *aesthetic* by stating that "aesthetic means embody concentrated, selective interactions between the constraints of the observed and the boundless possibilities of the imagined" (ibid., 11).

47. Recall that "academic respect" was one of the reasons Lindbeck encouraged the use of the cultural-linguistic method for use in a theory of religion and, ultimately, theology.

48. The relationship of secondary to primary texts is critical for Steiner. He argues this forcefully in *No Passion Spent*, 32.

49. Lindbeck confirmed the same developments, though for different reasons.

50. Ibid. The implication is not that one must be a poet to interpret poetry but that interpretation is best lived as a real encounter with an "other." See Steiner, *No Passion Spent*, 20.

51. Ibid., 13.

52. Steiner, *Real Presences*, 79. Cf. Lindbeck's observation that theology still employs a method at odds with most other sciences, which employ the cultural-linguistic method.

53. Proudfoot, *Religious Experience*, 219, and Lindbeck, *The Nature of Doctrine*, 34, 37.

54. "On this view, the means of communication and expression are a precondition, a kind of quasi-transcendental (i.e., culturally formed) *a priori* for the possibility of experience" (Lindbeck, *The Nature of Doctrine*, 36). Cf. "Emotions assume particular concepts and beliefs. They cannot be assimilated to sensations or simple internal events that are independent of thought" (Proudfoot, *Religious Experience*, 107).

55. For definitions of the "lexical," the "grammatical," and the "semantic," see Proudfoot, *Religious Experience*, pp. 157, 158, and 162.

56. Ibid., 81–82.

57. Ibid., 81. We might add "and the religious" for the purpose of inquiry here.

58. Ibid., 162.

59. Ibid., 163.

60. Ibid., 82–83.

61. Ibid., 165.

62. Ibid., 137.

63. For a careful study of Schleiermacher's epistemology, see Louis Roy, "Schleiermacher's Epistemology," *Method: Journal of Lonergan Studies* 16 (spring 1998): 25–46.

64. All reference for these terms were duly noted in the first chapter.

65. Friedrich Schleiermacher, *The Christian Faith*, ed. Mackintosh and Stewart, 48.

66. Ibid., 16. On the ego and external causality, see p. 12.

67. Ibid., 23.

68. Proudfoot, *Religious Experience*, 217.

69. Ibid., 229.

70. Ibid., 132.

71. Lindbeck, *The Nature of Doctrine*, 34.

72. Ibid. "Religious experiences in the sense of feelings, sentiments, or emotions then result from the new conceptual patterns instead of being their source" (ibid., 39).

73. Ibid., 37.

74. Ibid., 36.

75. Ibid., 11.

76. Steiner, *Real Presences*, 138.

77. Ibid., 137.

78. Ibid.

79. Ibid., 138.

80. Ibid.

81. Ibid., 139.

82. Ibid.

83. Ibid., 139–40.

84. Ibid., 140.

85. Ibid., 149. Steiner specifically refers to an "ethics of reception."

86. Ibid., 142.

87. Ibid., 163.

88. Ibid., 155.

89. Ibid., 163.

90. Ibid., 173.

91. Ibid., 174.

92. Ibid., 175.

93. Ibid., 227.

94. Ibid., 214. Steiner's affirmation and "wager on transcendence" to ensure the meaning of meaning is a deliberate contradiction to the deconstructive program (ibid., 123).

95. Ibid., 213. Descartes's *Third Meditation* is mentioned on pp. 91 and 138. The claims of deconstruction are compared to the "answerability in any Cartesian or Kantian way," which is further elucidated on p. 215. For further elaboration on the Cartesian and Kantian sense of Steiner's wager on transcendence, see Steiner, *No Passion Spent*, 31, 33–35.

96. Steiner, *Real Presences*, 216.

97. Ibid., 87.

98. Ibid., 102–3.

99. Ibid., 104. Ultimately, Steiner does view Wittgenstein as at least contributing to the deconstruction of language (ibid.). For more on Steiner's interpretation of Wittgenstein, see George Steiner, "Retreat from the Word," in *Language and Silence: Essays on Language, Literature, and the Inhuman* (Athenaeum Press, 1967), 12–35.

100. Steiner, *Real Presences*, 225.

101. Richard McKeon, "Experience and Metaphysics," in *Proceedings of the 11th International Congress of Philosophy*, vol. 4, Brussels, August 20–26, 1953 (North Holland Publishing Co., 1953), 85–86. This article is helpful for analyzing the various understandings of the term *experience* in the history of thought.

102. Steiner, *Real Presences*, 143.

103. Ibid. Steiner cites Derrida's assertion that "the age of the sign is essentially theological" (120) and contends the same himself (119).

104. Steiner, *Real Presences*, 96.

105. Ibid., 121.

106. Ibid., 120.

107. Steiner employs this term to describe his own approach and states that "'verification transcendence' marks every essential aspect of human existence" (214).

108. This is to disagree with Peter Phillips when he minimizes the influence of Descartes. See Peter Phillips, "George Steiner's Wager on Transcendence," *Heythrop Journal* 39 (April 1998).

109. Steiner, *Real Presences*, 91.

110. Ibid., 213.

111. James Collins, *God in Modern Philosophy* (H. Regnary, 1959), 378–79.

112. Ibid., 379.

113. Ibid.

114. This is confirmed in recent autobiographical reflections by Steiner. See George Steiner, *Errata: An Examined Life* (Yale University Press, 1997), 185.

115. Ibid., 186.

5. KARL RAHNER'S THEOLOGY OF MYSTERY

1. Rahner, *Foundations of Christian Faith*, trans. William V. Dich (Crossroad, 1983), 2. This foundational level of inquiry is further specified in the preface (xii). Rahner later adds further distinctions (9).

2. Ibid., 2. Rahner was acutely aware of what it meant to do theology contextually. See also Karl Rahner, "Reflections on Methodology in Theology," in *Theological Investigations*, vol. 11, trans. David Bourke (Seabury Press, 1974), 68–114; Karl Rahner, "The Concept of Mystery in Catholic Theology," in *Theological Investigations*, vol. 4, trans. Kevin Smith (Seabury Press, 1974), 36–73; Karl Rahner, "The Human Question of Meaning in the Face of the Absolute Mystery of God," *Theological Investigations*, vol. 18, trans. Edward Quinn (Crossroad, 1983), 89–104; Karl Rahner, "The Experience of God Today," *Theological Investigations*, vol. 11, trans. David Bourke (Seabury Press, 1974), 149–65. For insight on how he understood himself and his work, see Karl Rahner, "On Becoming a Theologian: Interview with Peter Pawlowsky for Radio Austria [July 11, 1980]," in *Karl Rahner in Dialogue: Conversations and Interviews 1965–1982*, ed. Paul Imhof and Hubert Biallowons (Crossroad, 1986), 256.

3. Fergus Kerr, *Immortal Longings: Versions of Transcending Humanity* (University of Notre Dame Press, 1997), 178.

4. Rahner, *Foundations*, 1.

5. Ibid., 7–8. For the German, see Karl Rahner, *Grundkurs des Glaubens Einfürung in den Begriff des Christentums* (Herder, 1984), 19. German references for *Foundations* are supplied for any who wish to check the original language.

6. Rahner adds: "These sciences no longer bow before philosophy's claim that they are to be mediated by philosophy or clarified by philosophy, or even that they are able to be clarified by philosophy" (Rahner, *Foundations*, 8).

7. Rahner, "Reflections on Methodology," 70. In addition to being an excellent resource for the method of transcendental theology employed by Rahner, the first ten pages give an overview of how he understands theology in the contemporary world, especially over and against earlier understandings (ibid., 74).

8. Kerr, *Immortal Longings*, 179.

9. Kerr, *Immortal Longings*, 180. Kerr refers to Karen Elizabeth Kilby's work "Vorgriff auf Esse: A Study in the Relation of Philosophy to Theology in the Thought of Karl Rahner" (Ph. D. diss., Yale University, 1994).

10. For further inquiry into the debate as to how Rahner's theology is characterized, especially by readers who tend to read him outside the typical foundationalist designation, see Fergus Kerr, *Theology after Wittgenstein* (Basil Blackwell, 1986); Kerr, *Immortal Longings;* Michael Purcell, "Mystery and Method: The Mystery of the Other, and Its Reduction in Rahner and Levinas" (Ph. D. diss., University of Edinburgh, 1996); Rusty Reno, *The Ordinary Transformed: Karl Rahner and the Christian Vision of Transcendence* (W. B. Eerdmans, 1995); Ann Riggs, "Rahner, Self, and God: The Question of the Cartesian Ego in the Theology of Karl Rahner" (Ph. D. diss., Marquette University, 1998).

11. Kerr, *Immortal Longings*, 182.

12. Rahner, *Foundations*, 10. One cannot emphasize the mutuality, the perichoresis, of the three moments enough. For the purposes of individual consideration these moments are separated, but their essence is in relation to each other.

13. For this reason, both philosophy and theology are considered together. For more, see Rahner, *Foundations*, 24–25.

14. Ibid., 11.

15. The focus here will be on Rahner's understanding of language and the relationship of language to "original experience." While this insufficiently captures what Rahner intends with the second moment of his method, it presents what is necessary for the current task.

16. Rahner, *Foundations*, 11.

17. Ibid. (Rahner, *Grundkurs des Glaubens*, 23).

18. Rahner, "Reflections on Methodology," 110. For the same statement put another way to emphasize the informing function of doctrine through language to reveal a particular experience, see Rahner, *Foundations*, 12.

19. Rahner, *Foundations*, 12. For comments on a common misunderstanding of mystery in the contemporary world, see Rahner, "Reflections on Methodology," 101.

20. Rahner, *Foundations*, 2 (Rahner, *Grundkurs des Glaubens*, 14).

21. The distinction between original and secondary knowledge or experience (*knowledge* and *experience* are used interchangeably) is posited at the beginning of the introduction and is a key presupposition for Rahner's theological project.

22. Rahner, *Foundations*, 26 (Rahner, *Grundkurs des Glaubens*, 37).

23. Rahner, *Foundations*, 26 (Rahner, *Grundkurs des Glaubens*, 37).

24. Rahner, *Foundations*, 28. Rahner mentions the regional anthropologies of biochemistry, biology, genetics, and sociology, which "tr[y] to explain man from particular data, by reducing him to his elements and then reconstructing him back together again from this particular data." Unfortunately, says Rahner, "[u]sually every such anthropology is also motivated by the secret desire not only to understand man, and not only to analyze and reconstruct him, but also really to control him thereby" (ibid., 28). This, of course, is a similar ethical concern of postmodernity in its view of "modernist conceit."

25. Ibid., 29.

26. Ibid. (Rahner, *Grundkurs des Glaubens*, 37).

27. Rahner, *Foundations* (Rahner, *Grundkurs des Glaubens*, 37).

28. Rahner adds, "A finite system cannot confront itself in its totality (ibid., 30).

29. Ibid.

30. For more on rejecting this responsibility, see ibid., 31.

31. Ibid.

32. Ibid. (Rahner, *Grundkurs des Glaubens*, 42).

33. Rahner, *Foundations*, 32 (Rahner, *Grundkurs des Glaubens*, 42–43).

34. Rahner, *Foundations*, 32 (Rahner, *Grundkurs des Glaubens*, 43). For a more in-depth discussion on the infinite horizon of human questioning with concrete examples and accessible analysis, see Michael J. Buckley, "Transcendence, Truth, and Faith," *Theological Studies* 39 (December 1978), esp. 642–43.

35. Buckley employs the helpful Bonaventurian distinction here between apprehension and comprehension. See Buckley, "Transcendence, Truth, and Faith," 646.

36. Rahner, *Foundations*, 33 (Rahner, *Grundkurs des Glaubens*, 43).

37. Rahner, *Foundations*, 33.

38. Ibid., 34.

39. Ibid., 34–35 (Rahner, *Grundkurs des Glaubens*, 45). For more on this, see Rahner, "Reflections on Methodology," 88.

40. Rahner, *Foundations*, 34 (Rahner, *Grundkurs des Glaubens*, 45).

41. See Rahner, "The Concept of Mystery," 46. For further distinctions and nuances in Rahner's theology of grace, see pp. 56, 61, and 66.

42. Rahner, *Foundations*, 35.

43. Ibid. (Rahner, *Grundkurs des Glaubens*, 46).

44. According to Rahner, there are three general ways one can evade transcendental experience. See Rahner, *Foundations*, 32–33. For this reason, an appeal to transcendental experience as the ground for theological reflection is *possible* even though such experience might not be *actualized* by all.

45. Paradoxically, any attempt to escape this responsibility affirms a person's freedom and responsibility. See Rahner, *Foundations*, 33.

46. Ibid., 38 (Rahner, *Grundkurs des Glaubens*, 490).

47. Rahner, *Foundations*, 39 (Rahner, *Grundkurs des Glaubens*, 49–50).

48. Rahner, *Foundations*, 41.

49. Ibid., 131.

50. For more on "divine self-communication," see Rahner, *Foundations*, 119–20.

51. Rahner includes a particular and careful distinction when conceptualizing this reality. For how he distinguishes *formal* causality from efficient causality, see Rahner, *Foundations*, 121.

52. Ibid., 52 (Rahner, *Grundkurs des Glaubens*, 61–62).

53. Rahner, *Foundations*, 58.

54. Some possibilities include "in anxiety, in the subject's absolute concern, in love's unshrinking acceptance of responsibility in freedom, in joy, and so on" (ibid., 59).

55. For why Rahner bypasses designations such as "absolute being," "being in the absolute sense," and the "ground of being," see Rahner, *Foundations*, 60–61.

56. Ibid., 61 (Rahner, *Grundkurs des Glaubens*, 70). See also Rahner, "The Concept of Mystery," 50.

57. Rahner, *Foundations*, 61.

58. Ibid., 64.

59. For a critical distinction on this topic, see ibid., 52.

60. Ibid., 64.

61. Rahner remarks on this "horizon" elsewhere. See Rahner, "Reflections on Methodology," 105.

62. Rahner, *Foundations*, 65.

63. Ibid. Rahner elaborates more clearly on this idea of love. See Karl Rahner, "Thomas Aquinas on the Incomprehensibility of God," *Journal of Religion* 58, suppl. (1978): S123–24.

64. It is impossible to give this topic of how knowledge moves into love adequate treatment in the space allotted for this chapter. I can only note that for Rahner such is the case and that this is important for understanding holy mystery.

65. Rahner, "Thomas Aquinas," S122.

66. Ibid., S123. For Rahner's comments on the ultimacy of love over knowledge, see ibid., S124.

67. Ibid. Cf. the seventh step of Bonaventure's *Itinerarium Mentis in Deum*, introduction and commentary by Philotheus Boehner (The Franciscan Institute, Saint

Bonaventure University, 1990), 100. The translator comments in the endnotes on the four kinds of wisdom and the precise sense of what Bonaventure intended for the seventh step (Bonaventure, *Itinerarium Mentis in Deum*, 130). This is clearly not univocal to the argument Rahner makes in the *Foundations*, but there is a similarity that can be seen in the "release" of intellectual and scientific activity that Bonaventure requires for mystical unity with God and the self-surrender that Rahner describes as necessary for knowledge to move into love so that the experience of absolute mystery can be the experience of holy mystery.

68. For the designation and explanation of *holy*, see Rahner, *Foundations*, 66.

69. Rahner, "Reflections on the Unity of the Love of Neighbour and Love of God," in *Theological Investigations*, vol. 6, trans. Karl H. Kruger and Boniface Kruger (Seabury Press, 1974), 247.

70. Rahner, *Foundations*, 43. It is important to emphasize here that none of the reflections summarized by this quote are to be understood in an absolute sense, as this would ignore the self-imposed limitations of transcendental theology. Rahner speaks precisely to this point in "Reflections on Methodology in Theology," 99.

71. Rahner, *Foundations*, 15 (Rahner, *Grundkurs des Glaubens*, 26–27).

72. Proudfoot and Lindbeck adhere to a kind of rationalism in the priority they give to concepts as formative of experience.

73. Rahner, *Foundations*, 15.

74. Ibid.

75. Ibid., 15–16. The translator offers this additional comment:

The two spellings, "existential" and "existentiell," follow the German usage. "Existential," as in Rahner's phrase "supernatural existential," refers to an element in man's ontological constitution precisely as human being, an element which is constitutive of his existence as man prior to his exercise of freedom. It is an aspect of concrete human nature precisely as human. "Existentiell," as in Rahner's phrase "existentiell Christology," refers to the free, personal and subjective appropriation and actualization of something which can also be spoken of in abstract theory or objective concepts without such a subjective and personal realization. (ibid., 16)

76. Ibid. Rahner illustrates this elsewhere; see Rahner, "The Experience of God Today," 151.

77. For more on Rahner's understanding of the relationship between language and experience, see Rahner, "The Experience of God Today," 152.

78. Rahner, *Foundations*, 16.

79. Rahner, "The Experience of God Today," 153.

80. Rahner, *Foundations*, 73 (Rahner, *Grundkurs des Glaubens*, 81).

81. Rahner, *Foundations*, 16 (Rahner, *Grundkurs des Glaubens*, 27–28). But it must be kept constantly in mind that this movement is not static but fluid, and in tension with the opposite direction as well.

82. Rahner, *Foundations*, 16–17.

83. Rahner, "The Experience of God Today," 151.

84. Ibid.

85. Rahner develops the nuances of this argument further in "The Experience of God Today," 152.

86. Rahner develops this distinction in more detail elsewhere. See Karl Rahner, "Experience of Self and Experience of God," *Theological Investigations*, vol. 13, trans. David Bourke (Seabury Press, 1975), 124.

87. Karl Rahner, "Interdisciplinary Dialogue and the Language of Theology," in *Karl Rahner in Dialogue*, 309. In another interview, Rahner comments on the positivistic Vienna Circle and the young Wittgenstein. See Karl Rahner, "The Language of Science and the Language of Theology," in *Karl Rahner in Dialogue*, 307, 315.

88. Rahner, "The Language of Science," 307, 315. For further nuances of this reflection upon language, see Rahner, "Interdisciplinary Dialogue," 313.

89. This quote is from written comments on this chapter given by Richard Miller, Ph. D. candidate, Boston College.

90. Karl Rahner, "What Is a Dogmatic Statement?" in *Theological Investigations*, vol. 5, trans. Karl H. Kruger (Seabury Press, 1975), 46.

91. Rahner, *Foundations*, 127.

92. Rahner, "What Is a Dogmatic Statement?" 60.

93. Ibid., 47. Rahner identifies this as the "difference between the truth which is grasped in a properly personal act and the truth which is present in the objective-conceptual truth—implied transcendentally or in some other way—and which is grasped in a personal spiritual act" (ibid.).

94. Ibid., 47–48.

95. Ibid., 48.

96. Ibid.

97. Ibid.

98. Ibid., 48–49.

99. Karl Rahner, "The Nature of Theology," in *Encyclopedia of Theology: The Concise Sacramentum Mundi*, ed. Karl Rahner (Seabury Press, 1975), 1689. For an extensive discussion on the kerygmatic element of a dogmatic statement, see Karl Rahner and Karl Lehmann, *Kerygma and Dogma* (Herder & Herder, 1969). For how Rahner and Lehmann designate kerygma, see ibid., 15.

100. Rahner, "What Is a Dogmatic Statement?" 50.

101. Ibid., 53.

102. Ibid., 52.

103. Ibid., 53.

104. Ibid.

105. Ibid., 54.

106. Ibid.

107. Rahner summarizes the twofold nature of what he designates as the highest theological designation—dogma. See Karl Rahner, "Dogma," in Rahner, *Encyclopedia of Theology,* 352.

108. Rahner, "What Is a Dogmatic Statement," 58–59.

109. Ibid., 59.

110. Ibid., 60.

111. Ibid., 60.

112. Ibid.

113. Ibid., 61.

114. Ibid., 62.

115. Ibid.

116. Rahner, "The Nature of Theology," 1686.

117. For preliminary remarks prior to the discussion on the nature of theology, on the intersubjectivity of truth, see ibid., 1687.

118. Rahner, "The Theological Dimension of the Question about Man," *Theological Investigations,* vol. 17, trans. Margaret Kohl (Crossroad, 1981), 55–56. Rahner reinforces this point elsewhere. See Karl Rahner, "Theology and Anthropology," *Theological Investigations,* vol. 9, trans. David Bourke (Herder & Herder, 1972), 28.

119. Rahner, "The Nature of Theology," 1687.

120. Ibid., 1686.

121. This definition is an attempted summary of the critical points on this topic made by Eberhard Simons in his article "Kerygma," in Rahner, *Encyclopedia of Theology,* 797–800.

122. Ibid., 797–98.

123. Rahner and Lehmann, *Kerygma and Dogma,* 18.

124. Rahner, "Nature of Theology," *Sacramentum Mundi,* 1689.

125. Ibid. Elsewhere, Rahner states the necessary connection between theocentrism and anthropocentrism. See Rahner, "The Theological Dimension," 55.

126. For the importance of the ecclesiastical nature of theology, see Rahner, "Nature of Theology," 1689.

127. Ibid.

128. Once again this is necessarily so, given the principle of intersubjectivity for Rahner's dogmatic theology. For more on this, see Rahner, "Theology and Anthropology," 35.

129. Rahner, "The Nature of Theology," 1690.

130. Ibid.

131. Ibid., 1691.

132. One could argue that Schleiermacher, Lindbeck, and Rahner share the *motive* for critical reflection upon the traditional doctrine of the Trinity: to communicate a received truth in such a way that it can be understood as critical to one's Christian existence. Statements by Rahner speak specifically to his concerns. See Rahner, "Theology and Anthropology," 40–41.

133. Ibid., 21.

134. Ibid.

135. Ibid., 22.

136. Ibid.

137. Ibid., 24.

138. Ibid., 32–33.

139. Ibid.

140. Ibid., 33. See n. 30. For more on the nature of "humanity," see ibid., 29.

141. Ibid., 34–35.

142. Ibid., 35.

143. Ibid., 40.

144. Ibid., 46–47.

145. Rahner, *Foundations*, 11. For how Rahner designates two general kinds of dogmatic statements, see Rahner, "What Is a Dogmatic Statement?" 61.

146. Leo O'Donovan, ed., *A World of Grace: An Introduction to the Themes and Foundations of Karl Rahner's Theology* (Crossroad, 1991), "Glossary," 194. This is contrasted with "ontic: a mode of conceptualizing reality through basic categories or paradigms drawn from the impersonal world of things" (ibid.).

147. Rahner, *Foundations*, 11–12.

148. Rahner, "Theology and Anthropology," 29.

6. The Retrieval of Experience

1. Karl Rahner, *Foundations of Christian Faith* (Crossroad, 1983), 21–22.

2. Karl Rahner, *The Trinity*, trans. J. Donceel (Herder & Herder, 1970), 22.

Select Bibliography

Altizer, Thomas J., et al., eds. *Deconstruction and Theology.* New York: Crossroad, 1982.

Anscombe, G. E. M. *An Introduction to Wittgenstein's Tractatus.* 2d, rev. ed. New York: Harper & Row, 1959.

Anselm of Canterbury. *The Prayers and Meditations of St. Anselm with the Proslogion.* Translated by Benedicta Ward. New York: Penguin Books, 1973.

———. *Proslogion.* German-Latin edition. Translated by P. Franciscus Salesius Schmitt. Abtei Wimpfen, Stuttgart-Bad Cannstatt: Friedrich Frommann, 1962.

———. *S. Anselmi Cantuariensis Archiepiscopi Opera Omnia.* 2 vols. Edinburgh: Thomas Nelson & Sons, 1946, 1961.

———. *Saint Anselm: Basic Writings.* Translated by S. N. Deane. Introduction by Charles Hartshorne. 2d ed. La Salle, Wis.: Open Court Publishing, 1968.

Aristotle. *Nichomachean Ethics.* Translated by and with introduction and notes by Martin Oswald. New York: Macmillan, 1962.

Augustine. *On Christian Doctrine.* Translated by D. W. Robertson, Jr. New York: Macmillan, 1958.

Barth, Karl. *Anselm: Fides Quarens Intellectum.* Richmond, Va.: John Knox Press, 1960.

———. *Church Dogmatics.* Edited by G. W. Bromiley and T. F. Torrance. 4 vols. Edinburgh: T. & T. Clark, 1936–1960.

Bonaventure. *Itinerarium Mentis in Deum.* Introduction and commentary by Philotheus Boehner. New York: The Franciscan Institute, Saint Bonaventure University, 1990.

Buber, Martin. *I and Thou.* Translated by Walter Kaufmann. New York: Charles Scribner's Sons, 1970.

Buckley, Michael J. *At the Origins of Modern Atheism.* New Haven, Conn.: Yale University Press, 1987.

———. "Experience and Culture: A Point of Departure for American Atheism." *Theological Studies* 50 (September 1989).

———. *Motion and Motion's God: Thematic Variations in Aristotle, Cicero, Newton, and Hegel.* Princeton, N. J.: Princeton University Press, 1971.

———. "Transcendence, Truth, and Faith: The Ascending Experience of God in All Human Inquiry." *Theological Studies* 39 (December 1978).

Boyd, Tom W. "Is Spirituality Possible without Religion? A Query for the Postmodern Era." In *Divine Representations: Postmodernism and Spirituality*, edited by Ann W. Astell. New York: Paulist Press, 1994.

Clements, Keith, ed. *Friedrich Schleiermacher: Pioneer of Modern Theology*. Minneapolis: Fortress Press, 1991.

Collins, James. *God in Modern Philosophy*. Chicago: H. Regnary, 1959.

Connor, Steven. *Postmodernist Culture: An Introduction to Theories of the Contemporary*. 2d ed. Cambridge, Mass.: Blackwell, 1997.

Dewey, John. *Logic: The Theory of Inquiry*. New York: H. Holt, 1938.

Doyle, Dennis M. "Lindbeck's Appropriation of Lonergan." *Method: Journal of Lonergan Studies* 4 (1986).

Feuerbach, Ludwig. *Lectures on the Essence of Religion*. Translated by Ralph Manheim. New York: Harper & Row, 1967.

Freud, Sigmund. *Civilization and Its Discontents*, Translated and edited by James Strachey. Biographical introduction by Peter Gay. New York: W. W. Norton, 1989.

———. *The Future of an Illusion*. Translated and edited by James Strachey. Biographical introduction by Peter Gay. New York: W. W. Norton, 1989.

Fries, Heinrich. *Fundamental Theology*. Translated by Robert J. Daly. Washington, D. C.: Catholic University of America Press, 1996.

Gadamer, Hans-Georg. *Truth and Method*. 2d, rev. ed. Translated and revised by Joel Weinsheimer and Donald G. Marshall. New York: Crossroad, 1989.

Gerrish, Brian A. *A Prince of the Church: Schleiermacher and the Beginnings of Modern Theology*. Philadelphia: Fortress Press, 1984.

Griffin, David Ray. "Introduction: Varieties of Postmodern Theology." In *Varieties of Postmodern Theology*, edited by David Ray Griffin et al. Albany: State University of New York Press, 1989.

Guarino, Thomas. "Between Foundations and Nihilism: Is Phronesis the *Via Media* for Theology?" *Theological Studies* 54 (March 1993).

Hefling, Charles. "Turning Liberalism Inside-Out." *Method: Journal of Lonergan Studies* 3 (1985).

Hume, David. *The Natural History of Religion*. Edited by H. E. Root. Stanford, Calif.: Stanford University Press, 1993.

James, William. *The Varieties of Religious Experience*. Edited with an introduction by Martin E. Marty. New York: Penguin Books, 1982.

Jasper, David. "Introduction: Religious Thought and Contemporary Critical Theory." In *Postmodernism, Literature and the Future of Theology*, edited by David Jasper. New York: St. Martin's Press, 1993.

Kant, Immanuel. *Critique of Practical Reason*. Translated by Lewis White Beck. 3d ed. New York: Macmillan, 1993.

———. *The Philosophy of Kant: Immanuel Kant's Moral and Political Writings.* Edited by Carl J. Friedrich. New York: Random House, 1979.

Kerr, Fergus. *Immortal Longings: Versions of Transcending Humanity.* Notre Dame, Ind.: University of Notre Dame Press, 1997.

Lash, Nicholas. *Easter in Ordinary.* Notre Dame, Ind.: University of Notre Dame Press, 1986.

Lawrence, Fred. "The Fragility of Consciousness: Lonergan and the Postmodern Concern for the Other." *Theological Studies* 54 (March 1993).

Lindbeck, George. "The Church's Mission to a Postmodern Culture." In *Postmodern Theology: Christian Faith in a Pluralist World,* edited by Frederic B. Burnham. San Francisco: Harper & Row, 1989.

———. *The Future of Roman Catholic Theology.* Philadelphia: Fortress Press, 1970.

———. *The Nature of Doctrine: Religion and Theology in a Postliberal Age.* Philadelphia: Westminster Press, 1984.

Lonergan, Bernard. *Method in Theology.* Minneapolis: Seabury Press, 1972.

McGrath, Alistair E. *The Genesis of Doctrine: A Study in the Foundation of Doctrinal Criticism.* Grand Rapids, Mich.: W. B. Eerdmans, 1997.

McKeon, Richard. "Experience and Metaphysics." *Proceedings of the 11th International Congress of Philosophy.* Vol. 1. Brussels, August 20–26, 1953. Amsterdam: North Holland Publishing Co., 1953.

Miller, James B. "The Emerging Postmodern World." In *Postmodern Theology: Christian Faith in a Pluralist World,* edited by Frederic B. Burnham. San Francisco: Harper & Row, 1989.

Niebuhr, Richard R. *Schleiermacher on Christ and Religion.* London: SCM Press, 1964.

———. *Schleiermacher on Christ and Religion: A New Introduction.* New York: Charles Scribner's Sons, 1964.

O'Donovan, Leo, ed. *A World of Grace: An Introduction to the Themes and Foundations of Karl Rahner's Theology.* New York: Crossroad, 1991.

Palmer, Richard E. *Hermeneutics.* Evanston, Ill.: Northwestern University Press, 1969.

Phillips, Peter. "George Steiner's Wager on Transcendence." *Heythrop Journal* 39 (April 1998).

Proudfoot, Wayne. "Attribution Theory and Psychology of Religion." *Journal for the Scientific Study of Religion* 14 (1975).

———. *God and Self: Three Types of Philosophy of Religion.* Lewisburg, Pa.: Bucknell University Press, 1976.

———. "Peirce on Natural Belief in Religion." In *Faithful Imagining: Essays in Honor of Richard R. Niebuhr,* edited by Sang Hyun Lee et al. Atlanta: Scholars Press, 1995.

———. *Religious Experience.* Berkeley: University of California Press, 1985.

Rahner, Karl. "The Concept of Mystery in Catholic Theology." In *Theological Investigations*, vol. 4, translated by Kevin Smith. New York: Seabury Press, 1974.

———. "The Experience of God Today." In *Theological Investigations*, vol. 11, translated by David Bourke. New York: Seabury Press, 1974.

———. "Experience of Self and Experience of God." In *Theological* Investigations, vol. 13, translated by David Bourke. New York: Seabury Press, 1975.

———. "Experience of Transcendence from the Standpoint of Catholic Dogmatics." In *Theological Investigations*, vol. 18, translated by Edward Quinn. New York: Crossroad, 1983.

———. *Foundations of Christian Faith.* Translated by William V. Dych. New York: Crossroad, 1983.

———. *Grundkurs des Glaubens Einfürung in den Begriff des Christentums.* Freiburg: Herder, 1984.

———. *Hearer of the Word.* Translated by Joseph Donceel. New York: Continuum, 1994.

———. "The Human Question of Meaning in the Face of the Absolute Mystery of God." In *Theological Investigations*, vol. 18, translated by Edward Quinn. New York: Crossroad, 1983.

———. "An Investigation of the Incomprehensibility of God in St. Thomas Aquinas." In *Theological Investigations*, vol. 16, translated by David Morland. New York: Crossroad, 1983.

———. *Karl Rahner in Dialogue: Conversations and Interviews 1965–1982.* Edited by Paul Imhof and Hubert Biallowons. New York: Crossroad, 1986.

———. "The Mystery of the Trinity." In *Theological Investigations*, vol. 16, translated by David Morland. New York: Crossroad, 1983.

———. "Nature and Grace." In *Nature and Grace: Dilemmas in the Modern Church*, translated by Dinah Wharton. London: Sheed & Ward, 1963.

———. "Nature of Theology." In *Encyclopedia of Theology: The Concise Sacramentum Mundi*, edited by Karl Rahner. New York: Seabury Press, 1975.

———. "Reflections on Methodology in Theology." In *Theological Investigations*, vol. 11, translated by David Bourke. New York: Seabury Press, 1974.

———. "Reflections on the Unity of Love of Neighbor and the Love of God." In *Theological Investigations*, vol. 6, translated by Karl H. Kruger and Boniface Kruger. New York: Seabury Press, 1974.

———. "The Theological Dimension of the Question about Man." In *Theological Investigations*, vol. 17, translated by Margaret Kohl. New York: Crossroad, 1981.

———. "Theology and Anthropology." In *Theological Investigations*, vol. 9, translated by David Bourke. New York: Herder & Herder, 1972.

———. "Thomas Aquinas on the Incomprehensibility of God." *Journal of Religion* 58, suppl. (1978).

———. *The Trinity.* Translated by J. Donceel. New York: Herder & Herder, 1970.

―――. "What Is a Dogmatic Statement?" In *Theological Investigations,* vol. 5, translated by Karl-H. Kruger. New York: Seabury Press, 1975.

Rahner, Karl, and Karl Lehmann. *Kerygma and Dogma.* New York: Herder & Herder, 1969.

Raschke, Carl A. "The Deconstruction of God." In *Deconstruction and Theology,* edited by Thomas J. Altizer et al. New York: Crossroad, 1982.

Redeker, Martin. *Schleiermacher: Life and Thought.* Translated by John Wallhausser. Philadelphia: Fortress Press, 1973.

Roy, Louis. "Schleiermacher's Epistemology." *Method: Journal of Lonergan Studies* 16 (spring 1998).

Schleiermacher, Friedrich. *Brief Outline on the Study of Theology.* Translated by Terrence N. Tice. Richmond, Va.: John Knox Press, 1966.

―――. *The Christian Faith.* English translation of 2d ed. Edited by H. R. Mackintosh and J. S. Stewart. Edinburgh: T. & T. Clark, 1989.

―――. *The Christian Faith.* Edited by H. R. Mackintosh and J. S. Stewart. Vol. 1. New York: Harper Torchbooks, 1963.

―――. *Der Christliche Glaube.* 3 vols. Edited by Hermann Peiter. 1821–1822. Reprint, New York: Walter de Gruyter, 1980.

―――. *Der Christliche Glaube.* 2 vols. Edited by Martin Redeker. 1831. Reprint, Berlin: Walter De Gruyter, 1960.

―――. *Der Christliche Glaube nach den Grundsätzen der Evangelishchen Kirche im Zusammenhange Dargestellt.* Berlin: Bei G. Reimer, 1830.

―――. *Hermeneutics: The Handwritten Manuscripts.* Translated by James Duke and Jack Forstman. Missoula, Mont.: Scholars Press, 1977.

―――. *The Life of Jesus.* Edited by Jack C. Verheyden. Translated by S. Maclean Gilmour. Philadelphia: Fortress Press, 1975.

―――. *The Life of Schleiermacher as Unfolded in His Autobiography and Letters.* Translated by Frederica Rowan. 2 vols. London: Smith, Elder, 1859.

―――. *On Religion: Speeches to Its Cultured Despisers.* Translated by Richard Crouter. Cambridge, England: Cambridge University Press, 1993.

―――. "On the Discrepancy between the Sabellian and Athanasian Method of Representing the Doctrine of the Trinity." Translated by M. Stuart. *Biblical Repository and Quarterly Observer* 19 (July 1835).

―――. *On the Glaubenslehre: Two Letters to Dr. Lücke.* Translated by James Duke and Francis Fiorenza. Ann Arbor, Mich.: Scholars Press, 1981.

Smart, Ninian et al., eds. *Nineteenth Century Religious Thought in the West.* New York: Cambridge University Press, 1985.

Steiner, George. *The Death of Tragedy.* New Haven, Conn.: Yale University Press, 1996.

―――. *Errata: An Examined Life.* New Haven, Conn.: Yale University Press, 1997.

―――. *Language and Silence: Essays on Language, Literature, and the Inhuman.* New York: Atheneum Press, 1967.

———. *Martin Heidegger.* Edited by Frank Kermode. New York: Penguin Books, 1982.

———. *No Passion Spent: Essays 1978–1995.* New Haven, Conn.: Yale University Press, 1996.

———. *Real Presences.* Chicago: University of Chicago Press, 1989.

———. *Tolstoy or Dostoevsky: An Essay in Contrast.* Boston: Faber & Faber, 1960.

Taylor, Mark C. "Text as Victim." In *Deconstruction and Theology,* edited by Thomas J. Altizer et al. New York: Crossroad, 1982.

Thiel, John E. *Imagination and Authority: Theological Authorship in the Modern Tradition.* Minneapolis: Fortress Press, 1991.

Tracy, David. *Plurality and Ambiguity: Hermeneutics, Religion, Hope.* London: SCM Press, 1987.

———. "Theology and the Many Faces of Postmodernity." *Theology Today* 51 (April 1994).

———. "The Uneasy Alliance Reconceived: Catholic Theological Method, Modernity, and Postmodernity." *Theological Studies* 50 (September 1989).

Welch, Claude. *Protestant Thought in the Nineteenth Century.* Vol. 1, 1799–1870. New Haven, Conn.: Yale University Press, 1972.

Wittgenstein, Ludwig. *Tractatus Logico-Philosophicus.* Frankfurt: Suhrkamp, 1968.

Index

aesthetic experience, 99–101, 108–9, 114–15, 156, 164n35

Anselm of Canterbury, Saint, 11–12, 27, 46, 67, 152

Aristotle, 56

attribution theory, 76, 102

Barth, Karl, 85, 86

Berger, Peter, 76

Bonaventure, Saint, 188n67

Browne, Thomas, 182n34

Cassirer, Ernst, 54

Church as community, 14–15, 23–26, 28, 33–35, 139–40, 144–45

Collins, James, 116–17

"common humanity," 24, 29–30, 47–49, 51–52, 58–62, 65, 72, 74–75, 77–78, 80, 86, 89, 92, 96, 113, 115, 151, 154

concepts, 58–59, 64, 107, 189n72

conceptual attribution theory, 76, 102. *See also* emotion

Crouter, Richard, 163nn7, 18

cultural-linguistic method, 72, 75–80, 84–85, 154, 183nn47, 52

deconstruction, 2–3, 9, 94–97, 110, 181n2, 184n94

dependence, 12, 21–22, 24, 26–27, 31–34, 38, 48, 57, 104–5, 129, 153

Derrida, Jacques, 185n103

Descartes, René, 99, 111, 116–17

Dewey, John, 173n62

divinatory interpretation. *See* technical/divinatory interpretation

doctrine, 54, 72, 73–80, 102, 122–24, 134. *See also* Trinity

dogmatic statements, 137–42. *See also* doctrine

dogmatic theology, 12, 25–38, 123–24, 142–46, 151, 180n78

doing, 29–30, 33, 105

doubt, theory of, 58–62

Durkheim, Emile, 76

ecumenism, 71–72, 81, 89, 154

Eliade, Mircea, 173n72

emotion, 52, 55–57, 61, 68, 98, 102, 112, 171n24, 175n5, 181n3

experience: "common humanity" and, 24, 29–30, 47–49, 51–52, 58–62, 65, 72, 74–75, 77–78, 80, 86, 89, 92, 96, 113, 115, 151, 154; emotion and, 52, 55–57, 61, 68, 98, 102, 112, 171n24, 175n5, 181n3; interiority and, 15, 20, 23–24, 61, 68; language and, 20–21, 24, 49, 51–58, 77–80, 92–93, 101–12, 123, 127, 133–42, 153; mystery and, 123, 124–33; priority of, 24, 31, 35, 47, 52, 135, 166n99; privateness of, 54, 76, 77, 79; theory and, 62–64